HARVARD STUDIES IN ADMINISTRATIVE LAW

VOLUME VI

LONDON: HUMPHREY MILFORD
OXFORD UNIVERSITY PRESS

JUDICIAL ASPECTS OF FOREIGN RELATIONS

IN PARTICULAR OF THE RECOGNITION OF FOREIGN POWERS

BY

LOUIS L. JAFFE

CAMBRIDGE
HARVARD UNIVERSITY PRESS
1933

PRINTED AT THE HARVARD UNIVERSITY PRESS
CAMBRIDGE, MASS., U. S. A.

TO

A. H. FELLER

FOREWORD

I WISH to thank two men: Professor Felix Frankfurter and Mr. A. H. Feller. To sit alone and to rear in dead silence a continuous and consistent growth of thought of any complexity whatever demands a goodly amount of self-starting energy and a stout confidence. The fruits of intellectual singleness are born of a too-fearful travail. Yet to find someone with whom in slow patience ideas may be generated, tried out, and welded into a growing structure can only be the result of a happy chance. It is, then, with due credit to happy chance that I thank Mr. Feller. His knowledge of international law, his easy mastery of the mechanics of scholarship and research, and his unfailing enthusiasm in the exploration of ideas were always equal to, and at the disposition of, my persistent demands upon them. I do not wish to implicate him in any particular conclusion reached in this essay, but I think that he will permit me to say that together we tried to deal out true justice, not too unaware, I hope, of the dangers of academic irresponsibility.

My debt to Professor Frankfurter in connection with this essay does not arise merely from what I, as one of his students, have drawn up out of the stimulating and sparkling wells of his wisdom and learning. No, here I salute him as chief member of the Opposition. It was his challenge to many of the conclusions reached here which prodded me once more along the hard and crooked path of my thinking, which forced me to dig out the probable biasses which may have determined its direction. Briefly, I have chafed at the restrictions which the courts, in deference to the executive, place upon themselves when dealing with questions relating to foreign affairs, particularly in the so-called recognition cases. Professor Frankfurter believes that many of these restrictions are wise. His intensive study of the musculature of government both as practitioner and student, his sensitivity to the subtle and impalpable demands of administration, have created in him a firm conviction of the value of specialization and its necessary complement, self-limitation, which means modesty and deference to other specialists. He is not alone, of course, in the belief that our judiciary has too often overstepped decent bounds in its treatment of matters primarily entrusted to other organs, particularly the legislature. With these, his major premises, I agree, and yet the challenged conclusions will still be found here. Do I thereby do lip-service, and no more? I hope not. It is my present conviction that "reasonable men" may differ as to whether the general attitude of Professor Frankfurter should control the particulars here in dispute. Yet I should not be surprised if the years to come and distance from Academe were to convince me that the greater wisdom was with the challenge of Professor Frankfurter.

L. L. J.

WASHINGTON, D. C.
October, 1933

CONTENTS

ABBREVIATED TITLES

A. J. .... American Journal of International Law.

Anzilotti .... Anzilotti, Cour de Droit International (French translation based on the 3rd Italian ed. 1929).

Brierly .... Brierly, The Law of Nations, An Introduction to the International Law of Peace (1928).

Fiore .... Fiore, International Law Codified (Borchard it., 1918).

Goebel .... Goebel, The Recognition Policy of the United States, Columbia Studies in History, Economics and Public Law No. 158, Vol. 66 (1915).

Hervey .... Hervey, The Legal Effects of Recognition in International Law (1928).

Holdsworth ..... Holdsworth, A History of English Law (3d ed., 1922–26).

J. D. I. .... Journal du Droit International (Clunet).

Le Normand .... Le Normand, La Reconnaissance Internationale et ses diverses application (1899).

Lorimer .... Lorimer, The Institutes of the Law of Nations (1883).

Noël-Henry...... Noël-Henry, Les Gouvernements de Fait Devant les Juges (1927).

Paxson .... Paxson, The Independence of the South American Republics (2d ed. 1916).

Warren .... Warren, The Supreme Court in United States History (1924).

Wright .... Wright, Control of American Foreign Relations (1922).

JUDICIAL ASPECTS OF FOREIGN RELATIONS

INTRODUCTION

FROM the Russian Revolution, from the long-drawn-out sequel of non-recognition, there has arisen in our courts, like the crop of armed warriors which sprang from the dragon's teeth, a formidable host of profound and perplexing problems. The radical reconstitution of the Russian social order, crossed with the refusal of our Government to recognize the new regime, has given birth to a situation so novel as to be unprecedented, at least in extent, in the administration of justice in our courts.

Too often, in the opinion of the writer, the courts have failed to rise to the high levels of judicial law-making demanded by the situation. They are hindered in their flight by the deadweight of formulas which they conceive as absolutes, formulas which they apply rigidly to materials whose fluidity and complexity resent the torturing mold.

The basic issue lies deep. It is nothing less than the claim that, as far as possible and as consistent with claims of equal validity, the continuity of the social and economic order be preserved from the shocks of war, of revolution, of international dissension and difference.[1] In the treatment of the cases turning on the non-recognition of foreign powers, the courts often fall into a series of assumptions which obscure this great underlying theme, which cut off the very

[1] In The Sophie Rickmers, 45 F (2d) 413 (S. D. N. Y. 1930), Judge Mack held that a treaty between the United States and Germany for reciprocally favorable tonnage duties was merely suspended by the War, and came into force again as soon as trading with Germany was permitted. Judge Mack did a tall job of distinguishing the very recent decision of Karnuth *v.* United States, 279 U. S. 231 (1929), which held that the War of 1812 had terminated the provisions of the Jay Treaty allowing free passage across the Canadian border. Judge Mack said:

"Such parts of treaties of commerce as affect at least the transportation of goods should, in my judgment, be so interpreted, if reasonably possible, as again to bring about for that time the status which prevailed before the war. The resumption of trade relations marks a resumption of the ways of peace. The processes of law, at least in the absence of a contrary determination by the executive branch of the government, should favor rather than retard the early restoration of pre-war conditions. . . . The war is, as has been aptly said, 'an interlude of savage life,' and its rigors ought not to be unduly prolonged by judicial construction." (*Id.* at 419.)

approaches to it. The first of these is the assumption that between the national and the international social order there is a clear line of cleavage; that it is possible to insulate the order of the forum from other national orders, and from the international order, which, properly considered, is the sum and synthesis of all these. As a corollary, the national courts take the attitude that only in the exceptional case where "comity" exists are they concerned with the maintenance of other national orders. This idea, largely inarticulate, finds its complement in the doctrine, by contrast iterated and reiterated, that executive procedures in the conduct of international or (as the courts seem to regard them) *extra-national* affairs are superior to the judicial process of being valued and weighed, of being entered in the competition with other claims and interests.

These assumptions, if they were valid, would be relevant to all cases in which the courts have before them litigation which impinges on international relations; more particularly to cases where the actual conduct of foreign affairs is involved. The judicial problems arising out of the recognition and non-recognition of foreign powers are but a phase of this larger issue; it is our particular purpose, here, to develop a technique for resolving, or at least determining, the conflict between executive and judicial purposes in recognition cases. But to this end we shall first "take a view" of the broader field; of the relation, generally, between the conduct of foreign affairs and the administration of justice by courts. There is no space to treat that subject in encyclopedic fashion. We shall adopt a frankly argumentative approach. In other words, we shall select a few segments of the whole in order to test the validity of the assumptions on which, as we have said, so many of the recognition cases seem to be based. This method may be criticized, since those cases will be selected which prove that the assumptions are faulty and those omitted which support them. But the purpose is simply to disprove that the assumptions are absolutes. Undoubtedly they are based on claims which are entitled to their day in court; once having destroyed them as mechanical determinants, we can block out tentative areas within which they are supreme, beyond which they must compete with other worthy claims.

It is not orthodox for a writer on the law to lay bare his prejudices; it is presumed that he has none, and that he is but a glass to reflect the true, clear image of the law. It is becoming respectable, however, to expose the subjectivity of legal doctrine, at least when a judge expounds it; and why should not the critics concede that they are no better (or rather no different) than their victims? After a preliminary survey of the field, this writer found himself already biassed. He disliked the cases which gave a very broad effect to the policy of non-recognition, and applauded those which somehow or other got around the policy, i. e. which considered the fact of non-recognition as irrelevant in the context of the given case. He set out to justify these preferences, and this essay is a record of the attempt. But why confess this sin against Science? Because, in the opinion of the writer, there was the same undercurrent running through the work of other Americans who had written on the subject. When the reasons pro and con had been set down and weighed, "it was submitted that the better view" or "it *seemed* that the more desirable view" was to ignore the fact of non-recognition. Beneath the ripples of logic there was a secret spring of judgments. This concealed source should be more thoroughly explored, more frankly faced; issues which are really worth bothering about are not decided by measuring the opposing "reasons" with a scales or a yardstick. Certainly we should canvass painstakingly the reasons on both sides. That is the stage of illumination, of planting and fertilizing the inscrutable mind. But into the judgment itself there will surely enter something more subtle, more uncontrolled. When we find that the judgments tend to move in one direction, we must seek further to find what lies behind, for there, perhaps, is the true battleground.

Consider, for example, what has been written about the case of *Luther* v. *Sagor*.[2] The Soviet Government confiscated some plywood belonging to the plaintiff and sold it to the defendants. The British court, in an action of trover, held that no effect would be given to the Soviet decree as long as the Soviet was unrecognized by the British. When the case reached the upper court, the Soviet had been recognized. The court decided that the recognition — so far as British courts were concerned — reached back to make valid the Soviet decrees prior to the recognition. But the Court of Appeals approved the opinion of the *nisi prius* judge. Professor Dickinson "submits"[3] that the view of the lower court (concurred in, as it was, by the Court of Appeals) is "erroneous." "The unfortunate results which ensue when private rights may be thus tossed about in the eddying current of international politics are too obvious to

[2] [1921] 1 K. B. 456; [1921] 3 K. B. 532.

[3] *The Unrecognized Government or State in English and American Law*, 22 Mich. L. Rev. 118, 131 (1924).

require emphasis." Fraenkel[4] vividly pictures, if *Luther* v. *Sagor* is to be good law, the vicissitudes that a piece of plywood may undergo as it floats from country to country, the first a recognizing state, the second not, and so forth. "A rule of law producing results so variable in time and space is entitled to little respect, and should not be persisted in." Yet a French writer, Noël-Henry,[5] endorses *Luther* v. *Sagor* unreservedly and gives very good reasons. The courts, he argues, must support the foreign policy of the government. If the Soviet is defeated in its attempts to sell confiscated goods, it will press harder for recognition, and it will meet the demands of the French Government. Individuals may suffer, titles may play hide-and-go-seek, but what of it? Is it for the court to say that the gains of the policy are not greater than the losses? Is it so deplorable that this or that citizen should pay a price for national security?

The American writers do not answer these questions. They do not even ask them. Implicitly, of course, they have rejected the Frenchman's reasons by preferring their own. But these questions are at the very heart of the problem. We want to know why they have not been asked, or, in so far as they have been, how the answers bear upon the specific results reached.

Have we Americans been moved to our conclusions because of dissatisfaction with the recognition policy of our Government? To some degree, perhaps, "Yes." Is there not a delicate trace of it in Professor Dickinson's concluding sentence, "It is a serious matter when the executive uses recognition as a bludgeon in the contests of diplomacy, but the situation may become doubly serious if courts feel constrained thereby to ignore what is going on abroad in a rather intricately integrated world"?[6] We should be unwilling to admit, of course, that all our reasonings are at bottom a badly disguised distaste for American foreign policy. If we could find nothing better than that, we should be compelled to scrutinize our results very closely and ask ourselves whether we would arrive at the same conclusions if we approved of the foreign policy involved in the cases.

This writer believes that there is something more tenable underneath it all, something that will at least warrant serious controversy. Professor Dickinson hints at it in his phrase "a rather in-

[4] *The Juristic Status of Foreign States*, 25 Col. L. Rev. 544, 563 (1925).

[5] Noël-Henry, p. 138.

[6] *Loc. cit.* (*supra*, note 3) at 134.

tricately integrated world." In "a rather intricately integrated world," organization and order are best placed on an international basis, are best secured when released from the opportunistic pressures of national policy. It is not unusual for an international lawyer to feel that there are international allegiances which, under certain circumstances, may legitimately compete with immediate national allegiances; allegiances which, if cultivated, are not unpatriotic since, in the greater and more universal security, there is balm for each of the nations. Nor, again, is it unusual for an American lawyer to feel a certain confidence in the impartiality of the courts, even if by impartiality we mean nothing more than a comparative freedom from the professionalism of the bureaus, a habit of regarding the particular in terms of the general, an appeal to which might secure a willingness to throw over such traditions and attitudes of diplomatic intercourse as cut off the broader views. We must take account of these points of view. These, the writer believes, are the submerged postulates which have moved him and, if it is not too bold to surmise, other American writers who arrive at similar results in the recognition cases. If that is so, it is not difficult to see why the Frenchman Noël-Henry with his intense nationalism has arrived at very different results; to see why he preferred "reasons" which we reject as not sufficiently weighty or compelling.

These postulates should be turned up into the light. In part, at least, it is on that ground that the battle must be fought. Our conclusions will lack inherent strength if we continually pay lip-service to the hegemony of the executive in foreign affairs, and at the same time work out results which challenge that hegemony, disingenuously ignoring the existence of the challenge or covering it with a phrase. This problem is not a question merely of finding the "right" "rule of law," as Fraenkel would imply. The courts must move about in the spacious and dangerous realms of policy and statesmanship; they are called upon to make a choice from among conflicting attitudes. Such a choice will not only answer implicitly the given problem, but will also transcend the results in individual cases. Unless, then, a writer admits that below the reasoned surfaces there is a question of attitudes, his objective legalism will rest on a quicksand of subterranean compulsions.

CHAPTER I

POLITICAL QUESTIONS IN CASES INVOLVING INTERNATIONAL RELATIONS

Constitutional Powers and Constitutional Understandings

The truth embedded in the aphorism "a government of laws and not of men" does not stir us deeply as it did our forefathers. Administration was comparatively a simple matter, and the young nation was rich in well-trained men. Tyranny, not inefficiency, haunted men's minds. Today, we are impressed with the truism that government is the resultant tension of the interreaction of laws and men; we do not presume to say which is more important. Faith in the pure value of words has, to some extent, gone out of us; Mr. Justice Holmes' beautiful figure that "a word is not a crystal, transparent and unchanged; it is the skin of a living thought and may vary greatly in color and content, according to the circumstances and the time in which it is used," [1] reflects the relativism of the age. It is our experience that a paper government may be realized in infinite and ever changing variety.

Into our Constitution has been written the dogma of the separation of powers, buttressed with a system of "checks and balances." When in 1793 Washington issued his history-making Proclamation of Neutrality, a debate [2] arose as to his power to make such a proclamation. Hamilton ("Pacificus") defended the President. The executive has the right to receive ambassadors; he is the organ of intercourse between the United States and foreign nations. Also he is charged with the execution of the laws, among which are treaties. Therefore, it is proper for him to declare to foreign nations what attitude toward them our laws require. But Madison ("Helvidius"), urged on by Jefferson, declared that Washington's action interfered with the power of Congress to declare war, which in-

[1] Holmes, J., in Towne *v.* Eisner, 245 U. S. 418, 425 (1918).

[2] This debate is minutely considered in Corwin, *The President's Control of Foreign Relations* (1917), pp. 1–32.

cluded equally the power to declare that we were not at war. Hamilton agreed that Congress had such power, but so, he claimed, did the President in exercising his function. Furthermore, he argued that the power to declare war was executive in nature, and being an exception to the general grant of executive power to the President must be strictly construed.

This argument was a leaf out of his opponent's own book. In the notable Congressional debate of 1789 over the President's removal power, Madison had maintained that the power both of appointing and of removing officers was executive; that the executive power was granted to the President in general terms; that the Senate's concurrent power in appointments was in express derogation from the executive power and excluded the possibility of any other restrictions on the power over officers; and that therefore participation by Congress in removals was unconstitutional. But in answer to any argument of this sort, it is usually possible to derive a contrary one from some other source of power which will sound equally good. Congress has the power to create offices; it can limit the terms of office; it can therefore prescribe the qualifications of office, and the conditions and termination of tenure.[3]

Such controversies are inevitable under our system. The Constitution may divide the field of power into legislative, executive, and judicial, but that simple trichotomy does not inhere in the nature of things, where notoriously there are no clear lines of division at all. In the process of articulating the powers of government, there is on one hand the task of distributing these powers, and on the other the problem of coordinating their exercise.

Congress alone can declare war and appropriate money. The President and Senate, sometimes the President alone, are exclusively competent to make treaties. Probably a treaty declaring that under certain circumstances war should automatically exist would derogate from the Congressional prerogative. But what of a treaty obligating us to make war on stated occasions? No doubt it would seriously impair the discretion of Congress in the exercise of the war power. Yet, legally, if not morally, it leaves Congress free to act. In the Jay Treaty, the United States agreed to indemnify the expropriated loyalists. A Congressional appropriation

[3] In Myers *v.* United States, 272 U. S. 52 (1926), this great constitutional issue was resolved in favor of the President's exclusive power over removals. The debate of 1789 was variously interpreted in majority and dissenting opinions.

was necessary. Did the House have a "right" to pass on the merits of the treaty before making the appropriation? There was, of course, nothing to stop them from acting as if they had such a "right" and refusing the appropriation. In fact, though the "right" has always been verbally asserted by the House, the appropriation has never been refused. Publicists differ on the existence of the "right." [4]

Abdication of independent judgment in deference to other organs is generally in accordance with an accepted principle of political action, a so-called constitutional understanding. Attempts to buttress desirable constitutional understandings by "legal" compulsions deduced from the Constitution have not succeeded. Quincy Wright says:

> The constitutional understandings are based on the distinction between the possession of a power and discretion in the exercise of that power. The law of the constitution decides what organs of the government possess the power to perform acts of international significance [*inter alia*], but the understandings of the constitution decide how the *discretion or judgment*, implied from the possession of power, ought to be exercised in given circumstances.[5] (Italics mine.)

The President in making a treaty has presumably passed judgment on its value, and has committed the country advisedly. Should not Congress accept the matter as *fait accompli*, as judgment made in the exercise of undoubted competence; is not their discretion foreclosed? Yet cannot Congress, with equal justice, ask

[4] "In general it may be said that where the cooperation of Congress is necessary to carry out a treaty, Congress ought to act, exercising discretion only as to the means most suitable for attaining the ends contemplated by the treaty, and the duty is none the less binding in international law and constitutional understanding from the fact that the Constitution furnishes no power to compel it. The entire system of the Constitution demands that each department accept in good faith and cooperate in carrying out the undertakings of the other departments. But such cooperation cannot be relied upon unless the treaty power has given due consideration to the attitude of Congress before making the commitment." Wright, p. 356; also see *ibid.*, § 54.

But cf. Corwin, *op. cit.* (*supra*, note 2), p. 30: "Madison was among the foremost of those who insisted upon the right of the House . . . to pass upon the merits of the Jay Treaty, preliminary to voting the money necessary to carry it into execution. He was unquestionably correct in his position. . . ."

Ibid., p. 97: "The conclusion, therefore, that we must come to is that neither treaties nor acts of Congress can curtail the discretion which constitutionally belongs to an organ of Government. . . ."

[5] Wright, § 7.

to be consulted by the treaty-making power before it is pledged to cooperation? To these questions there is no easy answer. Though appropriations for the performance of a treaty have never been refused, Congress has frequently passed laws impairing the operation of treaties. Here, as elsewhere, the doctrine of separation of powers is not very satisfactory as an interpretive device; that the foreign relations organ is solely intrusted with the making of treaties, and the subordinate judgments necessarily involved, points to one conclusion; that Congress has the exclusive power of making appropriations and passing laws points to the other. Furthermore it is not even clear that the doctrine of separation of powers is to be used as an interpretive device. In *Myers* v. *United States*[6] Mr. Chief Justice Taft said:

> From this division on principle, the reasonable construction of the Constitution must be that the branches should be kept separate in all cases in which they were not expressly blended, and the Constitution should be expounded to blend them no more than it affirmatively requires.[7]

But the same judge has said:

> These are some instances of positive and negative restraints possibly available under the Constitution to each branch of the government in defeat of the action of the other. They show that the independence of each of the others is qualified and is so subject to exception as not to constitute a broadly positive injunction or a necessarily controlling rule of construction. The fact is that the Judiciary, quite as much as Congress and the Executive, is dependent on the co-operation of the other two that government may go on.[8]

Generally, constitutional understandings should operate to promote a maximum of efficiency and to place reliance in the organ best fitted for the task; where the action of an appropriate organ creates a status such as diplomatic or treaty relationship, war or termination of war, the other organs should hesitate to destroy it by denying the implied judgments upon which it is based.[9] The extent to which one organ should defer to another before acting

[6] 272 U. S. 52 (1926). [7] *Id.* at 116.

[8] Ex parte Grossman, 267 U. S. 87, 120 (1925).

[9] "Where two organs enjoy concurrent powers to produce a status, the one acting first, of course, effects the result. . . . 'In short, it frequently happens that the same legal result may be produced by very different powers of government; nor need the fact lead to confusion, since as soon as any of the competent powers has acted, the result is produced.'" Quoting Corwin, *Power of Congress to Declare Peace*, 18 Mich. L. Rev. 669, 672 (1920); Wright, p. 341, n. 6.

will vary with the urgency of the issue and the feasibility of co-operation. President Lincoln declared a blockade of the Southern states before Congress had declared war. The Supreme Court held[10] that this was within his power as Commander-in-chief. The President thus may not declare war, but by exercising war powers in defense of the realm he may effectually carry us into war. Undoubtedly this action fettered the discretion of Congress. Lincoln apparently considered the matter too urgent to defer to Congress. In the making of treaties cooperation may not be feasible, though this would be more true of so-called executive agreements, particularly armistices, than of ordinary treaties, as to which it would be simple enough to take the sense of the House.

Efficiency is not an end in itself. The Fathers devised an elaborate system of checks and balances to temper the tyranny of government and the presumption of anointed persons. "It is," declared John Adams, "by balancing each of these three powers against the other two that the efforts in human nature toward tyranny can alone be checked and restrained, and any degree of freedom preserved." [11] Efficiency, then, is *prima facie* the vital principle of constitutional understandings, but not necessarily the be-all and the end-all.

The Formal and the Dynamic Aspects of the Theory of "Political Questions"

Over a number of controversies the courts refuse jurisdiction *in toto*. They will not hear a suit against a foreign nation without that

[10] The Prize Cases, 2 Black 635 (1862).

[11] Quoted by Bondy, *The Separation of Governmental Powers, Columbia Studies in History*, etc. (1896), v, 17.

And Mr. Justice Brandeis has said in Myers *v.* United States, 272 U. S. 52 at 292 (1926): "Checks and balances were established in order that this should be 'a government of laws and not of men.' . . . The doctrine of the separation of powers was adopted by the Convention of 1787, not to promote efficiency but to preclude the exercise of arbitrary power. The purpose was, not to avoid friction, but by means of the inevitable friction incident to the distribution of the governmental powers among three departments, to save the people from autocracy."

Cf. Pollard, *The Evolution of Parliament* (2nd ed. 1926), p. 253: "Nor does the separation of powers prevent that arbitrary exercise of them which the framers of the American Constitution dreaded so intensely. It is rather thereby facilitated, for within its sphere each authority is irresponsible and unchecked, and each department is, under the Constitution, the final and exclusive judge of its own competence." (Reference is made to the fact that the legislature is the

nation's consent. They will not undertake to insure to a state the constitutional guarantee of a republican government. Somewhat different are cases in which the court takes jurisdiction but refuses to decide certain facts on its own judgment. Of such cases we must distinguish two types. Of one sort are cases where, for example, the legislature and the executive exercise powers of government over a territory in the name of the United States; where the War Department requisitions neutral property claiming it needful to the national defense; where the treaty power "recognizes" an Indian tribe as an autonomous "nation" not subject to the laws of the state in whose midst it dwells. In all these cases there has been positive executive action. Not only the validity of such acts, but the fact basis on which they purport to rest, the court will not question. In the other class are cases where the court may be asked to decide that an unrecognized state is independent; that a treaty is no longer operative; that a government of one of the United States is not republican and that hence its legislation is invalid: all cases in which at the time of judgment the executive has taken no action, but in which it is claimed that the fact determinations necessary to settle the issues can in no case be properly decided by the court.

These three types of cases are often generalized under the head of "political questions." This phrase does no more than express the fact that the court leaves them to be decided by the legislature or the executive. Maurice Finkelstein [12] calls them cases of "judicial self-limitation," a phrase of pregnant implications. The courts have the power to decide but decline to exercise it. Thus they perform a free act of abdication, an act political rather than legal in its nature. In terminology already developed, these restrictions spring from constitutional understandings. This conception, like the kindred one that judges make law, sounds "dangerous" to the lawyer. Lusty attack has not been wanting. Melville Weston in a thoughtful article maintains that in deciding that a question is "political" the court is deciding that the determination of a certain issue *has been delegated by the Constitution* not to the court but to the "political" organs.[13]

arbiter of its own elections, and that the President and legislature stay out their terms regardless of consent of one by the other.)

[12] Finkelstein, *Judicial Self-Limitation*, 37 Harv. L. Rev. 338 (1924).

[13] Weston, *Political Questions*, 38 Harv. L. Rev. 296 (1925). This article is an attack on Finkelstein's (*supra*, note 12).

While to some extent they [the courts] thus [by using the word "political" argumentatively] import their own notions of what ought to be delegated, a comparison of the cases shows that they have chiefly in mind that the power relates to a subject usually dealt with by political as contrasted with judicial methods, and is at one with, or included in matters unquestionably and unequivocally delegated to, the executive and legislative departments.[14]

The author himself admits that his argument does not establish "judicial inevitability flowing from the Constitution." But does it, at least in the difficult cases, do any more than provide the formal dressing up of a decision which must be reached by other methods? Of course the Constitution is the formal source of the law, and if you are careful to remember that classification is not reasoning, it is permissible to assign to every decision of the court, even every act of government, its ultimate source in the Constitution.[15] In certain cases the method of argument from the Constitution, particularly when vitalized by infusions of history, is valuable. It may locate "fundamental powers." Thus, from the powers expressly conferred upon the executive we derive its power over foreign affairs; and we exclude the judiciary from the power (here the method is inverted) because it relates to matters "usually dealt with [i.e. in the Constitution] by political as contrasted with judicial methods." This method is perhaps sufficient to account for cases in which the court refuses jurisdiction completely, as in suits against foreign nations or to guarantee republican government.

The method also is of some help in the second class of cases, sometimes grouped under the doctrine of "acts of state" or "acts of government." No doubt all "acts of state" come within the proposed formula, but unfortunately (for the formula) many which fit

[14] *Id.* at 331.

[15] Kelsen builds his whole "pure theory of law" on the self-sufficiency of formal constitutional sources: "Legislation and custom . . . rest upon the constitution, which in the sense of legal logic is the ultimate norm, the final source of the system of law. The decisive element for the positivity of law which gives law the character of a self-sufficient system, distinct from all other systems of norms, independent, and closed within itself, lies in this norm [i. e. the Constitution] as the highest, derivable from nothing beyond, through the quality of sovereignty lent by this ultimate norm to the whole system of law raised out of it." Kelsen, *Das Problem der Souveränetät* (1920), p. 94, as translated by Dean Pound, *Progress of the Law: Analytical Jurisprudence*, 41 Harv. L. Rev. 174, 175 (1927). Of this and like attempts to isolate "what law is" from "what it ought to be" Dean Pound says (*id.* at 177): "Thus, we are to get a universal science of law rid of all the doubts and difficulties which make a science of law worth having."

into it have not been held to be "acts of state." Consider the decisions dealing with confiscation of enemy property during war. Now, on its highest ground an "act of government" is equivalent to a law enacted by a proper legislative organ; the incompetency of the court to question it is thus formally established. Clearly that is so of a declaration of war by Congress. Congress in time of war may authorize the President to seize property which he believes to be enemy-held; it is sufficient for constitutionality that *after* seizure a method is provided of rectifying mistakes as to ownership.[16] In *Commercial Trust Co.* v. *Miller* [17] it was held that even after a proclamation of peace such a law continued to be valid.

> A court cannot estimate the effects of a great war and pronounce their termination at a particular moment of time, and that its consequences are so far swallowed up that legislation addressed to its emergency had ceased to have purpose or operation with the cessation of the conflicts in the field.[18]

Here, then, the power of determining the fact of war and the penumbra of war is inextricably interwoven with the power of enacting law. Neither the law nor the fabric of fact on which it is set will be questioned.

As we have seen, even without Congressional action the President may declare a state of war to exist, declare a blockade, and so by his fiat make the marine-going property of enemy and neutral alike subject to confiscation; [19] all this from his power to conduct foreign affairs, to command the army and navy, to execute the laws. None of these acts, any more than those of Congress, do the courts presume to question.

But there are cases which burst the symmetrical patterns. In *Brown* v. *The United States* [20] the Court decided that the executive could not in time of war confiscate alien property on land without the authorization of Congress. Chief Justice Marshall said:

[16] Central Union Trust Co. *v.* Garvan, 254 U. S. 554 (1921); Stoehr *v.* Wallace, 255 U. S. 239 (1921).

[17] 262 U. S. 51 (1923). Also cf. Hamilton *v.* Kentucky Distilleries, 251 U. S. 146 (1919). Congress could pass an act prohibiting the sale of intoxicating liquors as a war measure, though an armistice had been declared, and the act was not to be effective until eight months after the cessation of hostilities.

[18] Commercial Trust Co. *v.* Miller, 262 U. S. 51, 57 (1923) (per McKenna, J.). Cf. Miller *v.* United States, 11 Wall. 268 (1870) (for confiscation purposes rebels can be constitutionally treated as "public enemies" and their property confiscated without the usual guarantees).

[19] The Prize Cases, 2 Black 635 (1862).

[20] 8 Cranch 110 (1814).

When war breaks out, the question, what shall be done with enemy property in our country is a question of policy rather than of law. The rule which we apply to the property of our enemy will be applied by him to the property of our citizens. Like all other questions of policy, it is proper for the consideration of a department which can modify it at will; not for the consideration of a department which can pursue only the law as it is written. It is proper for the consideration of the legislature, not of the executive or judiciary.[21]

Mr. Justice Story, dissenting, said:

Independent of such express authority, I think that, as the executive of the nation, he must, as an incident of the office, have a right to employ all the usual and customary means acknowledged in war, to carry it into effect.[22]

The implication in Marshall's statement that the executive is not an organ of policy is indeed surprising and cannot have been well considered. But the decision is a warning. We must not accept too freely the idea that conduct of a "political" nature is immune from judicial scrutiny. Another case is *The Paquete Habana.*[23] Here the Prize Court decided upon general principles of international law that fishing smacks owned by enemy civilians and operating out of blockaded ports were not legitimate prize. But said the Court:

The exemption, of course, does not apply to coast fishermen or their vessels, if employed for a warlike purpose, or in such a way as to give aid or information to the enemy; nor when military or naval operations create a necessity to which all private interests must give way.[24]

Admiral Sampson was of the opinion that it was necessary to keep these fishermen, good material for the Spanish Navy, from getting back to Cuba.[25] So under this decision, at least, the court rather than the military or admiralty makes itself the judge of the necessity. However, perhaps too much emphasis must not be put on this case or the famous case of *The Zamora,*[26] in which it was held that the King in Council could not lay down rules of law for the Prize Court. The Prize Court is specially designed to pass independent judgment on the action of the war power in cases of capture.

[21] *Id.* at 128–129.
[22] *Id.* at 145.
[23] 175 U. S. 677 (1900).
[24] *Id.* at 708.
[25] *Id.* at 712.
[26] [1916] 2 A. C. 77. The Prize Court is considered in detail below. See *infra,* p. 41 et seq.

Furthermore, in *The Paquete Habana* there is an intimation [27] that if expressly authorized by order of the President, the capture might have been upheld. And in other cases there are hints that express presidential sanction will validate action otherwise held to be outside the power of the executive. In this there is significant reminder of the royal prerogative, a residuum of the once great powers of royal legislation, and it shows the close affiliation between the concept of the "act of state" and enactment of law.

There are, then, acts of the executive, decisions, and more particularly opinions in the course of performing a peculiarly "political" function which, even so, the courts will not accept as binding; which, for various reasons, the courts will not toss into the hopper of "political questions" and thus remove from judicial scrutiny. To be sure, such cases are exceptional. It is in the third class of cases that there is most debate and uncertainty — cases in which there has been nothing equivalent to an act of state, but in which it is urged that some matter to be determined is a "political question" beyond the competence of the court. Here Weston's characterization as "political" of subjects "at one with, or *included,* in matters unquestionably and unequivocally delegated to the executive and legislative departments" is completely deceptive, and could only have been arrived at by excluding as many cases as it includes.

Principal reliance for Weston's point is found in *Luther* v. *Borden* [28] and a line of cases following it, typical of which is *Pacific States Telephone and Telegraph Co.* v. *Oregon.*[29] The famous case of *Luther* v. *Borden* involved the civil uprising in Rhode Island in 1842. Luther sued Borden for trespass. Borden's defense was that he had acted on the authority of the Government, which had in fact prevailed, and which the President by offering aid to it had "recognized." Here undoubtedly was an "act of state" binding on the Court. But Chief Justice Taney went further. The Court, he said,

[27] 175 U. S. 677, 711 (1900); cf. Mitchell *v.* Harmony, 13 How. 115 (1851). In MacLeod *v.* United States, 229 U. S. 416 (1913), military officials in possession of Manila required the plaintiff to pay duties on goods imported into a certain locality claimed by the United States, but in fact in the control of hostile forces. The Court ordered the payment to be refunded, as having been exacted contrary to principles of international law. However, the presidential order did not call for customs payments under such circumstances, and the indication is that the decision might have been different if the tax were collected under an unequivocal presidential order.

[28] 7 How. 1 (1849).

[29] 223 U. S. 118 (1912); also Ohio *v.* Hildebrant, 241 U. S. 565 (1916); Mountain Timber Co. *v.* State of Washington, 243 U. S. 219 (1917).

was not competent to question the authority upon which a government rested, nor could it enforce the constitutional guarantee to the states of a republican form of government. In the *Pacific States Telephone and Telegraph Co.* case the plaintiff asserted the unconstitutionality of a statute on the ground that Oregon having adopted the referendum was no longer a republican government and was consequently bereft of the power to govern. This fanciful argument was rejected. Whether Oregon's government was republican was a "political question," said the Court. Now in both of these cases there was jurisdiction of the controversy; in neither was the Court asked to enforce directly the constitutional guarantee. But the Court refused to determine the fact of republican government, however it might be raised, even where incidental to an ordinary action of trespass. In other words, this is a case where the Court bars itself not only from *exercising certain powers* called "political" over certain objects, but, in addition, from *determining any fact* or forming any opinion upon which the exercise of the particular power would depend. These cases, then, seem to bear out Weston's analysis.

On the other hand, it is an interesting fact that though the case of *Cherokee Nation* v. *Georgia* [30] is widely cited as a prime example of a "political question," *Worcester* v. *Georgia*,[31] which followed hard upon it, is discreetly overlooked; it does not fit so easily into schematization. In the first case the Cherokee Nation sought to enjoin the state of Georgia from passing and enforcing laws which assumed to exercise jurisdiction over it. The majority dismissed the action on the ground of failure of proper party plaintiff, but Marshall doubted the justiciability of the issue, in any case. Mr. Justice (William) Johnson, in his usual forceful and emphatic manner, was much more certain:

> . . . The contest is distinctly a contest for empire. It is not a case of meum and tuum in the judicial but in the political sense. Not an appeal to laws but to force.
>
> There is then a great deal of good sense in the rule laid down in the Nabob of Ascot's case, to wit, that as between sovereigns, breaches of treaty were not breaches of contract cognizable in a Court of justice.[32]

The bearing of these words is manifest if it be remembered that the current political situation was charged with electric-

[30] 5 Peters 1 (1831). [31] 6 Peters 515 (1832).

[32] 5 Peters 1, 28, 29 (1831). Cf. Georgia *v.* Stanton, 6 Wall. 50 (1867); Rhode Island *v.* Massachusetts, 12 Pet. 657 (1838) (Taney dissenting).

ity.[33] Georgia had defied both the nation and the Supreme Court to interfere with her assertion of power over the Cherokees. President Jackson, to put it conservatively, had shown no intention of interfering with Georgia. And now the Court had said, "It is none of our business." Georgia then arrested two missionaries in the Cherokee country, convicted them, imprisoned them. From the Supreme Court there went down a writ of error to "the judges of the Supreme Court . . . in the State of Georgia." And barely, precariously, the record came up, certified to by the clerk, ominously lacking the signature of the judges. The record was held to be before the Court (Baldwin dissenting). The conviction was reversed: the acts of Georgia violated the treaty rights of the Cherokees; the treaties were "laws of the United States"; the acts were unconstitutional and void. Let Georgia release the missionaries! Thus, in a controversy over the rights of a private party, and clearly within its jurisdiction, the Court decided the very "political question" it had abjured the previous session. It interpreted certain documents containing agreements between the United States and the Cherokees; it decided that these documents were "treaties"; that by these treaties the United States had guaranteed the political autonomy of the Cherokees; that the acts of Georgia were violations of the treaties. The executive was not consulted, and legend has it that he might have decided otherwise. Be it noted, however, that Mr. Justice Johnson was at home sick in bed.[34]

The conceptions of "political question" and "act of state" are preeminently dynamic formulas. It is futile to attempt to fill them in by analysis from the Constitution conceived as a fixed or static organization. It obscures their real nature. These conceptions are shorthand statements of the relations between the executive and the judiciary, the resultants of the conflicting claims of competence. History is our witness that these relations have changed as a consequence of an intricate and continuous readjustment of many factors. This was so prior to the adoption of the Constitution, and that instrument could not, was not intended to still these restless forces. In the words of Mr. Justice Holmes:

> When we are dealing with words that are also a constituent act, like the Constitution of the United States, we must realize that they have called

[33] The background of these cases is set forth in Warren, vol. II, ch. XIX, "The Cherokee Cases and President Jackson."

[34] 6 Peters (page listing the judges).

into life a being the development of which could not have been foreseen completely by the most gifted of its begettors. It was enough for them to realize or to hope that they had created an organism. . . . The case before us must be considered in the light of our whole experience and not merely in the light of what was said a hundred years ago.[35]

In the Norman beginnings of the English Constitution, the separation of powers was unknown. The King ruled through his Council or *curia.*[36] This body, however, was feudal. It was not an instrument of central or national government. Here the King met his lords and took their advice. Here the relations between the King and his great feoffees were adjusted. Out of this body grew the Parliament, the courts, the administrative departments, and the modern Privy Council. But, as Baldwin has said, "they were brought forth not by any inherent tendency in the court itself, but by the strong and persistent assertion of the royal prerogative."[37] The strength of the King's position as head of the feudal hierarchy enabled him to cut through the whole feudal fabric, to offer governmental services directly to all individuals, and to formulate and execute his policy on a national scale.

Chief among the services which the King extended to the nation was the administration of justice. Petitions could be addressed to the Council, from which the King would issue his personal order, commanding the presence of the party claimed against. And as the King's power grew, disobedience of his personal summons became dangerous. In time, the Council sent commissions to go about the country and represent it in the trial of specified matters. There is no place here to trace from the beginnings the rise and growth of the courts of justice. It is important only to note that for hundreds of years they were simply meetings or committees of the Council itself, sitting to do judicial business. Their jurisdiction was fed — in derogation of the jurisdiction of the feudal lords — from the waxing royal prerogative.[38]

[35] Missouri *v.* Holland, 252 U. S. 416, 433 (1920).

[36] Baldwin, *The King's Council* (1913), p. 4: "Another essential characteristic of the King's Council during the feudal age is found in its lack of differentiation or specialization. This was not incompatible with a high degree of centralization and an effective control of all the agencies of government. It means that the same body, whether large or small, was a royal council, a court of justice, or a general assembly, according to the needs of the moment. . . ." See also Pollard, *The Evolution of Parliament* (2nd ed. 1926), pp. 238–246.

[37] Baldwin, *op. cit.* (*supra*, note 36), p. 6.

[38] "To use a metaphor, Feudalism, a spirited and somewhat unruly charger,

Ghose has said: "Was it not the King's judges who invented the doctrine, 'The King can do no wrong'? It was they who found for the King that undefined reserve of discretionary powers which was sanctified by the name of 'Prerogative.' The common law laid the foundation in England of both State and Individual rights." [39] But the prerogative was a political fact before the King's judges turned it into a common-law concept. The judges were simply exercising the prerogative jurisdiction of the King. They could not deny it without destroying themselves.

In Magna Carta it was provided that "common pleas shall not follow our court but shall be had in some certain place." This assured the continuity of the Court of Common Pleas as a separate institution. But it was still under the complete control of the Council. Over one hundred years later, in the twenty-fifth year of Edward III, the Commons demanded that no man should answer for his freehold or for matters of life and limb before the Council. The King consented to the restriction only as regards freeholds.[40] During the fourteenth and fifteenth centuries there was apparently a growing feeling, in part among the lawyers and courts, and even more strongly among their conservative clients, that the common law should not be set aside by the exercise of the prerogative. And Professor Vinagradoff finds evidence in the Year Books that the judges, while assigning the Prerogative a very wide range, yet considered it as "legal institution subject to definite rules and limitations." [41] But this point of view did not find consistent or

was first broken by the military power of the Norman and Angevin Kings, and then ridden by the Royal judges." Ghose, *Comparative Administrative Law* (1919), p. 94.

[39] *Ibid.*

[40] Baldwin, *op. cit.* (*supra*, note 36), p. 279. The Council itself during Lancastrian times passed many self-denying ordinances to the effect that matters "touching the common law" should be determined by the common-law courts. But there was always a saving clause "unless it were against such high personages that right could not be obtained elsewhere" or "unless there be too much might on the one side, and too much unmight on the other." *Ibid.*, p. 280.

In the first year of James I's reign the Council resolved to interfere only upon an "extraordinarie occasion."

[41] *Constitutional History and the Year Books*, 29 Law Q. Rev. 273, 280 (1913), quoted in Holdsworth, II, 435; and Holdsworth adds: "There is no doubt that Coke's emphatic words on this topic represent both the letter and the spirit of his authorities." But it should be said that these authorities speak only for the judges' views. Whether these views prevailed is another matter. There is an instance in Dasent, *Acts of the Privy Council*, III, 159, in the year 1550, when the

continuous expression until Parliament and the courts under Coke used it to refute the Stuarts' claim of an unlimited Prerogative; and even then it prevailed only upon the successful issue of the Revolution.

Until this time the Council maintained an elaborate supervision over the administration of justice. In scope, in vigor, in utility, the activities of the Council reached their height under the Tudors.[42] The minutes which we have of the meetings of the Privy Council show the variety and the detail of their work.[43] Upon petition by one of the parties, the Council would interfere in the conduct of pending trials. The court might be ordered to expedite a trial,[44] to refrain from issuing execution in "commyseracion of the defendant's decaying estate," [45] to forbear proceedings until "upon their perfect understanding . . . they shall make personal report" to the Council.[46] The Council acted as a court of conflicts, ordering one tribunal to relinquish jurisdiction in favor of another. These orders were, above all, necessary to protect the newer "administrative" tribunals of Admiralty [47] and Star Chamber [48] from the pretensions of the older, more autonomous common-law courts.

judges, asked why they had proceeded in the Bishop of Bathe's matter of *pre munirie* after a letter of restraint from the Council, answered "that thei were sworen to suffer the lawes to have their due courses, so that withoute violatinge of their othes thei could staye no proces." The upshot does not appear. See Holdsworth, v, 347–348.

[42] Holdsworth, IV, 80, 105–106.

[43] The records of the Privy Council during the reigns of Henry VIII and Elizabeth have been made available in thirty-two volumes edited by J. R. Dasent under the title *Acts of the Privy Council*, published between 1890 and 1907. These will be referred to as "Dasent." References to the judicial business of the Council are collated in Holdsworth, IV, 84–85.

[44] Dasent, XI, 59; XIX, 62 (to expedite a trial so that the defendant can go to Ireland in the Queen's service); XXI, 95 (asking the Court to make counsel get to the issue on their pleading); XXII, 250 (to expedite a matter already much heard, in interest of the impoverished plaintiff).

[45] Dasent, XIX, 18.

[46] Dasent, VIII, 14; XI, 63 (a letter to the judges not to prosecute a murder with so much "extremitie," to try with "indifferency and uprightnes," and if guilt were found to forbear judgment until the Queen's pleasure); XIX, 101, 111 (stay of suit).

[47] Dasent, XXVII, 31 (rebuke to King's Bench for allowing trover of goods which admiralty had allowed to be seized as pirate goods).

Characteristically the common-law courts, particularly under Coke and after, sought to drain off the jurisdiction of the Admiralty courts, though the procedure of the common-law courts was unfitted to the business. Holdsworth, I, 553–558.

[48] Dasent, XX, 37; also XXII, 52 (order not to interfere with suit in Court of Requests).

Of more immediate interest to us are cases in which the Council suggested or dictated the decision of the court. A specialized form of such interference was exercised in those cases in which the writ *de non procedendo Rege inconsulto* was invoked. Causes in which the interests of the Crown were involved, either directly or indirectly, were not subject to the jurisdiction of the common-law courts. Should such an interest appear in the course of the litigation, the King would command the court to discontinue until he had been consulted, or the judges themselves might desist of their own motion.[49] During the Middle Ages there was a confusion between *dominium* and *imperium*. The organization of political power was not much more than an aspect of the system of land tenures. The cleavage between economic power and political rights, so generally asserted in modern times, and so precariously maintained, was almost non-existent. It is not surprising that the personal, landed interests of a ruler, and interests which as head of the feudal system might be called public, were not well differentiated. Typically, the writ *de rege inconsulto* was used to protect proprietary interests of the Crown.[50] But many interests today considered public were then treated as proprietary. In the case of *Brownlow* v. *Mitchell*,[51] argued on behalf of James I by his Attorney-General, Sir Francis Bacon, the contest was over the asserted right of the Crown to create and appoint to an office "for the sole making of writs of *Supersedeas quia improvide emanavit* in the Common Pleas."

The potentialities of the decision to be made in *Brownlow* v. *Mitchell* were in everyone's mind at the time. That the writ *de rege* was valid under certain circumstances no one, including Chief Justice Coke, denied. Fortescue,[52] when Chief Justice, had once disobeyed the writ, but against this lonely challenge Bacon was able to marshall "a cloud of precedents, *nubem testium*." [53] But if the right to appoint to office were a right of the Crown such that the court could be foreclosed from questioning the existence of the power or the validity of its exercise in any case, it might be possible to insin-

[49] Baldwin, *op. cit.* (*supra*, note 36), p. 270.

[50] Bacon in his argument on the writ, Bacon's *Works* (Spedding's ed. 1879), VII, 683, 706, lists nine sorts of cases where it is applicable. Most of them involve a possible loss to the King of a feudal "proprietary interest" (possession, rents, reversion, etc.). But a few, such as loss of power to appoint to office and question raised as to a charter or patent granted, verge on the political.

[51] 3 Bulstrode 32, 33 (1616).

[52] Bacon, *op. cit.* (*supra*, note 50), VII, 703.

[53] *Ibid.*, p. 706.

uate into that category any power of government. Nor was Bacon slow to see this probability. He wrote to the King:

> The writ is a mean provided by the ancient law of England to bring any case that may concern your Majesty in profit *or power* from the ordinary Benches, to be tried and judged before the Chancellor of England by the ordinary and legal part of this power. And your Majesty knoweth your Chancellor is ever a principal councillor and instrument of monarchy, of immediate dependence on the King; and therefore like to be a safe and tender guardian of the regal rights.[54] (Italics mine.)

Furthermore, Bacon contended that the court must obey the command of the writ without enquiring whether a matter of Crown right was in fact involved. And for this proposition he was able to cite precedent.[55] But Coke and the Court rejected this contention. They saw well enough that if it were allowed the writ would be available to the Crown without limit. Coke said that this is a "legall courte, and this writ also is ancient, and legall." [56] The case, after elaborate argument, was eventually settled, so that the material scope and flexibility of the writ was not determined. But the preliminary decision definitely located the writ as existing within the common-law system, for in that judgment the Court claimed the power to determine whether the writ lay. This judicial control of the writ was undoubtedly a later-day development, since originally the writ was but one species of the mass of undifferentiated and plenary orders which the Council might issue to the courts. Originally obliged to accept the writ, the judges rationalized it into the common-law system; so much so that they might of their own motion take notice of the Crown's interest, as today our courts, without any pressure from the executive, will refuse to decide a "political question."

The Council dictated decisions, however, on a much broader, a much less clearly defined, front. For example, Elizabeth granted a monopoly of the trade to Spain. She gave the patentee power to punish interlopers. The Council wrote to the Queen's Bench and the Common Pleas, warning them not to issue out any habeas corpus in favor of one whom the patentee should choose to hold or punish.[57] Of particular interest to us is a litigation which indirectly

[54] Quoted in Moore, *Act of State* (1906), p. 18.

[55] The case of Arden *v.* Darcy given by Bacon in his argument, *op. cit.* (*supra*, note 50), VII, 719.

[56] 3 Bulstrode 33.

[57] Dasent, X, 37. Directions as to the decision were probably more frequent in the Admiralty Court. *Ibid.*, XIV, 238; XIX, 251. In one case the Admiralty was

involved the conduct of foreign affairs. An English merchant had committed acts of piracy against some Dutch merchants, had stolen their ship and their cargo, and thrown their sailors overboard. To save the Englishman from punishment by the United Netherlands, Elizabeth gave the Dutch merchants leave to seize the Englishman's ships. The Dutch merchants accordingly did. The Englishman brought an action of trover in the Queen's Bench and recovered. The Council wrote to the Lord Chief Justice, requesting that the suit go no further. "We doubt not but you and the rest will thincke our request reasonable and take order therein accordingly." [58]

There seems to be little doubt that the King's Council up to, and more particularly during, the time of the Tudors considered that the Prerogative, at least in the administration of justice, was plenary. Anything and everything was a matter of state, was a "political question" if the Council thought it so. That was the opinion of James I and of his apologist Lord Bacon. There was nothing particularly radical or unconstitutional in their claims. They could find precedent in the reigns of Henry VII, Henry VIII, and Elizabeth. But the Tudors had not drawn the bit too tight in the mouth. Nor had they talked so much about their rights. Bacon identified the King with the *salus populi*. He held that it was the duty of the judges to consult with "the King and State" whenever "there is matter of law intervenient in business of State. . . . For many times the things deduced to judgment may be *meum* and *tuum*, when the reason and consequence thereof may touch to point of estate: I call matter of estate not merely the parts of sovereignty, but whatsoever introduceth any great alteration or dangerous precedent, or concerneth manifestly any great portion of people."[59] The King, in his turn, was to consult the judges in matters of law. But as to who was to ride the horse there was no question. "Let judges also remember that Salomon's throne was supported by lions on both sides: let them be lions, but yet lions under the throne." [60]

Even more exalted are the words of James:

> Encroach not upon the prerogative of the Crown. If there falls out a question that concerns my prerogative or mystery of State, deal not with

instructed to retain money owing to French merchants until goods of English merchants held in Normandy were relinquished. *Ibid.*, XIV, 297.

[58] Dasent, XXVII, 31.

[59] Essay of Judicature, *Works* (Spedding's ed. 1878), VI, 509–510.

[60] *Ibid.*

it till you consult with the King or his Council, or both, for they are transcendent matters. . . . That which concerns the mystery of the King's power is not lawful to be disputed, for that is to wade into the weakness of princes and to take away the mystical reverence that belongs to them that sit in the throne of God.[61]

Lord Coke apparently did not appreciate the exhortation, and had to be cashiered from the bench. In 1636 Charles I asked his judges whether "when the good and safety of the kingdom in general is concerned and the whole kingdom in danger" he might compel his subjects to furnish him ships and also whether "the King is the sole judge both of the danger and when and how the same is to be prevented and avoided." The judges answered both questions in the affirmative.[62] This gave the Crown unlimited power in war or peace to declare the country to be in a dangerous state, and to take any steps it chose in its exercise of the Prerogative of defense, including, as in this case, taxation without the consent of the Commons. Parliament was quick to legislate this case and all its reasoning into limbo.[63] In the years since, this so-called Prerogative of defense has shrunk mightily. In times of peace, acts of the Crown deriving from the Prerogative of defense which are in contravention of common right must be justified on grounds of necessity and imminent danger. And the sufficiency of the showing is for the Court.[63a]

It is not quite as clear from the cases what the limits are in time of war. It is often and generally said that whether a given act is necessary as a measure of defense is for the executive to decide. Yet there are cases which show that the courts will, on occasion, control the exercise of this power. In *Brown* v. *United States*,[64] discussed

[61] Quoted in Moore, *op. cit.* (*supra*, note 54), p. 18.

[62] Case of Ship Money, 3 State Trials 826, 843 (1636).

[63] 17 Car. I. c. 14 (1641): "An act for the declaring unlawful and void the late proceedings touching ship-money, and for the vacating of all records and process concerning the same."

[63a] Sterling *v.* Constantin, 287 U. S. 378, 400 (1932).

[64] 8 Cranch 110 (1814). In Mitchell *v.* Harmony, 13 How. 115 (1851), the plaintiff, a military officer, arrested property belonging to an American citizen who was following the army in Mexico. He justified on the ground that he feared that it would otherwise fall into enemy hands. The Court held that there must be a reasonable belief that the danger is urgent, immediate, and impending, that being a question of fact for the court or jury. "It is not for the court to say what protection or indemnity is due from the public to an officer who, in his zeal for the honor and interest of his country, and in the excitement

above, the Court held that the executive could not in time of war confiscate alien property on land without the authorization of Congress. And it is doubtful that a merely formal claim of necessity would have changed the decision. It is very rare that during the course of a war the presumption in favor of the executive will fail. In an English case decided in 1915 (later referred to as the *Shoreham* case),[65] the war authorities sought to confiscate property for an aerodrome, offering compensation as of grace rather than as of right. Military men testified that the taking was necessary for defense. This opinion, said the Court, should be conclusive provided that the military was acting "reasonably and in good faith." And since this property was on the coast and the Court had been duly impressed with the fact that long-range guns made attack "imminent," it was easy to find that these conditions had been met. But in the *De Keyser's Hotel* case,[66] which reached them after the war, the House of Lords was unwilling to apply this decision to an attempt to expropriate a London hotel for war offices. Lord Sumner said:

> The statement that no court ought, in time of war, to require of the officers of the Crown proof (ex hypothesi public proof) of the reasons of State which had led them to hold that in a particular case a certain course should be taken, seems to me to be an obvious statement. It is not in conflict with what seems to me to be an equally obvious proposition — namely, that when the Court can see *from the character and circumstances of the requisition itself that the case cannot be one of imminent danger*, it is free to inquire whether the conditions, resting on necessity, which were held to exist in the *Shoreham Case*[67] are applicable to the case in hand.[68] (Italics mine.)

But these "equally obvious" propositions do seem to be in conflict. A case which on its face "cannot be one of imminent danger" may, for all of that, be a case of imminent danger, and the Crown would have to give reasons (possibly secret) why it was. The Court apparently wants to save for itself the power to overrule the executive in cases of flagrantly excessive use of the Prerogative, but is not frank enough to say so, nor to give us the reasons which would enable us to judge the value of their claim to the power.

of military operations, has trespassed upon private rights. That question belongs to the political department of the government" (per Taney, C. J., *id.* at 135).

[65] In re A Petition of Right (The Shoreham Case), [1915] 3 K. B. 649.

[66] [1920] A. C. 508.

[67] In re A Petition of Right, discussed *supra*, note 65 and text.

[68] [1920] A. C. at 565.

In *The Zamora*,[69] decided during the World War, the Privy Council considered whether the Government had the right to commandeer (with compensation) neutral property in the custody of the Prize Court before final adjudication and upon the posting of bond. The Court decided that such a right existed where the goods "were urgently required for use in connection with the defense of the realm," and that the judge "ought, as a rule, to treat the statement on oath of the proper officer of the crown" to that effect as conclusive. "Those who are responsible for the national security must be the sole judges of what the national security requires." [70] Yet the Court did lay down one limit on the Prerogative power. The claim of the Crown will be denied if the capture of the property at sea was without reasonable suspicion that the neutral was violating the law; otherwise, it would be open to the Crown to exercise eminent domain over all the seven seas as and when it wished. Thus, if on the preliminary hearing it appears that there is no issue to be tried, the vessel will be released to the neutral owner, despite the claim of the Crown.

With respect to that particularly drastic exercise of the Prerogative, the trial of civilians by military courts,[71] there has been something of an attempt to build up a criterion of necessity. In the famous Civil War litigation of *Ex parte Milligan*,[72] the Supreme Court required the executive to make an affirmative showing of necessity. The President had proclaimed that "during the existing insurrection, and *as a necessary means for suppressing the same*, all rebels and insurgents, their aiders and abettors within the United States . . . shall be subject to martial law, and liable to trial and punishment by courts martial or military commission." Milligan, a civilian and a citizen of Indiana, was tried before a military court for inciting insurrection and was sentenced to death. Milligan petitioned the Federal Court to issue a writ of habeas corpus. He based his petition on an act of Congress which provided that if any person were arrested for treason, and the grand jury should terminate its

[69] [1916] 2 A. C. 77.

[70] *Id.* at 107.

[71] Trial of civilians by military courts in time of war, rebellion, etc., is usually called "martial law," but Sir Frederick Pollock insists that the term is broader. "So-called 'martial law,' as distinct from military law, is an unlucky name for the justification by the common law of acts done by necessity for the defence of the Commonwealth when there is war within the realm. Such acts are not necessarily acts of personal force or constraint. They may be preventive as well as punitive." *What is Martial Law*, 18 Law Q. Rev. 152, 156 (1902).

[72] 4 Wall. 2 (1866).

session without returning an indictment against him, the judge of the court should order his release. The case came up to the Supreme Court after the termination of the War. The Court took judicial notice that the Federal Court in Indiana had been open for business during the entire War. But the Government contended that Indiana was the seat of a vast conspiracy of rebellion, and that it was only the presence of the military which enabled the courts to stay open.[73] Furthermore, the charges against Milligan laid the offense in Indiana, "a State within the military lines of the army of the United States, and the theatre of military operations, and which had been and was constantly threatened to be invaded by the enemy." The petitioner had not denied this. Would the Court, the Government asked, take judicial notice that these facts were not so?[74] But the Court did not care whether they were so or not. "Martial law cannot arise from a *threatened* invasion. The necessity must be actual and present; the invasion real, such as effectually closes the courts and deposes the civil administration."[75]

The right of jury trial "cannot be frittered away on any plea of state or political necessity."[76] And it is exactly in seasons of civil

[73] "If the court takes judicial notice that the courts were open, must it not also take judicial notice how, and by whose protection, and by whose permission they were so open? that they were open because the strong arm of the military upheld them; . . . if the soldiers of the United States, by their arms, had not held the State from intestine domestic foes within, and the attacks of traitors leagued with such without; had not kept the ten thousand rebel prisoners of war confined in the neighborhood from being released by these knights and men of the Order of the Sons of Liberty [an alleged rebel order in Indiana to which it was claimed Milligan belonged]; there would have been no courts in Indiana, no place in which the Circuit Judge of the United States could sit in peace to administer the law." Argument for the United States, *Id.* at 87. See also *Id.* at 17.

[74] *Id.* at 85.

[75] *Id.* at 127.

[76] *Id.* at 123. The majority held that Milligan's trial offended constitutional guarantees, and so implied that not even Congressional authorization of the military tribunal would in this case have been legal. The minority protested this limitation on the power of Congress. The courts might be open, they agreed, and yet be incompetent to avert threatened danger. Congress was the judge of this danger, and if it thought necessary could authorize military courts. Its failure to exercise the power indicated its belief that they were not necessary; indeed the provisions of the statute under which Milligan petitioned showed that Congress intended a civil trial. But the issue cannot thus be resolved as one of statutory construction, since the question was whether the public danger was not so great that the laws must be superseded. Furthermore, though the reasons given by the minority for Congressional power may be

commotion when passion runs high that the right is to be most zealously protected. In the *Jamaica* case, Lord Chief Justice Cockburn, in a charge to the grand jury, said that "there are considerations more important even than shortening the temporary duration of an insurrection. Among them are the eternal and immutable principles of justice — principles which can never be violated without lasting detriment to the true interest and well-being of a civilized community." [77] The effect of the *Milligan* case, then, is to throw upon the executive the burden of justifying martial law by showing "a controlling necessity."

The Judicial Committee of the Privy Council in *Ex parte Marais* [78] rejected this solution: ". . . Where actual war is raging, acts done by the military authorities are not justiciable by the ordinary tribunals," [79] and "the fact that for some purposes some tribunals had been permitted to pursue their ordinary course is not conclusive that war was not raging." The Boer War was being fought at the time, but from the report of the case it is impossible to

good, it is not clear why they are not applicable as well to the power claimed for the executive. Perhaps the argument would be that the power of Congress to declare war is more general than the power of the President as Commander-in-chief.

[77] Quoted by Counsel in Rex *v.* Allen, [1921] 2 I. R. 241, 253; and cf. J. S. Black *arguendo* in the Milligan case, 4 Wall. at 81: "A violation of law on pretence of saving such a government as ours is not self-preservation, but suicide."

[78] [1902] A. C. 109.

[79] *Id.* at 114. A number of writers hold that while "proceedings against military men . . . for acts done under so-called martial law" cannot be entertained during war, there may be post-bellum liability for excessive acts. Dicey, *Law of the Constitution* (8th ed. 1915), p. 546. Pollock, *loc. cit.* (*supra*, note 71) at 157: "The judgment in *Ex parte Marais* involves the further position that neither an application for summary release from extraordinary arrest nor an action for anything done as an extraordinary act of necessity will be entertained by the Ordinary Courts during the continuance of a state of war in the jurisdiction, when the Court is satisfied that a responsible officer acting in good faith is prepared to justify the act complained of." See also Cyril Dodd, *The Case of Marais*, 18 Law Q. Rev. 143, 148 (1902); Rex *v.* Allen, [1921] 2 I. R. 241, 269.

But Moore, *op. cit.* (*supra*, note 54), pp. 58–64, believes that there should be no difference between cases during and after war. If, for example, a sentence of death is illegal, it must not be executed though war is raging. But where, as in Ex parte Marais, the military authority claims to supersede the civil authority, no question, he says, arises as to the legality of a particular act; if the assumption of jurisdiction is justified by a state of war, the acts of the military tribunal cannot be questioned either during or after war, for under the circumstances "it is a system of authority with its own organs of justice." See also H. Erle Richards, *Martial Law*, 18 Law Q. Rev. 133, 140 (1902).

gather whether there was any fighting, disturbance, or even threat of invasion at the place of arrest and trial. The implication is that there was not. Does this mean that war was "raging" throughout the British Empire? Throughout the entire colony in some part of which there was fighting? The Privy Council apparently did not mean to deny that the court is itself to decide on the existence of war, but it must be confessed that the case gives no clue as to what order of ideas will be employed to make the decision.[80] Sir Frederick Pollock says: "There may be a state of war at any place where aid and comfort can be effectually given the enemy, having regard to the modern conditions of warfare and means of communication,"[81] which to us seems to be almost anywhere. Professor Moore suggests as a test: "Wherever the circumstances of the war have made the military authority predominant in fact so that all other organs are plainly subordinate to them."[82]

The Prerogative of defense thus still exists, and in its content is a formidable instrument. But formally, at least, the common law, amoeba-like, purports to have absorbed it completely within its system, and of course the common-law courts assume to define its limits. David Dudley Field, arguing in the *Milligan* case, said that "our system knows no authority beyond or above the law. We may therefore dismiss from our minds every thought of the President's having any prerogative as representative of the people, or as interpreter of the popular will."[83] "Much confusion of ideas has been produced by mistaking executive power for kingly power. Because in monarchial countries the kingly office includes the execu-

[80] In a recent Irish case, Rex *v.* Allen, [1921] 2 I. R. 241, growing out of the Civil War, the area in question was one in which rebellion was active, though due to its intermittent, guerilla character the courts were still functioning. The Court, upholding the death sentence of a military court, was careful to affirmatively set up the hostile character of the area in question.

[81] *Loc. cit.* (*supra*, note 71) at 157. H. Erle Richards seems also to go very far when he says that the commander should have the powers of martial law "in districts occupied by his troops." He pleads that many of the offenses are not against the ordinary law but against some rule which for military reasons the commander has found it necessary to enact. Quick action, special information are needed. The civil courts are inadequate. *Loc. cit.* (*supra*, note 79) at 138. But this simply means that whatever the military believes to be good to win a war, is *ipso facto* good for the country. This may be nearer the view that prevails in practice than we or the courts like to think.

[82] *Op. cit.* (*supra*, note 54), p. 63. This is more or less the test advanced by counsel for the United States in Ex parte Milligan and rejected by the Court.

[83] 4 Wall. at 30.

tive, it seems to have been sometimes inferred that conversely the executive carries with it the kingly prerogative. Our executive is in no sense a king, even for four years." [84] But in England, too, at least lawyers and courts would probably insist that all the powers of the executive were included within the common law, and were no greater for being identified with the royal Prerogative. Lord Camden in *Entick* v. *Carrington* says that "with respect to the argument of State necessity or a distinction that has been arrived at between State offences and others, the common law does not understand that kind of reasoning, nor do our books take notice of any such distinction." [85]

We set out to investigate the problem: when is a question "political"; when is litigation or a question of fact not to be decided by the courts? And we received the answer: the Constitution will tell us. We found that this was only a partial explanation; that often it was merely a formal method of stating results. And now we have turned up another answer: the common law will tell us. The law is supreme. It governs ruler and ruled alike. But the important point about this explanation, however much lawyers labor to conceal it, is that the common law means the courts. To speak of the common law as itself giving us the answer leads to somewhat the same fallacies as the argument from the Constitution. We are given the idea of a fixed body of principles from which deductions are constant. Such and such a question is said to be "political" as if it were "political" in the nature of things, always was, and always will be. But when we perceive that the real kernel of this explanation lies in the fact that the courts announce the law, so that in effect it is not the law but the courts which are supreme, we have a theory which is at once more plausible and more concrete, however much we may doubt its truth. We are brought face to face, not with an improbable body of self-generating principles, but with a living, a functioning organization, which can and continually does give answers. Is the common law supreme? It decides, for example, that the Crown has the power and the right to declare war. It may give reasons showing that this should be so; and that, therefore, for these reasons, it is so. But, of course, normally it has no choice in the matter, no effective choice, that is, since its decision to the contrary would be successfully ignored. The supremacy of the law,

[84] *Id.* at 32.

[85] 19 State Trials 1030 (1765). Quoted by Moore, *op. cit.* (*supra*, note 54), p. 22.

like the supremacy of the Constitution, is a formal generalization, though it is without doubt a conception of immense importance.

The relation between the judiciary and the executive is too complicated, too variable, too subtle to find adequate expression in these formulas. Too often we make the mistake of thinking of the courts and the executive as if they always had been and always would be essentially the same thing. Continuity of terminology conceals important changes. We saw that at one time the courts were mere appendages of the King. They were what has been called "thought organizations." [86] They advised the King, who was a "will organization." Gradually the pressure of business, the values of specialization, set them off. They, too, became will organizations, but still subject to executive supervision in any fashion that the executive saw fit. But the courts, as is natural in persons endowed with will, sought "to find themselves": to secure their autonomy. It would appear that in the fifteenth century the judges were powerful; "the class legislation of Parliament was defeated by the national legislation of the judges." [87] Subsequently, however, the Tudors subjected the courts once more to active supervision. The Council became an administrative organization of unlimited jurisdiction, which dealt *ad hoc* with private and public controversies, which interfered freely in pending lawsuits. Today this would be considered a deplorable usurpation. Such matters, we would say, are for the court. But to sample the cases in which the Council had to interfere is to become convinced that the courts were simply not doing their work properly. Their process was tortuously slow and ruinously expensive. Their law was obsolete. And apparently they had no flexibility, no conception of themselves as one of the organs of government, and hence no vision. They no longer deserved their autonomy; they lost it because they were not good enough to keep it.[88]

Of the Council (Star Chamber) it has been said that "it was . . . admirably calculated to be the support of order against anarchy, or of despotism against individual liberty. During the Tudor period,

[86] Wallas, *The Great Society* (1914).

[87] Scrutton, *The Land in Fetters* (1886), p. 76. Quoted in Pollard, *op. cit.* (*supra*, note 36), p. 252. Pollard gives other instances of the influence and independence of the judges. "Statutes, indeed, were still regarded as measures to give effect to the law as interpreted by the judges."

[88] Cf. *ibid.*, p. 245.

it appeared in the former light; under the Stuart, in the latter." [89] It is not that the activities of the Council in Stuart times were so very different than in Tudor times, but that the great work of establishing order had been done.[90] Star Chamber procedures grew more irksome as they became less necessary.

> The change [says Professor Holdsworth] from the feudal monarchy of the Middle Ages to the territorial state of the present day left the extent of all kinds of political authority very obscure. The Tudors made use of this obscurity to assume the powers which they considered necessary for the maintenance of the peace. The Stuarts assumed similar powers, but not so much with the bona fide desire to keep the peace as in pursuance of their design to make themselves absolute kings.[91]

We emphasize this point because it shows how a particular branch of government may vary in its use and its usefulness, depending on the need of the epoch and the spirit of the men who control it.[92]

Under the Tudors, the common-law courts had given ground to the Council, and the newer prerogative Courts of Chancery, Admiralty, Star Chamber, and Requests. Yet they, in common with all central institutions, profited by the strengthening of central government. Under Coke, they were ready to undertake a new rôle. The popular cause was personal liberty, and Coke laid it down that the common law was the bulwark of personal liberty, that it was prepared to defend it even against the Crown. This proposition involved not only the autonomy of the courts, their power to decide cases free from interference, but in some instances their supremacy, their power to control the Crown when it overstepped

[89] Prothero in *Encyclopedia Britannica* (1910–11), xxv, 796. Quoted by Baldwin, *op. cit.* (*supra*, note 36), p. 306.

[90] "The establishment and maintenance of internal peace and effective government was the lasting work of the Tudor dynasty. . . . Its honesty and impartiality, its tact and skill, earned for it the gratitude of thinking and law-abiding citizens, and go far to explain why the nation as a whole acquiesced in the large powers it assumed in other directions." Holdsworth, IV, 80. See also *ibid.*, p. 106.

[91] *Martial Law Historically Considered*, 18 Law Q. Rev. 117, 123 (1902). During the Lancastrian regime the council was an instrument of the nobility, and was used to exploit the power of the Crown for their profit. Its criminal jurisdiction (so often directed against the great lords) was allowed to lapse. Baldwin, *op. cit.* (*supra*, note 36), pp. 421, 428–429.

[92] "In respect of the work accomplished, the council was always a power most vital to the history of England. Free from the usual trend of constitutionality, of the common law and formalism, it was also industrious, persistent and watchful. . . . In relation to the courts of common law the council was a constant recourse in solving points of difficulty; it gave advice and issued orders

certain bounds. These ideas were, of course, grounded by Coke in precedents immemorial. But in all except words and as programs for action, they were new. They did not prevail under him; but they rode in on the crest of the Revolution of 1688.

Since that time the executive has never given orders to the courts, and courts frequently do give orders to the executive. We can see to what limits this development has gone when Chief Justice Marshall can write that a question of policy is not a matter for the executive since it is a "department which can pursue only the law as it is written;" [93] the executive, in that case, was not acting contrary to any express legislation. It sought in time of war to confiscate enemy property, and the Court told the executive that international ethics were against the practice, and, as a consequence, that it must not act without express authorization from Congress. And toward the end of the century the courts began to tell Congress itself what it could and could not do.

In the present century, the courts still had the power and the will to govern, but not the vision. Too often their credo of liberty has meant the exaltation of the arrogance of property and privilege. And in many other things they have failed, perhaps inevitably, to meet the challenge of change. The regulation of important private and governmental services has fallen into the hands of executive organizations. The present era has come to bear certain resemblances to the Councilar government of the Tudors, though comparatively the courts have lost very little ground.

The courts then, just as other political institutions, are subject to growth, to atrophy, and to decay of function. Many functions which the courts perform at one moment of history may be performed by the executive (or the legislature) in another. A court may label an issue "political," and so refuse to decide it because of any one of a number of reasons: it believes that the Constitution or the laws expressly or by reasonable implication forbid; it has no machinery to decide the matter itself; the executive has better machinery; it is afraid that its decision will have unfortunate consequences; it knows or fears or is unwilling to take the chance that its decision will be ignored. Any of these factors may vary with re-

that were necessary to assist the ordinary legal processes. Above all, in cases of the utmost difficulty and danger the council was the one court capable of meeting the emergency, and during one period of history, one may fairly claim, was instrumental in saving the kingdom from utter destruction." Baldwin, *op. cit.* (*supra*, note 36), p. 463.

[93] Brown *v.* United States, 8 Cranch 110, 128–129 (1814).

spect to any given matter. They may vary not only with changes in the structure and procedure of the organizations concerned, but with the needs of the time, and with the vision, the awareness, and the courage of those who control the organization.[94]

The administration of justice by the common-law courts is not then necessarily and at all times the best or the most to be preferred. What we are seeking is an organization which is trained in the technique of impartial judgment (or, as W. A. Robson would say, possessed of the "judicial spirit"), and which has a frame of desirable values, objectives, biases, prejudices, or what you will, within which that technique may be worked. Robson is of the opinion that the advance of civilization is predicated on the conquest by the judicial temper of those fields of activity in which social judgments must be made.

> No single change in the life of the world [he says] is needed more urgently or would bring about a greater improvement than that mankind should exhibit a more judicial frame of mind in certain departments of life. All our efforts at securing international peace by means of an organization which shall prevent civilization being once again turned into a wilderness of internecine strife; all our attempts at producing industrial agreement by some method less inevitably impoverishing than the long-protracted economic conflict which now casts a blight over our productive capacity; . . . all such efforts as these may be reduced to a single plea that men and women should act in a more judicial spirit. . . .
>
> . . . We are inclined to go so far as to suggest, indeed, that the whole modern conception of economic and social democracy involves the exercise of discretions which shall be "judicial" in that they are not to depend on individual caprice and shall be free from personal favor and individual self-interest. . . .[95]

Going on to define the "judicial frame of mind," Robson remarks that

> the administration of justice was the first activity in which it became essential to obtain the kind of impartiality which is based on a suppression of

[94] "The general principle contended for by Bacon, of a fundamental distinction in law between matters of state and government, the *jus publicum*, on the one hand, and matters of *meum* and *tuum*, the *jus privatum*, on the other, is one which the English system rejected. What is matter of state and government, what is public or private, what concerns the welfare of the community and what the rights of individuals varies from age to age. It has its place in the sphere of political wisdom or of constitutional propriety. It is essentially a political question and one which should not lightly be put in legal fetters." Moore, *Executive Commissions of Enquiry*, 13 Col. L. Rev. 500, 520 (1913).

[95] Robson, *Justice and Administrative Law* (1928), p. 38.

personal emotion, and a willingness to suspend judgment until a systematic exploration of the ground has been made; but the psychological processes involved have spread with the rise of civilization from one field to another. The "artificial" methods of thought employed by all who have to make sound judgments, whether in courts of law or in laboratories or on wholesale produce markets, or elsewhere, are rooted in a desire to attain the impersonality which is a necessary accompaniment of the judicial spirit.[96]

Fully as important as a judicial frame of mind, in fact the very condition of its operation, is a set of values, a sense of direction. Impartiality in the cosmic sense of regarding as equally valuable every claim that ever has been or will be made is as non-existent as it would be useless. Impartiality, in essence, is judgment which has its being in none but the relevant facts, but it is just as vital to the process of making desirable social adjustments that *all* the relevant facts be considered. A judge (using the word in its broadest sense) cannot do his work without standards of preference. In many instances these will be determined for him by authority, but where authority fails to cover the case he will adopt (or intuitively absorb) standards which are held by the social group which it is his duty to represent, or, perhaps, by its "better" or its dominant elements. But further than this,

> It is not enough [to quote Mr. Robson again] for the judge merely to endeavor to discover and follow the deeper and more permanent loyalties of the community. He must also seek to promote the progressive evolution of society, to manifest what Judge Learned Hand calls "the half-framed purposes of his time." . . . Stress is always laid on the duty of a judge to be a trustee of the past, but in reality it is far more important that he should be a prophet of the future, in so far as that is compatible with the faithful administration of the existing body of law.[97]

Since "the half-framed purposes" of the time are never much more than conjecture, this must mean that the judge will draw upon his own convictions or those of a minority with whom he agrees. In such cases, whether his work be prophecy or creation will be a poser for the metaphysician.

These ideas find embodiment in the history of our common-law courts. Their reputation for impartiality is high. Indeed it may, perhaps, be said that the judicial spirit abides, among our governmental organizations, most consistently and to the largest degree in our courts. That, at least, is their reputation, and that, in part, is the basis for whatever claims of competence we make for them here.

[96] *Ibid.*, p. 213.

[97] *Ibid.*, p. 244.

But their greatest triumphs have needed more than this. Coke and the lawyers of the Revolution had an impassioned prejudice against prerogative government; they placed an exalted value on individual freedom from governmental interference. They seized upon the machinery and the processes of the courts to further their purposes.

The courts did not succeed alone, but with the help of Parliament they eventually set substantial "legal" limits in a field which was once unrestrictedly "political." It fell out in later years that in a number of fields their machinery for gathering facts was too crude; their idea of what facts were relevant too narrow and uninspired. These matters were taken from them and placed in the hands of the executive, but, even so, not the undifferentiated "political" executive but so-called administrative boards, boards which were intended to act "judicially." The conquest of the field by the "judicial spirit" was thus not lost; if anything, it received a needed reinvigoration by the infusion of purposes and perspectives more responsive to current and future demands. In fact, this transference and re-transference of function from one to another department of government is one of the modes of our continuous search, to use William James' phrase, for "the more inclusive order."

There is a vital need, a splendid opportunity, for the conquest of international politics by the judicial temperament. The arbitration tribunals, the Permanent Court, the League of Nations, the recent consultative pacts, are, of course, tangible responses. But there are numerous intra-national decisions which bear on the peaceful ordering of the international community. Some of them come before our courts, one of the most important of which is the chief subject under discussion: the effects of non-recognition. But in this preliminary survey of "political" questions we shall discuss others. In no other field are the courts so quick to shy from an issue as when it touches upon the international order — or, more specifically, on the conduct of foreign affairs. And this attitude, sometimes unreasoning, has been carried very far in the recognition cases. It is, no doubt, closely bound up with the overpowering prestige of the doctrine of sovereignty which, in our next chapter, we shall consider in its relation to the theory of recognition. We believe that the courts should retreat from this position; that purposefully, wilfully, intentionally, they should inquire whether the application of their technique to a given type of issue would not in the long run give valuable results. There are limited regions where the courts may bring into the domain of international law and politics a fresher, broader point of view, one freed from the professional predilections and limitations of the foreign office, one that will anticipate and so build up the social values of the future.

We do not purpose that the courts should annex the foreign office. Usually the issue touching on foreign affairs will be involved only incidentally in a litigation in which the court is ultimately responsible for the judgment. In such case it is a matter of increasing what we have called the autonomy of the court. Only rarely will there be an issue of direct interference with the executive, of "the supremacy of the law." But in neither sort of case do we hold a brief for unthinking intermeddling, or even for indirectly weakening an avowed executive policy without a reasonable hope of advantage. An examination of some of the cases does show, indeed, that the courts have not always and in all matters rigidly excluded themselves from the considerations of issues bearing on foreign affairs. These cases will show us what we already found in our general consideration of political questions: that a formulistic résumé will not succeed. The Constitution grants to Congress, the Senate, and, above all, to the President, powers which are the keys to the conduct of foreign affairs. Yet it will be found impossible — and undesirable — to argue that the judiciary is thereby incompetent to decide any question which might arise for decision in the exercise of the various powers over foreign affairs. The field of incompetence is extensive, but it is too often and too easily exaggerated.

It is the proud boast of our courts that they administer the law of nations as part of the law of the land, and surely it cannot be denied that many of the rules of international law are being worked out and applied in the courts. This alone establishes the court as an organ of international relations. It is true that most of the litigation in which the rules are applied is between private parties. But decisions adjudicating the rights of a national of a foreign state may involve the rights of the state itself, so that an unfair or mistaken decision may directly affect foreign relations.

There is considerable debate over the claim of the courts that they administer international law. It is argued that international law has no force in the courts as such; that it is only a "source" of law, effective as and when the courts incorporate it into the system of municipal law.[98] The argument is not very pertinent here, since

[98] "The true view would seem to be that so far from International Law being in any sense whatever a part of the Common Law of England it is merely a

the important thing is that the courts do apply rules of international law and do settle controversies which may have repercussions on our relations with other countries. A French commentator, seeking to establish the complete subserviency of the courts to the foreign office, minimizes the rôle of municipal courts as organs of international law: "In truth," he says, "customary international law is utilized by the national courts only to complete national legislation when it is silent, or to interpret it when it is obscure." [99] Of this statement we would say, first, that it is misleading. The national legislation is nearly always silent about matters which the nations normally regard as governed by a universal code, whether they arise in a court or a foreign office. The legislature, just as the court, feels that this code is not made by its will, nor is it alterable by its will. It is this feeling, by the way, which constitutes a partial answer to the proposition that international law is merely a "source" of municipal law. But in the second place, if Noël-Henry means no more than that the court is bound to follow the legislature if it changes the rule of international law, then this — though an occasional writer holds otherwise [100] — is merely a

source of law, and that this fundamental confusion between cause and effect has initiated the whole controversy." Picciotto, *The Relation of International Law to the Law of England and the United States* (1915), p. 105. And Professor Dickinson has lately stated much the same view in *Changing Concepts and the Doctrine of Incorporation*, 26 A. J. 239, 260 (1932).

Cf. Quincy Wright, *Conflicts of International Law with National Law and Ordinances*, 11 A. J. 1, 2 (1917). "The question whether international law is a part of municipal law, remains . . . a question of point of view and definition.

"Define international . . . and municipal law from the standpoint of the authorities which can repeal or amend their respective rules, and hence in a certain sense have commanded them, and they have nothing in common. Define them from the standpoint of the actual sources used in administering the two branches of the law, and they overlap."

[99] Noël-Henry, p. 74: "A la vérité, le droit international coutumier n'est utilisé par les tribunaux nationaux qu'en vue de compléter la législation nationale, lorsqu'elle est muette, ou de l'interpréter lorsqu'elle est obscure. . . ."

[100] The Belgian Prize Court has stated in The Agiena, Moniteur Belge 405 (1920), that it is not bound by national law where it conflicts with international law. 16 A. J. 117 (1922). Lord Stowell was reluctant to follow statutes contrary to international law, and only did so when he could not possibly "interpret" or avoid them. See The Recovery, 6 C. Rob. 341 (1807), and *infra*, note 105. In The Zamora, [1916] 2 A. C. 77, 93, Lord Parker says: "A British Prize Court would certainly be bound by Acts of the Imperial Legislature. But it is none the less true that if the Imperial Legislature passed an Act the provisions of which were inconsistent with the law of nations, the Prize Court in giving effect

truism.[101] The conflict is on a different plane. It is between the foreign relations power (executive or executive plus Senate) and the judiciary. How far will executive "acts of state," executive claim of prior or paramount jurisdiction, executive exercise of the residual prerogative ordinance power, postpone or supersede the application of international law?

International Law in the Prize Courts

This question has been peculiarly acute in the Prize Court. In language of assurance and some audacity, Lord Stowell (then Sir William Scott) said in *The Maria* [102] that he considered himself

> . . . as stationed here [in the Prize Court] not to deliver occasional and shifting opinions to serve present purposes of particular national interest, but to administer with indifference that justice which the law of nations holds out, without distinction to independent states, some happening to be neutral and some to be belligerent. The seat of judicial authority is, indeed, locally *here*, in the belligerent country according to the known law and practice of nations, but the law itself has no locality.[103]

Lord Stowell apparently had qualms over his own boldness. In *The Fox* [104] he stated that the King in Council had legislative powers over the Prize Court. When confronted with his own pronouncement that prize courts "do not deliver occasional and shifting opinions to serve present purposes of particular national interest" but administer the law of nations, he replied that such Orders in Council would declare international law to the courts and that "its own [the Court's] observation and experience attest the general conformity of such orders and instructions to its principles of unwritten law." [105]

to such provisions would no longer be administering international law. It would in the field covered by such provisions be deprived of its proper function as a Prize Court."

Potter, *International Law and National Law in the United States*, 19 A. J. 315, 318–320 (1925), takes the view that the American decisions giving paramount effect to later legislation over earlier treaties are unsound.

[101] Picciotto, *op. cit.* (*supra*, note 98), chap. III; Wright, *loc. cit.* (*supra*, note 98) at 9.

[102] 1 C. Rob. 340 (1799).

[103] *Id.* at 349.

[104] Edw. Ad. 311 (1811). This case concerned the Orders in Council retaliating for Napoleon's blockades. Stowell refused to pass on the propriety of the measures or whether they should no longer be applied by reason of Napoleon's retraction. All these questions, he said, were for the Council.

[105] *Id.* at 314. In all fairness, it should be said that within the frame he

This synthesis, so reminiscent of the device of the schools both of the natural law and the historical jurists of reconciling the ideally or historically valid law with positive law, whatever it might be,[106] was rejected by the Privy Council in the remarkable case of *The Zamora*.[107] The Court quoted *The Maria* with approval; the dictum in *The Fox* it found inconsistent and unacceptable.

In all these cases there is much talk as to whether the Prize Court administers international law or municipal law, and the arguments proceed as if this were the crux of the matter. This logomachy is

allowed himself, Lord Stowell administered the law with considerable independence and impartiality. In his rulings on the blockade, for example, he demanded from the British naval authorities that they take all the measures necessary to establishing a real, as distinguished from a fictitious, blockade. See The Betsey, 1 C. Rob. 93 (1798); The Henrick and Maria, 1 C. Rob. 146 (1799). The Success, 1 Dod. 131, 134 (1812). And see his liberal interpretation of one of the Reprisal Orders in Council of 1807 in The Lucy, Edw. Ad. 122 (1809).

In The Stert, 4 C. Rob. 65 (1801), Lord Stowell held that a blockade could not be imposed on neutral ports even though these ports were available to the enemy by transhipment over land. He admitted that this might partially defeat the blockade, but held that under the existing legal limits of blockade the result was unavoidable. This was followed in The Peterhoff, 5 Wall. 28 (1866), where the Court said: "We administer the public law of nations, and are not at liberty to inquire what is for the particular advantage of our own or another country." *Id.* at 57. The previously existing legal limitations on blockades were almost entirely ignored during the World War. See Colombos, *The Law of Prize* (1926), §§ 215–219.

Indeed, Lord Stowell refused to apply statutes phrased in general terms to aliens, where to do so would violate international law, holding that a prize court is a court of international law, and so must not apply municipal law. The Recovery, 6 C. Rob. 341 (1807) (violation of navigation laws by alien ships does not make good prize).

106 See The Kim, 3 Lloyds Prize Cases 167, 223 (1915), where Sir Samuel Evans, the President, said ironically that "Lord Stowell's view, apparently, as far as I have been able to gather, can be pretty shortly stated as this: If an Order in Council was clearly in violation of international law it would not bind the Prize Court but it is inconceivable that any Order in Council made in this country would be inconsistent, and, therefore, the Prize Court will obey every Order in Council."

But Holdsworth, I, 567, n. 1, says that Lord Stowell's position was not inconsistent; that in The Maria, where he said that the Court applied international law, he had under consideration a case where there was no Order in Council and his remarks were intended for such a situation.

Picciotto, *op. cit.* (*supra*, note 98), p. 36, believes that Stowell did not make his presumption of the legality of the Order in Council irrebuttable, and would have ignored it — and even an act of Parliament — in an extreme case.

107 [1916] 2 A. C. 77.

illusory. Both Lord Stowell in *The Fox* and Lord Parker in *The Zamora* insisted that the Prize Court administers international law, yet arrived at opposite results. Lord Stowell considered it his duty to apply international law as it was understood by the King in Council; Lord Parker, as he himself understood it. Otherwise, argued Lord Parker, we are executing not international law but the will of the King, a proposition which rests on the assumption — quite natural for a lawyer — that only a court can expound "the law."

Equally two-faced are the arguments derived from the separation of powers. "Prior to the Naval Prize Act, 1864, jurisdiction in matters of prize was exercised by the High Court of Admiralty, by virtue of a commission issued by the Crown under the Great Seal at the commencement of each war." [108] If the Crown failed to issue the commission, there was no court in the land which could question the acts of its navy or its commissioned ships. Is not the Prize Court, then, a tribunal of departmental discipline to make sure that public ships do not violate the orders of the King in Council? This was the effect of Stowell's dictum, but to state it thus baldly was repugnant to his sense of the dignity of the Court. Apparently both the French and the Germans regard a prize court as "administrative," and its business merely to see that the orders of the War Department are properly executed.[109]

In *The Zamora* the Court, adopting a different premise, was able to reach the opposite result.

> The idea that the King in Council, or indeed any branch of the Executive, has power to prescribe or alter the law to be administered by Courts of law in this country is out of harmony with the principles of our Constitution.[110]

All courts, Lord Parker argued, originated in the exercise of the Prerogative. There was no reason to distinguish between the Prize Court and other courts. It is true that the force of this argument was considerably invigorated by the Naval Prize Act of 1864.[111] Under that act, the High Court of Admiralty has *ipso facto* prize jurisdiction. It no longer depends for its existence on the Crown. In the United States the prize jurisdiction is presumably part of the constitutional competence of the Federal courts.[112]

[108] *Id.* at 90.

[109] See Garner, *Prize Law During the World War* (1927), §§ 3, 133–136.

[110] [1916] 2 A. C. 77, 90.

[111] 27 and 28 Vict. c. 25.

[112] See Glass *v.* The Betsey, 3 Dall. 6, 16 (1794). "The Judges being de-

But the core of the problem is whether the Prize Court can pass on the validity of acts authorized by orders of the King in Council, highest organ of defense and foreign affairs. It by no means follows that because it is a true court not amenable to executive dictation, it can or should question the acts of the executive. The solution lies in the nature of the Court's function. The Prize Court is an instrument of the international legal order; there is nothing quixotic or altruistic in this function. National well-being and security are dependent on it; it is of utmost importance in time of war to maintain friendly relations with neutrals, and to assure them that their shipping is not being seized illegally. This work might be done by the foreign office. But a court is in certain respects superior to attain the desired ends. And the Court in *The Zamora* considered that its usefulness would be far greater if it could go behind the Orders in Council when it pleased.[113] Lord Parker, speaking for the Court, stated its position as follows:

It follows that but for the existence of Courts of Prize no one aggrieved by the acts of a belligerent Power in times of war could obtain redress

cidedly of opinion, that every District Court in the United States, possesses all the powers of a court of Admiralty, whether considered as an instance, or as a prize court. . . ." See Sayre, *Cases on Admiralty* (1929), p. 29 n.

[113] The matter never seems to have arisen in our courts as pointedly as in The Zamora. In The Paquete Habana, 175 U. S. 677 (1900), discussed above, the Court, sitting as a prize tribunal, declared its duty to apply international law to captures by the navy. However, there was an intimation of a different result if the capture had been authorized by the President. But since the legality of the prize in this case was said to turn on a question of military necessity, the Court may have meant merely that the President alone could judge of that in such a way as to foreclose the Court. Cf. also MacLeod *v.* United States, stated *supra*, note 27.

In Jennings *v.* Carson's Executors, 1 Pet. Adm. 1, 4n (D. Pa. 1792), it is said: "Its [the Prize Court's] proceedings are generally according to the law of nations; though in particular instances it is governed by local orders and occasional interference of the executive authority, of disputable character, as they respect the laws of nations."

In Maisonnaire *v.* Keating, 2 Gall. 325, 334 (C. C. Mass.), Story, J., remarked that "if, for instance, the sovereign should by a special order, authorize the capture of neutral property for a cause manifestly unfounded in the law of nations, there can be no doubt that it would afford a complete justification of the captors in all tribunals of prize." But Story was not referring here to the effect of executive orders in courts of the United States — in any case, is the executive equivalent to "the Sovereign"? — but to the point that neutral courts cannot sit in judgment on a condemnation of a prize court in a belligerent otherwise than through diplomatic channels and at the risk of disturbing international amity. An appropriate remedy is, however, provided by the fact that, according to international law, every belligerent Power must appoint and submit to the jurisdiction of a Prize Court to which any person aggrieved by its acts has access, and which administers international as opposed to municipal law — a law which is theoretically the same, whether the Court which administers it is constituted under the municipal law of the belligerent Power or of the Sovereign of the person aggrieved, and is equally binding on both parties to the litigation. It has long been well settled by diplomatic usage that, in view of the remedy thus afforded, a neutral aggrieved by any act of a belligerent Power cognizable in a Court of Prize ought, before resorting to a diplomatic intervention, to exhaust his remedies in the Prize Courts of the belligerent Power. A case for such intervention arises only if the decisions of those Courts are such as to amount to a gross miscarriage of justice. It is obvious, however, that the reason for this rule of diplomacy would entirely vanish if a Court of Prize, while nominally administering a law of international obligation, were in reality acting under the direction of the Executive of the belligerent Power.[114]

Marshall, writing to District Judge Peters, congratulating him on publishing his admiralty decisions, said:

If a great system of public law is ever to prevail on the ocean, it must, in analogy to the municipal system, result from decisions and reasonings, appealing through the press to the common judgment of the civilized world. Heretofore, admiralty proceedings have been concluded with too little publicity, and without disclosing the privileges on which they were founded. Naturally, they have been substituting for principles the capricious mandates of power and of belligerent policy. . . .[115]

Normally with the conduct of a war and of foreign affairs it is unwise to interfere. But here the continuum of international law

country, though the court has acted under executive ordinances contrary to international law.

Quincy Wright points out that the Federal courts in the time of the Civil War developed the doctrine of "continuous voyage" — at a time when it was disputed — in conformity with a current naval instruction authorizing seizure of ships and goods bound for insurgent ports either directly or "indirectly by transhipment." *Loc. cit.* (*supra*, note 98) at 16, n. 45. The Supreme Court, however, in the leading cases on the point, The Bermuda, 3 Wall. 514 (1865), The Springbok, 5 Wall. 1 (1866), did not mention the naval instruction. District Judge Betts in The Hart, Blatch. P. C. 387 (S. D. N. Y. 1863), mentioned it in passing as being in conformity with established international law, and the American view was subsequently sustained in arbitrations covering these cases. Moore, VII, 725; Moore, *International Arbitrations* (1898), IV, 3928–3935. See also The Peterhoff, discussed *supra*, note 105.

114 [1916] 2 A. C. 77, 92.

115 Quoted in Warren, II, 28.

and order, with the court the eventual referee of the system, is conceived to outweigh the value of unbridled executive action. There is nothing rigorous or uncompromising about the balance thus achieved. The court, no doubt, will think long before finding an Order in Council invalid, more particularly where it is alleged to be vital to proper defense; and at any time Parliament may reweight the scales, though its action may be less narrowly opportunistic than that of the Council, which may seize on any course which promises a gain, however temporary.

The Prize Court is a significant example of that process of change, action and reaction, progression and recession, which characterizes the relations between executive and judiciary. It illustrates so many of the typical tendencies and variations which have been pointed out as incident to the process. The origin of the prize jurisdiction seems to have been due in part to the breakdown of the common-law courts in dealing with illegal prize "piracy." [116] In more than one case the jury declared that the offense was not committed in their county and that they knew nothing of the matter or of the accused. The ordinary courts proving useless, the King and Council, before whom these foreign spoil cases usually came in the first instance, began early in the fourteenth century to appoint commissioners or arbitrators to deal with each case as it arose.[117] Jurisdiction over prize was conferred also on the Admiral, but for two centuries it was seldom used. Many of the important cases were dealt with directly by the King in Council. Cases of illegal prize were increasingly a matter of political importance, since they usually involved breaches of treaties or truces.[118] But even after the High Court of Admiralty was set up in the sixteenth century, it was subject to prerogative control in the exercise of the prize jurisdiction.

As a matter of history [says Holdsworth] it is certainly the fact that from the earliest times royal proclamations, Orders in Council, and treaties have played at best as great a part in shaping prize law as the decisions of the courts or statutes. As a matter of law it is obvious that the ascertain-

[116] Marsden, *Early Prize Jurisdiction and Prize Law in England*, 24 Eng. Hist. Rev. 675, 679 (1909).

And Holdsworth (I, 544) notes that the Admiral was given a disciplinary jurisdiction over the fleet in his command "owing to the diplomatic difficulties in which the King found himself involved, from the want of some efficient authority to coerce the marauding and piratical propensities of his subjects."

[117] Marsden, *loc. cit.* (*supra*, note 116).

[118] *Id.* at 681. And cf. Holdsworth as quoted *supra*, note 116.

ment of the contents of those rules of international law which have not been incorporated with the common law is intimately bound up with the prerogative of the Crown in relation to foreign affairs.[119]

This being the historic background of the Prize Court, *The Zamora* might well have been differently decided. But the common-law courts had had the same history, and they had outgrown it. Powerful impulses and purposes such as Coke had imparted to the courts augmented the driving force of the urge — more or less normal in will-organizations — to autonomy. But how is it that a question which for other courts had been settled for hundreds of years still remained open in 1917 for the Prize Court? For one thing, its jurisdiction was until 1864 dependent upon a special commission from the Crown at the beginning of each war. It functioned spasmodically. Such an organization could not be as full with the sense of itself as the normal courts. The tendency to autonomy was thus weaker. It comes into being in times of war to deal with the conduct of war, when even the strongest of the courts hesitate to interfere with Prerogative. But consider, too, that the common-law courts had to do with the personal liberty of the subject, whereas the Prize Court dealt with neutrals and enemies, "foreigners." The lag in the Prize Court is perhaps a measure, however crude, of the slow growth of any felt need for the strengthening and preservation of the international order. Only gradually has the ideal of international justice come to have even a small part of the power to drive men's minds which for hundreds of years has been immanent in the issue of personal liberty. We have suggested that strong belief in a cause is often necessary to induce a court to overcome executive resistance, to create in the court a conviction that its processes — which it believes, of course, to be superior in "judiciousness" and impartiality — should be introduced into a field formerly controlled by the executive.

The Zamora may be an indication of at least the beginning of such a conviction with regard to the Prize Court.[120] We say that it

[119] Holdsworth, I, 567.

[120] To be sure, Lord Stowell had a very strong sense of the international "values" which it was the business of the Prize Court to further and maintain. See note 105, *supra*. And so did Lord Mansfield before him. See his judgment in Lindo *v.* Rodney, 2 Doug. 612, 616 (1782), where he says:

"By the law of nations, and treaties, every nation is answerable to the other for all injuries done, by sea or land, or in fresh waters, or in port. Mutual convenience, eternal principles of justice, the wisest regulations of policy, and the

may be because, despite the rather uncritical praise [121] which has been lavished upon the decision, there are a number of factors which should put us on guard against an easy enthusiasm. In the first place, the effect of the decision itself was a compromise. The Court held that an Order in Council making property in custody of the Prize Court liable to requisition had no warrant in international law and was not binding on the Court. But if the goods were necessary to the defense of the realm the requisition would be honored, and on the issue of necessity the statement of the Crown was conclusive. Now at the time of this decision neutrals were complaining bitterly to the British Foreign Office of the treatment of their shipping. "In reply to the advice of the Foreign Office that their complaints should be taken to the Prize Court, they said in effect: 'What is the use of our going to a Court which is under the control of the Government?'" [122] The Judicial Committee of the Privy Council, highest tribunal of prize, were, of course, well aware of this. And in considering *The Zamora* we must not forget the incentive that there was to provide the Government with an answer to these criticisms, and yet not hinder any very important governmental policy. Subsequent to *The Zamora*, there were one or two occasions on which the Court declared that it was not bound by pertinent Orders in Council, but only to arrive at the same result, or even a more stringent one, than that indicated by the Order in Council.[123] Really important orders, such as the ones defining the liability of property to be taken as contraband, were followed. Thus, certain presumptions of the enemy destination of goods set forth in Orders in Council were applied because it was said that the interference was less than that allowed under international law and that the

consent of nations, have established a system of procedure, a code of law, and a court for the trial of prize. Every country sues in these courts of the others, which are all governed by one and the same law, equally known to each."

[121] See, for example, the uncritical eulogy by Professor Pierce Higgins of The Zamora and his toast to the Prize Court "independent and unfettered by State instructions." Introduction to Colombos, *The Law of Prize* (1926), pp. vi, xviii. See also Wright, *loc. cit.* (*supra,* note 98) at 1.

[122] Pierce Higgins, *op. cit.* (*supra,* note 121), p. vi. He does not, of course, intend any animadversion on the Court.

[123] Thus at the beginning of the war the Council adopted the Declaration of London with certain modifications. In The Hakan, [1918] A. C. 148, the Court stated that it was not bound to follow the Declaration of London because or as adopted by the Council, but it arrived at the result contended for by the Government.

In The Zamora it was stated that though the Council could not prejudice the

Orders were really concessions to neutral protests.[124] But most writers believe that the Crown asked and received under these orders powers unprecedented. A recent English writer concludes that, as a result of the decisions of the Prize Court, "the notion of contraband means in reality that the belligerent has the right to prevent all cargoes from reaching the enemy country, on the ground that the supply of any kind of goods enables his adversary to sustain or protract the war."[125] This was really the position of the

rights of neutrals under international law, the Crown might abandon or relinquish in favor of neutrals its own rights. Yet in The Proton, [1918] A. C. 578, where the order operated more favorably to the neutral than the rule of international law, the Court refused to apply it because it was intended, the Court said, to lay down the law to the Court, and this, of course, cannot be done.

[124] Thus, an Order in Council, while purporting to abolish the doctrine of continuous voyage for conditional contraband, made it applicable in certain cases; so that goods on a vessel bound for a neutral port were liable to capture (1) if the goods are consigned "to order" or (2) if the ship's papers do not show who is "the consignee of the goods," etc. These orders were treated by the courts as establishing presumptions of enemy destination and throwing the burden of proof on the owner of the goods. The Court went further, laying down that "the consignee" did not mean merely "a consignee"; "the consignee" must be someone buying the goods outright. As long as the shipper retained control over the goods, there was a presumption of enemy destination. The Louisiana, [1918] A. C. 461; also The Kim, [1915] P. 215; The Hellig Olav, [1919] A. C. 526.

In thus applying the Order in Council the Court claimed it was more favorable to neutrals than international law required, but Chandler P. Anderson protests that such a presumption is entirely contrary to the then understanding of prize law that neutral trade is not to be interfered with by a belligerent unless the belligerent can clearly establish its character as contraband intended to be supplied to the enemy. Furthermore, he argues that the facts which the orders declare controlling are insufficient to raise any such presumption. *British Prize Court Decision in The Chicago Packing House Cases*, 11 A. J. 251, 258 (1917). And Garner, *International Law in the European War*: VI, *Contraband, Right of Search, and Continuous Voyage*, 9 A.J. 372, 381, 391 (1915), finds no authority for the application to conditional contraband of the doctrine of "continuous voyage." He quotes Atherly-Jones, *Commerce in War* (1907), p. 257:

"It is impossible to regard without the greatest apprehension the concession of a license to belligerents to condemn goods all over the world on suspicion satisfactory to themselves that their enemies are ultimately intended to have the benefit of them."

But Pierce Higgins in his introductory chapter to Colombos, *op. cit.* (*supra*, note 121), p. xiii, finds that the decisions are a "logical development from existing principles of Prize Law." Higgins was of counsel for the Government in the prize cases. Colombos does not believe that they are logical developments of older views, but rather that they are departures from views no longer suited to actual conditions of warfare. His point is not so much justification as inevitability and universal practice. *Ibid.*, § 183.

[125] *Ibid.*, § 171.

Government, and the Court, while maintaining the older terminology but altering its substance, was able to give the Government the decisions it wanted.[126]

Yet though we have discounted *The Zamora* by realistic standards of what it has meant in action, there still remains an important residue of achievement and aspiration. Lord Stowell would not rule contrary to an express Order in Council, but he went very far in interpreting the Orders and the action under them, according to received principles of international law — further, it would seem, paradoxically, than the Prize Court which in *The Zamora* announced its freedom of Orders in Council. *The Zamora* enlarges the frame within which a courageous judge of Stowell's type can work. Furthermore, it may be used argumentatively — as we are here using it — to increase the range of judicial independence and effectiveness in matters international.

This example of the Prize Court, then, is important to refute the glib talk of judicial incompetency as to anything touching on or concerned with matters of state and the conduct of foreign affairs. Where international order may be served better by judicial than diplomatic action, a formula should not be enough to disqualify the court. And it should be remembered that, if prize adjudication is a

[126] Further decisions of importance are those dealing with the Reprisals Orders of March 11, 1915, and of February 16, 1917. In The Zamora, [1916] 2 A. C. 77 at 98, Lord Parker had said:

"An Order authorizing reprisals will be conclusive as to the facts which are recited as showing that a case for reprisals exists and will have due weight as showing what, in the opinion of His Majesty's advisors, are the best means of meeting the emergency; but this will not preclude the right of any party aggrieved to contend, or the right of the Court to hold, that these means are unlawful, as intailing on neutrals a degree of inconvenience unreasonable, considering all the circumstances of the case." But in The Stigstad, [1919] A. C. 279, and The Leonora, [1918] P. 182, [1919] A. C. 974, both reprisal orders were respectively upheld *in toto* and the Court refused to find any of the measures taken unreasonable. It held, also, that the orders being legal, neutrals were entitled to no reimbursement for the inconvenience (and in the second order, danger) entailed in obeying the Orders. The Court intimated that the profits of the neutral trade were great, and costs could be passed on to the customer — by implication, the enemy.

Baty, *Naval Warfare, Law and License*, 10 A. J. 42, 50 (1916), believes that the Reprisals Orders as applied to neutrals were without right. And at 45 he says: "The enormities (and they are many) of Germany are recounted to justify retaliation upon America, Spain, and Sweden. A freedom from judicial subtleties is claimed which might have satisfied Brennus or Lynch, Fouquier-Tinville or Bethmann-Hollweg."

field where the application of international law is traditionally expected, it is also a field in which the claim of the Prerogative to control defense and foreign affairs is put very high, so that a display of judicial independence here is of argumentative importance in other matters touching upon foreign affairs.

Questions of Sovereign Immunity

In another group of cases we may perceive the subtle interplay of executive and judicial action in a question intimately related to the conduct of our foreign relations. We speak of the situations in which certain privileges and immunities of foreign sovereigns are asserted. It is the general rule that courts will not decide cases against foreign states or sovereigns without their consent, and that in addition certain property, persons, and acts appertaining to sovereign states are withdrawn from the jurisdiction of the courts. This does not mean that a foreign state can commit no wrong, but that the controversy is more properly settled by diplomacy, or international courts or war.[127] Here, then, is a true judicial incompetency. But even here there is an intial exercise of judicial jurisdiction, for the vital question of whether there is or is not immunity is decided by the court. In many instances, as where the suit is directly against a state or an ambassador, the decision is automatic. In the case of *The Attualita*,[128] the question arose whether a ship under requisition by the Italian government was immune from attachment. The Court decided it was not:

> The steamship says that in any event her right to immunity is a political question, which has been passed upon by the executive branch of government. A comparison of the suggestion which was filed in *The Exchange*[129] [citation] with that in this case, shows quite clearly that, while in *The Exchange* the executive demanded the ship's release, it has in this case carefully refrained from doing anything of the kind.[130]

But in *The Exchange* the Court on general legal doctrine decided in favor of immunity and stated that it was unnecessary to pass on the question of whether the executive's request (through the district attorney) was binding on the Court.

[127] Noël-Henry, pp. 81–82.

[128] 238 Fed. 909 (C. C. A. 4th, 1916). [129] 7 Cranch 116 (1812).

[130] *Id.* at 911. Cf. The Adriatic, 258 Fed. 902 (C. C. A. 3rd, 1919), where a ship was libelled for breaking a charter-party which by its terms was to be null and void if requisitioned by the British Government. The British Ambassador "suggested" that it had been so requisitioned. The Court refused to consider whether the requisition was legal.

In the curious case of *The Florence H* [131] a libel in tort was filed against a United States Shipping Board vessel which had been loaned to the French Government and was operated at the time of collision by a French crew. To arguments of incompetency Judge Learned Hand answered:

> There can be no embarrassment *juristically* in undertaking a judgment upon them [acts of the French Government's crew].
>
> That there may be embarrassment *diplomatically* . . . is of course possible, but such considerations are not justiciable by courts. A suggestion from the Secretary of State would be one thing, since he is charged with the responsibility for our relations with other powers. But a court, which is not authorized to treat in any fashion with foreign powers, should be in consequence quite inaccessible to any suggestion which is based upon international considerations. I am aware that it has in some cases been said that, before assuming jurisdiction of causes involving aliens, the court may use its discretion. Whatever may be the grounds which may in any case control that discretion, *it appears to me plain that they should not include the possible diplomatic* adjustment which a decree might make necessary.[132] (Italics mine.)

This is a strong statement. The position is this: the court must decide controversies as they come before it, using the rules applicable generally in the administration of justice. This is its duty and function as a court. If its actions embarrass the executive in diplomatic matters, let the executive make the necessary adjustments. By the so-called doctrine of "political questions" we should arrive, of course, at the opposite result, namely, it is the court which must adjust itself to the needs of diplomacy.

Clearly it is not Judge Hand's meaning that "international considerations" do not enter into the making of general rules of law; rather it is the idea that rules once determined or rules of general value will not be warped to the woof of contemporary diplomacy. We would add that in cases in which there is no "rule" and the decision must be made, the needs of diplomacy though a legitimate interest are not an automatic determinant, as if nothing could compete with the sacred claims of diplomacy.

Judge Hand tempers his principle of strict separation by the intimation that the Secretary of State can suggest diplomatic embarrassment. Whether such suggestions are binding is not clear. There is no case bearing out the hint in *The Attualita* that the ex-

[131] 248 Fed. 1012 (S. D. N. Y. 1918).
[132] *Id.* at 1017.

ecutive's opinions on immunity, where expressed by a demand for release or dismissal, are binding on the Court. To be sure, if sovereign immunity were granted by the courts simply that the executive might not be diplomatically embarrassed, the latter's opinion ought to be considered as binding.[133]

In *The Pesaro*,[134] the Supreme Court granted immunity to a vessel of the Italian Government engaged in merchant shipping. In a prior proceeding against [135] the same ship, it appears of record that the Secretary of State did not consider such ships to be entitled to immunity; nevertheless immunity was granted by the Supreme Court. It would thus seem that the grant or denial of immunity has a broader ground than simply deference to the executive in the conduct of foreign affairs.

The courts consider that the grant of immunity from judicial process in given cases is prescribed as a state obligation by the law of nations, and does not depend on the current opinion of the foreign office. Undoubtedly at the base of the rule is also the regard for the

[133] The curious rule of Ex parte Muir, 254 U. S. 522 (1921), that the Court will not consider the sovereign immunity claim of a ship unless asserted by the executive on behalf of the foreign government or unless the foreign state or its authorized representative appears as a suitor, may proceed from a vague feeling that the immunity is largely a matter of deference to diplomatic organs. This is strongly suggested by Judge Mack's decision in The Pesaro, 277 Fed. 473 (S. D. N. Y. 1921), in which in denying immunity much is made of the point that the Department of State recognized no immunity (though the Court says that "immunity should not be refused in a *clear case* simply because the executive branch has failed to act") (*id.* at 480), and in which there is an intimation that a "suggestion" of immunity by the Department might have changed the result (*id.* at 482).

In Molina *v.* Comisión Reguladora del Mercado de Henequen, 91 N. J. L. 382, 103 Atl. 397 (1918), immunity from suit was denied to a governmental corporation of one of the Mexican states. The Court communicated with the Department of State, which replied that it would not advise the Attorney-General to appear, for the reason that it did not believe that the claim of immunity was well taken. The Court said: "This very sensible position of our government makes it clear that the present case is free from any political complications, and leaves it to be determined purely as a legal question" (at 385, Atl. at 398). For a study of the doctrine of Ex parte Muir see Feller, *Procedure in Cases Involving Immunity, etc.*, 25 A. J. 83 (1931).

[134] 271 U. S. 562 (1926).

[135] The Pesaro, 277 Fed. 473 (S. D. N. Y. 1921) at 479, footnote 3: "It is the view of the Department that government-owned merchant vessels, or vessels under requisition of governments whose flag they fly, employed in commerce should not be regarded as entitled to the immunities accorded public vessels of war." (In reply to inquiry by the Court.)

difficulties which might arise in the foreign office because of a *denial* of immunity; this is a factor to be weighed in making the general rule or, where there is no rule, in deciding particular cases, but that does not mean that it is the only factor, nor is it to be assumed that any one demand or any one opinion of the foreign office properly represents the position best fitted in the long run to diplomatic needs. As a matter of fact, the Department of State has itself indicated that the problems of immunity are best decided by the courts, and that at least its mere suggestion is not to be understood as a demand for release.[136]

Questions of Neutrality

Again consider the fashion in which our courts have built up the law of neutrality. Neutrality is purely an obligation between nations. Yet our courts, in the absence of any request by the executive, and at the suit of private persons, citizens, or strangers, have administered the obligation.[137] Such suits are usually libels to recover ships seized by belligerent privateers or public vessels. The libellant relies on the fact that at some time prior to the capture, though in the course of the same voyage, the capturing ship has violated in some manner our neutrality statutes. There is no statutory authority for the suit.[138] Judge Story held that such a capture was a maritime tort by the law of nations, and thus it lay within the

[136] Research in International Law, Harvard Law School, *Drafts of Conventions Prepared for the Codification of International Law* (1932), "Competence of Courts," Art. 20 and comment, pp. 684, 685. Recently, because the Department of State has not always been sympathetic to the claim of immunity, it has given up the making of "suggestions" and has certified merely to the diplomatic character of the officer who is to raise the issue for the foreign government. The failure of the Department to give an opinion will not be construed as an opinion against immunity. The Maipo, 252 Fed. 627, 628 (S. D. N. Y. 1918).

[137] Santissima Trinidad, 7 Wheat. 283, 348 (1822). See Warren, II, 29–46, for an appraisal of the services performed by the Supreme Court in building up and administering the Neutrality Law.

"The enforcement of the *obligations* of neutrals was a problem with which the Court dealt masterfully and effectively, and in such a way as to effect materially the foreign relations of the country. For many years, it became one of the most potent factors in preserving peaceful relations between the United States and Spain, and Portugal, amid the serious complications which had arisen out of the revolutions of the Spanish and Portuguese colonies in Central and South America." *Id.* at 30.

[138] The Neutrality Acts, U. S. C. Title 18, c. 2, provide specifically for only one case, i. e. capture within our territorial waters, where a private party may

power of the Admiralty Court to decree specific restitution. Thus, through the medium of a private right created for the purpose, the international obligation is enforced. But in the recent and remarkable case of *The Appam* [139] there was no violation of any specific provision of our Neutrality Law, and clearly the capture did not constitute a tort.

The Appam, a British ship, was seized by the Germans in 1916, put in charge of a prize crew, and led into the port of Baltimore, where the prize master announced his intention of laying up until the end of the war. The British owners libelled it. The Supreme Court held that to allow the vessel to remain in our ports would violate our obligation of neutrality, and gave judgment for the libellants. The dispute here is primarily between nations. At stake is the duty of the United States to the belligerents England and Germany. The libel by the owners throws the dispute into the form of a private litigation, making it possible for the Court to act easily upon and enforce its judgment. But it is the conduct of the German Government which is being judged, the rights and duties of states.

To the action of the Court in *The Appam* the German Government objected, proposing arbitration. Replied Secretary of State Lansing:

> Inasmuch as the Appam has been libeled in the United States District Court by the alleged owners, this Government, under the American system of government, in which the judicial and executive branches are entirely separate and independent, could not vouch for a continuance of the *status quo* of the prize during the progress of the arbitration proposed by the Imperial Government.[140]

Clearly this controversy might fitly have been dealt with by the organ of foreign affairs. The President by the Neutrality Act [141] is

move the court, apparently for restoration of the ship. In general the act specifies for criminal penalties, which, of course, are only applicable on motion of the executive. The President is given power to employ the militia, navy, etc., against foreign-owned vessels and their officers "in order to enforce the execution of the prohibitions and penalties of this chapter and the restoration of such prizes [i. e. prizes held by the foreign vessel] in the cases in which restoration shall be adjudged" (Sec. 26); but when and on whose motion, except in the case mentioned above, such adjudications shall be made does not appear.

[139] 243 U. S. 124 (1917).

[140] *For. Relations Supp.* (1916), p. 736. As Quincy Wright points out (Wright, § 247), the peculiarities of our constitutional system would be no defense to our inability to perform an international obligation; as an expression of international law, Lansing's reasons for refusing to arbitrate are rather irrelevant. We are here concerned with it as a statement of internal polity.

[141] U. S. C. Title 18, c. 2, sec. 27.

expressly authorized to compel the departure of foreign vessels whose presence violates the law of nations. It is Secretary Lansing's proposition that there is concurrent jurisdiction; by a constitutional understanding the first organ seized of the controversy will be suffered to proceed exclusively.

Questions Involved in International Controversies

The famous *McLeod*[142] case should be compared with *The Appam*. In 1837 the Canadian Government sent a force of men into New York to destroy the ship *Caroline*, which had engaged in hostile activities against Canada. One Durfee was killed, and McLeod, a soldier of His Majesty, was indicted by the New York authorities for the murder. The British Government protested the trial of McLeod:

> The transaction on account of which McLeod has been arrested, and is to be put upon his trial, was a transaction of a public character, planned and executed by persons duly empowered by Her Majesty's colonial authorities to take any steps and do any acts which might be necessary for the defence of Her Majesty's territories, and for the protection of Her Majesty's subjects; and that consequently those subjects of Her Majesty who engaged in that transaction were performing an act of public duty for which they cannot be made personally and individually answerable to the laws and tribunals of any foreign country.[143]

Distinct from the merits of the plea of justification is the question of the competency to judge the plea. Does the avowal of the act, and assumption of responsibility by the foreign government, automatically preclude judgment? The British contended that "this is a question especially of a political and international kind, which can be discussed and settled only between the 2 (*sic*) Governments, and which the courts of justice of the State of New York cannot by possibility have any means of judging or any right of deciding." [144] Secretary Forsyth at an earlier time had replied to the British Government that "the United States cannot deprive the State of New York of her undoubted right of vindicating, *through the exercise of*

[142] People *v.* McLeod, 25 Wend. 483 (1841).

[143] 29 British State Papers 1127 (1840–41). Also set out in the margin of People *v.* McLeod at *506.

[144] *Ibid.*

her judicial power, the property and lives of her citizens." [145] (Italics mine.) But Webster, who succeeded him, agreed with the British contention that in such a case the Court should by the law of nations discharge the prisoner. He pointed out, however, that the jurisdiction of the Court continued, and the executive, except where the law officer of the government might enter a *nolle prosequi*, was powerless to affect directly the status of the accused.[146] Webster here was referring to the fact that the Federal executive could not terminate a proceeding in a state court, a situation which was remedied the following year by a Congressional act [147] allowing *habeas corpus* to be issued by a Federal court to a state authority in a case where the prisoner claimed privilege as the agent of a foreign power. Thus, at present the executive may always supersede, if it wishes, the judiciary in the criminal aspect of such matters. The problem, however, still remains whether the court should assume jurisdiction in cases in which the executive does not choose to halt the proceedings, and civil cases in which it has not power to do so.[148]

Whether, as Webster maintained, the avowal of responsibility by the foreign power — sometimes called the defense of "act of state" — is a complete bar in all cases is a question on which we still have very little light from either the cases or international practice. Harrison Moore finds it difficult to believe that in cases of assassination or pilfering of state documents the defense would be good. It is, however, highly unlikely that in such cases the foreign power will avow responsibility, and such avowal is, of course, necessary.[149] "The case," he says, "for immunity has never been put higher than

[145] People *v.* McLeod, margin at *503.

[146] *Id.* at *508. And in 29 British State Papers 1130–32 (1840–41).

[147] Act of August 29, 1842. U. S. C. Title 28, § 452: "The writ of habeas corpus shall in no case extend to a prisoner in jail unless where he is in custody . . . for an act done or omitted under any alleged right, title, authority, privilege, protection, or exemption claimed under the commission, or order, or sanction of any foreign State, or under color thereof, the validity and effect whereof depend upon the law of nations. . . ."

[148] Thus Webster pointed out that though McLeod was held on civil process by the owner of the destroyed ship, Caroline, there was no power in the executive, either Federal or state, which could stop the proceedings. 29 British State Papers 1141 (1840–41). Also in People *v.* McLeod at *510.

[149] In the case of Horn *v.* Mitchell, 232 Fed. 819 (C. C. A. 1st, 1916), the defendant, indicted for carrying explosives, claimed that the blowing up of a Canadian bridge, the use to which they were to be put, was intended as an act of war. The defense was rejected, apparently because he failed to show any authorization from the German Government to commit the act.

the public and open employment of force." [150] And Calhoun, at the time of the *Caroline* incident, maintained that the defense was good only if the attack on the *Caroline* were justifiable internationally, for, if it were otherwise, then to the extent that the alien was exempt from the laws for acts done on our soil we should *pro tanto* surrender our territorial sovereignty.[151] The argument of the great state's righter obscures the fact that it is not a question of sovereignty that is involved but of the responsibility for an infringement of sovereign right, if it exists. Are the agent and principal both responsible or the principal alone? A distinction might be taken between the commission of acts which under certain circumstances are permitted by international law, and those which never are. Assassination and theft of documents would be in the latter class; reprisals, defense of frontiers, and comparable categories in the former. This treatment would seem fair enough to both the agent — who, in the first class of cases, is ordinarily a member of an armed force bound to take orders, and in the second is generally a volunteer — and to the foreign power, which should not complain that a municipal trial of its agent is an offense to its dignity where it has set on foot a crime. An analogous distinction is taken between a soldier and a spy:[152] in time of war the spy, if made a prisoner, is liable to execution; the soldier is not.

The act of state doctrine would apparently not be applied in cases of breach of neutrality. The statutes provide that "whoever" within the United States fits out a vessel, etc., for use against a friendly power is guilty of a crime.[153] And we have seen in studying

[150] *Op. cit.* (*supra*, note 54), p. 131. This was, perhaps, the extent of the claim made by the British in the McLeod case. "It would be contrary," writes Fox, the British Minister, to Webster, "to the universal practice of civilized nations to fix responsibility upon persons who with the sanction or by the orders of the constituted authorities of a State engaged in military or naval enterprises in their country's cause." 29 British State Papers 1127 (1840–41). Also in People *v.* McLeod at *506.

In Arce *v.* State, 83 Tex. Cr. 292, 202 S. W. 951 (1918), a conviction of murder was reversed in a case where a group of Mexican soldiers under Carranza's *de facto* authority raided Texas and killed a certain United States army officer (*inter alia*). The Court reversed on the ground that the fighting, if not a "complete or public war," was "a condition of war."

[151] Moore, *op. cit.* (*supra*, note 54), p. 130.

[152] The cases are not strictly analogous, since spying though held to be "dishonorable," is not "illegal," i. e. it is not illegal for the state to use spies. Hall, *International Law* (8th ed. 1924), § 188.

[153] U. S. C. Title 18, c. 2, §§ 23, 24. See note 138, *supra*, for comment on the act.

The Appam that a belligerent who captures a ship in violation of our neutrality will be forced to return it in a judicial proceeding. In such a case, however, the gist of the action is restitution, not punishment or damage.

If, then, the defense is admissible in some cases and not in others, who is to decide in any given case? When the question arises, the matter may already be in court. Must the court dismiss the action if the defense is raised, must it postpone the action until the foreign office has ruled, or should it decide for itself? It should be understood that the question at issue will not be whether the foreign power was justified in its action (whatever the court decides, that will remain for settlement between the foreign offices), but whether the action was within a category of measures which under international law might be justified under proper circumstances. It would seem that the courts are not unfitted to decide such an issue. It relates to the doctrinal aspects of the case in greater measure than to its politico-factual side. This solution seems particularly appropriate where our Government has taken no stand. Even where the Government disagreed with the foreign power and denied the immunity, and possibly is prosecuting the agent, it should be proper for the court to determine independently whether the suit should proceed. Conceivably the Government in prosecuting is yielding to some popular or special pressure. An additional and independent determination would be of value in maintaining our foreign relations on a sound basis. The Government might have denied immunity because, feeling that it was itself the cause of the foreign power's action, it wished to shift responsibility. Here again an enlightened regard for national good faith and international order should move the Court to decide for itself.[154]

In the *McLeod* case, however, Webster in an official communication to the British Government agreed in principle with that government. By admitting that McLeod should under the law of nations be released, he practically confessed judgment against the United States, in case he were not released. Webster's admission did not create a treaty; in form it was a mere expression of opinion.

[154] If it were a civil suit, the dismissal might place upon the executive the task of securing indemnity from the foreign power for the disappointed plaintiff. But if the Government has denied immunity because it considered the act unjustified, it should not object to pressing the plaintiff's claim as part of its own. If the denial was made to shift the responsibility of decision to the Court, the plaintiff, turned out of court, may find it difficult to get the Government to act.

But it was transmitted to the other government. It was an acquiescence in the contention of that government. In effect it lays down the rule of law to be applied in settling the dispute between the two nations; it is a formal act tending to establish a relationship between the states. The Court in *People* v. *McLeod* spurned the notion that such a diplomatic adjustment could supersede the criminal law of which the courts are the traditional guardians. Said he:

> Not only are our constitutions entirely explicit in leaving the trial of crimes exclusively in the hands of the judiciary, but neither in the nature of things, nor in sound policy, can it be confided to the executive power. . . . It has charge of the question in its national aspect only. It must rely on accidental information and may place the whole question on diplomatic considerations. These may be entirely wide either of the fact or the law as it stands between this state and the accused. The whole may turn on questions of national honor, national strength, the comparative value of national intercourse, or even a point of etiquette.[155]

Here, surely, is small faith in diplomatic justice. It is one of the most extreme expressions of judicial self-sufficiency and independence to be found in the books. The Court does indeed concede that the executive has power over the "national aspect" of the question, but by its decision fairly emasculates the stand taken by Webster. Webster, as did Forsyth before him and Lansing in *The Appam*, might have declined to act or even express an opinion, and have left the law to the Court. But he acted, and his action, in a matter definitely crying out for diplomatic treatment, should have been taken by the Court as decisive of an issue so closely related to it as to make cooperation desirable and necessary. The law is not thereby put aside; the act of government is constitutive, itself a source of law.

In *McLeod's* case we have seen a state court assert the primacy of its criminal jurisdiction in a matter which was at the time the immediate subject of international controversy. That case we have criticized because both interested countries had agreed in principle on a method of solution which would embrace all issues of the controversy. Such an agreement is closely akin to a treaty which, under our constitutional economy, the courts will respect as an act of paramount will. Of course, we use the word "will" here merely as a way of describing our result; in the nineteenth century, however, it was popular to speak of the state or the nation or "the

155 25 Wend. at 598.

people" as having a will much as the individual is conceived as having a will. Thus Tazewell, of counsel in *The Santissima Trinidad*, provided a formula for solving conflicts between governmental organs put in terms of locating *the* "will of the people":

> The people, although sovereign, can have but one will; and that will must be spoken by all their agents, or our government is a many-headed monster. The question, then, at last results in this: In what department of the government does this will, in relation to *foreign* states, reside? For wherever it does reside, that will must be uttered here, or we shall have two conflicting wills on the same matter.

Then, after stating that the "political" branches utter this will on questions of foreign affairs, he continues:

> This does not impugn judicial independence. The judiciary are not independent of the law. They utter the legislative will of the people when declared by the legislature. They pursue its executive will when communicated by the executive department.[156]

Today we should probably regard the concept of a "sovereign will" — conceived as a discoverable moral entity — as a convenient fiction to describe the counsel which in any given case ultimately prevails. It may be that at any one moment there is, or should be, but one operative will in the conduct of foreign affairs; yet it is evident that the expression of the "sovereign will" in these matters will not abide at all times and in all cases in the same organ of government. This is borne out, for example, by the relation between the Prize Court and the executive, where, as we have seen, sometimes one and sometimes the other speaks the final word. Yet Tazewell's statement does formulate nicely the idea that the judiciary does not necessarily abdicate its function by accepting a decision of the executive. In *McLeod's* case Webster's agreement on principle with the British Government created an agency capable of representing every interest and of integrating the solutions of all the questions involved. In such a case we have an expression that may justly be taken for the "will" of the nation, and which, accordingly, the judiciary would do well to recognize as such.

McLeod's case suggests a further question. If in a controversy between the United States and some other nation no agreement is

[156] 7 Wheat. 283, 304 (1822). Tazewell was one of the group of distinguished counsel including Webster, Wirt, Pinckney, Sergeant, Wheaton, etc., who between 1807 and 1822 assisted the Supreme Court in formulating a body of international law doctrine. See Warren, II, 27, 33–34.

reached, are the courts, where litigation raises the controversy before them, bound by the contentions of the executive? In other words, does the executive here represent *the* will of the nation in such fashion that the courts must abide by it?

The most important answers to the question have been given in cases where territorial sovereignty was in dispute, a consequence which creates a second question. Undoubtedly, if the legislature presumes to pass laws for a given territory, assuming it to be within its jurisdiction, it is not for a court to reason why. This was established by the eminent case of *Foster* v. *Neilson.*[157] By the treaty of Ildefonso (1800) Spain ceded Louisiana to France. France sold the same territory to the United States in 1803. After this date Spain granted a certain tract of land to a party from whom the plaintiff claimed. Not only did the United States maintain that this land was within the Ildefonso cession, but Congress had on numerous occasions assumed to govern the disputed area. For the Court to uphold the grant on the ground that Congress had construed the treaty improperly "would subvert," said Marshall, "those principles which govern the relations between the legislative and judicial departments and mark the limits of each." "The judiciary is not that department of the government to which the assertion of its interests against foreign powers is confided. . . ." [158]

By an act of Congress it was provided that, when any citizen of the United States shall "discover a deposit of guano on any island . . . not within the lawful jurisdiction of any other government," the island may "at the discretion of the President . . . be considered as appertaining to the United States." This same statute provided for the punishment of crimes committed on such islands as if committed on vessels at sea. Under this law the Navassa islands were proclaimed "to be appertaining to the United States." It appeared that Hayti claimed prior rights to the island. One Jones, indicted under this statute for murder, denied that the Court had any jurisdiction over him. He maintained that the President had acted in excess of the power conferred upon him by the statute. The Court refused [159] to investigate whether the President had properly exercised his discretion. It relied on *Foster* v. *Neilson.*

The cases differ somewhat. If the *Jones* case is closely analyzed

[157] 2 Peters 253 (1829). Followed in Garcia *v.* Lee, 12 Peters 511 (1838); United States *v.* Arrendondo, 6 Peters 691, 711 (1832).

[158] *Id.* at 307.

[159] Jones *v.* United States, 137 U. S. 202 (1890).

it appears that there are two important questions involved: first, whether Congress or the President or both have power to annex territory by discovery and occupation; and second, whether the President, in annexing the Navassas, acted within the statute which created the specific criminal jurisdiction under which Jones was being prosecuted. Conceivably both of these questions are "political"; conceivably only the first. In *Foster* v. *Neilson* the disputed territory had been acquired by treaty. There are authorities [160] who maintain that, there being no constitutional provision authorizing the Federal Government to acquire territory, such a power must be derived from either the power to make war or that to conclude treaties. Under this theory, they are much puzzled to find any source of power to annex by discovery and occupation as in the case of the Navassas.

Quincy Wright, however, says that in *Jones* v. *United States* the Court did not decide as to the existence of the power, since in any particular case whether a territory has been annexed is a political question. With this we agree. The President's declaration that the Navassas were part of the United States should be conclusive. On this issue the Court cannot ask whether the Federal Government has power to make such an annexation; and so, on this issue, whether the President has properly exercised the authority under the statute is immaterial; but this answers only the first question. The narrower issue in the case was whether the specific criminal jurisdiction created by the statute existed. On this issue the Court

[160] See Wright, § 72. The view has been expressed that over and above the specifically granted powers of the Federal Government relating to the conduct of foreign affairs that government possesses "all those powers which states in general possess with regard to matters of international concern." (Willoughby, *Constitutional Law* [1910], I, 451). Wright opposes this view on the ground that the Federal Government is a government of delegated powers, and by construction nearly any power over foreign affairs that is needed can be derived from the delegated powers. The case of Jones *v.* United States is a stumbling-block, since power to annex by discovery does not flow very obviously from, for example, power to make war or treaties, upon which power of annexation is usually placed. But Wright explains away the Jones case by saying that it turned upon the doctrine of "political questions," namely that the court cannot go behind a statement of the political branch as to the sovereignty of a territory, and so cannot test the power of the political branch in such cases; in other words, the action of Congress and the President was without constitutional authority, but there is nothing to be done about it. Willoughby's rationalization seems a good deal more honest and unsophistical than Wright's, though it may not fit as nicely into the closed constitutional system.

might have considered whether the President had acted under the statute so as to bring its criminal aspects into play. It might have done this without denying the *fait accompli* of the annexation. It could not, however, have done so without grave possibilities of paralyzing the government of the islands. The alternative to the statutory jurisdiction would have been martial law. The nature of the executive action taken under this statute was such, therefore, as to preclude interpretation by the judiciary. The incompetency proceeds not so much from the nature of the statute as from the kind of action which in this particular case had been taken under it. This is a distinction which as we proceed we shall attempt to clarify and reënforce.

In *In re Cooper* [161] the action of the executive was without express authorization. The case arose out of the Behring Sea controversy between England and the United States. Russia, when possessed of Alaska, had always claimed the whole Behring Sea, and purported to pass on to the United States its asserted rights. The executive applied the statute for the protection of the seal fisheries to the entire sea, and against the repeated protests of Great Britain maintained our jurisdiction over the sea. Congress had intentionally left the question open. The statute applied simply to "all the dominions of the United States in the waters of Behring Sea." The petitioner was a Britisher whose vessel had been apprehended in the disputed waters and had been confiscated. The Court was able to dispose of the case upon procedural grounds, apparently to its great relief. However, it inclined to the view that the action of the executive was binding upon it:

> The application calls upon the Court, *while negotiations are pending*, to decide whether the government is right or wrong, and to review the action of the political departments upon the question, contrary to the settled law in that regard.[162] (Italics mine.)

But counsel for the petitioner argued

> that without the clear authority of the law of Congress, the executive can never, by determining a so-called political question or by construing an act of Congress or a treaty, conclude the rights of persons or property under the protection of the Constitution and laws of the United States, or conclude the courts of the United States in a determination of these rights.[163]

[161] 143 U. S. 472 (1892). *Accord*: The James G. Swan, 50 Fed. 108 (Wash. N. D. 1892); The La Ninfa, 49 Fed. 575 (D. Alaska 1891).

[162] *Id.* at 503.

[163] *Id.* at 489, quoted by the Court on 499.

The Court, having already decided against the petitioner on an easy ground, could afford the luxury of looking both ways at once. Compare with its statement above the following:

> We are not to be understood, however, as underrating the weight of the argument that in a case involving private rights, the court may be obliged, if those rights are dependent upon the construction of acts of Congress or of a treaty, and the case turns upon a question, public in its nature, which has not been determined by the political department *in the form of a law* specifically settling it, or *authorizing* the executive to do so, to render judgment "since we have no more right to decline the jurisdiction which is given than to usurp that which is not given." [164] (Italics mine.)

Professor Quincy Wright believes [165] this was just such a case. Here was a dispute between the nations. Congress had left it open, thus inviting the Court to decide it. But Congress left it open, apparently, so as not to embarrass the negotiations of the executive. Furthermore, here, as in the *Jones* case, there is more than a dispute between nations and an assertion of a national claim by the executive: there is an exercise of sovereign authority. The sovereign assertion must not be gainsaid. That would be to encourage defection, martial law, and anarchy. This is so whether either Congress or the executive has acted in excess of treaty rights or even without constitutional warrant. The question in the Navassas case, it is true, is narrower than the validity of the sovereign claim. The President asserts the creation of a given criminal jurisdiction dependent on the proper exercise of Congressional authorization. But where he *purports* to act under the authorization, the court should not look behind his act; for he would thereby be deprived of the powers of administration and police upon which he has relied in making the annexation.

Therefore, in both the *Jones* and the *Cooper* cases the issue far transcended the bare question of whether the judiciary must follow the executive in every claim of right made against a foreign country. In *Williams* v. *Suffolk*,[166] however, on which both of those cases relied, the issue was simply that. The defendant insured plaintiff's sealing ships against loss. The captain of these ships, warned by the Government of "Buenos Ayres" not to seal off the Falklands, defied that Government, which promptly confiscated the ships. Our Department of State denied that Buenos Ayres had any dominion

[164] *Id.* at 503.

[165] Wright, p. 174.

[166] 13 Peters 415 (1839).

over the Falklands or any competency to regulate the fisheries. The Court gave judgment to the plaintiff. Said the Court:

Can there be any doubt, that when the executive branch of the government, which is charged with our foreign relations, shall in its correspondence with a foreign nation assume a fact in regard to the sovereignty of any island or country, it is conclusive on the judicial department? And in this view it is not material to inquire, nor is it the province of the Court to determine, whether the executive be right or wrong. It is enough to know, that in the exercise of his constitutional functions, he has decided the question. . . .

If this were not the rule, cases might often arise in which, on the most important questions of foreign jurisdiction, there would be an irreconcilable difference between the executive and judicial departments. By one of these departments, a foreign island or country might be considered as at peace with the United States, whilst the other would consider it in a state of war." [167]

It is doubtful that the opposite decision in the case would by a course of inevitable logic have led to such dire results. Here the United States did not assert any claims of sovereign jurisdiction as in the *Cooper* case. If the decision had been the other way, what harm would accrue? The executive, of course, would not be bound by the decision, but it will be said that the other state may cite it and greatly "embarrass" the executive. This answer is by no means conclusive. Before testing its validity in this case, it will be helpful to correlate some of the cases involving treaties which afford significant data for comparison.

Interpretation of Treaties

To contrast the treatment of treaties by French and American courts is interesting. From the same dogma of separation of powers have been drawn off such diverse brews that undoubtedly other materials have been put in the kettle.

Typical of the French "jurisprudence" is the following:

Though diplomatic treaties regularly promulgated have in France the force of law and ought by this token to be applied by the judiciary, it is not the business of the Courts to interpret them except in cases where the interpretation concerns itself with private interests, whose ordering is submitted to their judgment.[168]

[167] *Id.* at 420.

[168] Dalloz, Rec. pér. 78.1.137 (1877). Cited by Pic in a note on Ministère Public *v.* King (117 Arrêts de la Cour de Cassation en Matière Criminelle 189) in 19 Revue Gén. de Dr. Int. Pub. 355, 360 (1912).

"Si les traités diplomatiques régulièrement promulgués en France ont force

And another court adds: "When it is a question on the contrary of fixing the purport of a treaty from the point of view of international public law, treaties can be interpreted only by the very governments who are parties to them." [169] Professor Pic has attacked this dichotomy. He asserts "the impossibility of taking literally this restrictive formula since it is impossible to conceive of an application of any treaty whatsoever, which does not bring into play, at least indirectly, the sovereignty of one of the contracting states." [170]

These formulas are simply "the almost banal statement of an evident truth," namely, of the fact that the judicial interpretation of a treaty is "relative," i. e. effective only in the case before the court.[171]

de loi, et doivent à ce titre être appliqués par l'autorité judiciaire, il n'appartient aux tribunaux de les interpréter que dans le cas où cette interprétation se réfère à des intérêts privés, dont le règlement est soumis à leur appréciation."

[169] Ministère Public *v.* King (*supra*, note 168): "Que, s'il s'agît, au contraire, d'en fixer le sens et la portée au point de vue du droit international public, les conventions de cet ordre ne peuvent être interprétées que par les gouvernements mêmes entre lesquels elles sont intervenues. . . . "

[170] Pic, *loc. cit.* (*supra*, note 168): "Nous avon fait ressortir l'impossibilité de prendre à la lettre cette formule restrictive, attendu qu'il est matériellement impossible de concevoir une application quelconque d'un traité diplomatique qui ne mette en jeu, au moins indirectement, la souveraineté de l'un des États contractants."

The Italian courts have apparently adopted Professor Pic's logical attack, with the result that they refuse to interpret any treaty. A treaty, they say, is a political act between two nations. An interpretation by an Italian court would not bind a Brazilian court. Thus in a suit by an Italian under an Italo-Brazilian treaty providing for litigation of wrongs done to Italians, an interpretation was refused. Durazzo Adorno *v.* Minis. des affaires étrangères (Cour de Cass. Rome 1900), 32 J. D. I. 448 (1905).

Noël-Henry, p. 68, and De Visscher, *Les Gouvernements Étrangèrs en Justice*, 3 Rev. de Dr. Int. (3rd Série) 300, 331 (1922), both accept the stock formula without blinking an eyelash.

The Minister of Foreign Affairs, in a letter intended for the courts in the recent controversy over the rent laws, discussed below, says that interpretation is for the court as long as the controversy is limited to the parties before the court, but that once there is diplomatic intervention by the other party to the treaty the question becomes exclusively political. This letter is set forth in the report of Sanchez *v.* Gozland (Cour. de Cass. 1931), 59 J. D. I. 683, 688. This test avoids the specious distinction between private and public right based on the nature of the subject matter. But we have seen that the French courts will refuse, at times, to interpret a treaty even in advance of diplomatic intervention.

[171] Pic, *De l'Interprétation des Traités Internationaux*, 17 Rév. Gen. de Dr. Int. Pub. 5, 17 (1910): "Que reste-t-il donc des formules restrictives rapportées

Professor Pic, however, is fighting the hard facts of French judicial decision, which, like the windmills, persist unperturbed after the attack. The French courts have carried their incompetency to extreme lengths. By a customs treaty France and Spain granted certain rights to each other's nationals. A Spaniard was brought before a French customs tribunal, and made a claim of right under the treaty. The treaty was not clear; there was no official interpretation. The case was dismissed.[172] The Court held that measures of protection provided in a treaty for nationals of other countries are *d'ordre public*, and are acts of government which can only be interpreted by the governments themselves. In later instances the procedure is not to dismiss the case, but to continue it until an interpretation is vouchsafed to the Court. Thus, in a controversy over the rights under treaty of an Italian consul to administer the estates of Italian nationals dying in France this course was adopted.[173] The Court pointed out that if it had been a question only of rights of succession under the treaty, being a matter of the private right, the Court would have been competent to give an interpretation.

Clearly an interpretation concurred in by both countries would be binding on the court. It is on a plane with the treaty itself.[174] It

plus haut? Simplement la constatation presque banale d'une vérité évidente, à savoir que le droit d'interprétation des tribunaux se limite rigoureusement aux litiges qui leur sont soumis, et que l'interprétation, essentiellement relative, donnée à un traité par quelque juridiction que ce soit ne saurait, ne lier le gouvernement, ni à la plus forte raison porter une atteinte quelconque aux droits de l'autre partie contractante."

[172] Yter *c.* Administration des Douanes, 5 J. D. I. 166 (Cassation Crim. 1877) (1878).

[173] Chancelier de l'Ambassade d'Italie à Paris *c.* Desouches, 27 J. D. I. 616, 624 (Civil de la Seine 1900).

[174] Henry *v.* Tixier (Cour de Paris 1930), 58 J. D. I. 1058 (1931). In this case there was an interpretive agreement entered into by the foreign offices of Switzerland and France. The original treaty was of a type which under the French Constitution required approval by the Parliament. The interpretive agreement was not so approved. Considerable controversy has arisen whether such an agreement is binding on the courts, but if a unilateral interpretation by the foreign office is binding such an agreement would seem an *a priori* case. However, as a recent commentator has pointed out, an interpretation might amount to a modification and the foreign office might make agreements by this device to which Parliament is opposed. This, in fact, was the situation in Henry *v.* Tixier, which related to the rent laws (discussed below), and on this ground another French tribunal has refused to follow a similar agreement. Schreiber *v.* Ragorn (Trib. Paix Paris 1930), 58 J. D. I. 1073 (1931 *semble*). This

might be thought that the French courts base their incompetency on the reason that a unilateral interpretation could not bind the other state. But they hold themselves bound absolutely to follow their own foreign office even where there is a disagreement between the two nations on the interpretation.[175] Of a lower court not aware of this compulsion, an upper court said "that the Court has disregarded the principle of the separation of powers and has exceeded those which have been legally bestowed on it." [176]

An extensive controversy has arisen recently in France dividing jurists and courts,[177] and raising a question as to whether the traditional "jurisprudence" on treaty interpretation is undergoing a

view is given added support in that the Swiss-French interpretive agreement was by its terms to apply only to the future.

[175] Cf. Bigelow *v.* Princess Zizianoff, Gaz. du Palais, May 4, 1928 (No. 125). Translated in 23 A. J. 172 (1928) and in Hudson, *Cases on International Law* (1929), p. 876.

[176] Ministère Public *v.* King, *supra*, note 168. Of course, the very fact that the French courts do claim that where private interests are alone at stake they may interpret a treaty, means that it is within the competence of the French court to say when there is at stake a national right under the treaty and when merely a private interest; and as Professor Pic points out, even a matter of "private interest" under a treaty logically involves national right. Pic is able to point to a number of such cases (17 Rev. Gén. de Dr. Int. Pub. at 23–27).

However, the courts probably would not go behind an official pronouncement that the interests of state were concerned, whatever distinctions they might draw in the absence of a statement.

Of particular interest are two cases in colonial courts, Nguyen van Bao dit Ba Giao *c.* Nguyen Dihn Nguyen (Cour d'Appel d'Hanoi 1897), Dalloz 1902.2.305; Nguyon-Hun-Thin *c.* Thi-Lang (Trib. de Paix d'Hanoi 1898), Dalloz 1902.2.312. Both involved the question of whether under a treaty whereby the King of Annam gave to France a concession in certain territories, those domiciled in the conceded territories were subject to the jurisdiction of the French courts *qua* French nationals or *qua* nationals of Annam. In the first case the Court construed the treaty, in the second it refused and continued the case until an official interpretation was forthcoming. Professor Pic relies heavily on the first for his thesis, but the second seems far more in accord with the prevailing French "jurisprudence."

A very similar question arose in a German case in which under a German-Dutch treaty ceding certain territory to Germany it was held by a German court that the Netherlands had retained certain sovereign rights in the nature of an "international servitude." Aix-La Chappelle-Maastricht R. R. Co. A. G. *v.* Thewis and Royal Dutch Government, 8 Zeitschrift für Völkerrecht 437 (1914). Translated in 8 A. J. 907 (1914) and Hudson, *Cases on International Law* (1929), p. 492.

[177] See Sanchez *v.* Gozland, *loc. cit.* (*supra*, note 170), argument of the procureur general at 695. See a book review by Sack, 81 U. of P. L. Rev. 366, 367

change. In 1926 and 1927 laws were passed allowing tenants to prorogate their leases. Aliens were expressly excluded from the benefits of the law, unless French nationals were accorded the benefits of similar and existing laws in the alien country. The Minister of Foreign Affairs announced to the courts that aliens entitled under treaty to "national" or "most-favored" treatment had rights under the treaties to the benefits of the rent laws. In a recent case [178] the Court of Cassation rejected the foreign minister's interpretation. The decision was based on two grounds. It was held first that the law, as was made clear from its texts and from parliamentary debate, expressly excluded aliens, and, second, that the treaty (in this case with Spain) did not entitle the Spanish national to exceptional benefits (civil rights *strictu sensu*), though the treaty did stipulate that "the subjects of the two countries can voyage and reside in the respective territories *as nationals* . . . and rent shops [inter alia]. . . ." [179]

The Court in support of its second conclusion asserted the competence of a judicial tribunal having jurisdiction of a conflict of private interests to interpret a treaty, and undoubtedly this claim of competence does fit the terminology of the established rule. But there seem to be few, if any, instances where the intervention of the Foreign Office has not in itself established that the conflict transcended the private rights at issue.[180] It may be, however, as the procureur general argued, that if there was any interpretation to be made here "it was rather of the statute than of the international convention," [181] and that though the later law might be contrary to the earlier treaty, the Court had no option but to apply the law. The Foreign Office by its declaration to the courts and by informal interpretive agreements made with Great Britain and Switzerland was undoubtedly attempting to achieve a result which, as shown by the debates, Parliament did not want.[182] Yet the question which the case raises cannot be completely answered by a categorical state-

(1933). The details of this controversy as given here are taken from the argument of the procureur general.

[178] Sanchez *v.* Gozland, *loc. cit.* (*supra*, note 170).

[179] "Les sujets des deux pays pourront voyager et résider sur les territoires respectifs comme les nationaux . . . louer les magasins . . . qui leur seront nécessaires. . . ." Quoted in Sanchez *v.* Gozland, *loc. cit.* (*supra*, note 170) at 702.

[180] See note 170, *supra.*

[181] *Id.* at 695: "S'il y a interprétation à faire, c'est bien plutôt de la loi que de la convention internationale."

[182] See note 174, *supra.*

ment that an interpretation of a law, and not of a treaty, was at issue. Though Parliament was desirous of excluding all aliens from the benefits and phrased the exclusion in general terms, the President of the Commission of Legislation declared in the Senate that "if strangers allege that they are beneficiaries of treaties and claim rights under them, the courts will decide." [183] If this statement is taken as authoritative, the interpretation of the treaty was involved,[184] and this may account for the fact that the Court rested its decision on both grounds.

The case illustrates a phenomenon probably more familiar to us than to the French. A court will exclude itself from a potential competence in favor of another organ. Faced with what, in its opinion, is an extreme abuse of the relinquished power, it will discover or rediscover its own competence. Usually there will be a formula at hand to serve the occasion. Here it was the oft-asserted competence of interpreting treaties in cases of private right, applied, however, in novel fashion. This application may await a companion until the occurrence of another instance as extreme, or, on the other hand, it may impregnate the old formula with the germ of a new content.

From substantially the same formulas the courts of the United States have derived quite different rules. There seems to be no case where the court because of the absence of an official interpretation has refused to construe a treaty, nor any case in which the court has declared itself incompetent on the ground that the interests involved were public rather than private.[185] Some of the cases have included the rights and privileges of foreign nationals,[186] the immunities of consuls,[187] the jurisdiction of our consular courts,[188] and—a

[183] *Id.* at 703: "Si les étrangers allèguent qu'ils sont bénéficiaires de traités et font valoir lesdits traités, les tribunaux apprécieront."

[184] But see Sack, *loc. cit.* (*supra*, note 177).

[185] Dickinson, *International Political Questions in the National Courts*, 19 A. J. 157, 161 (1925), says that "how a treaty shall be construed, at least in respect to matters of public right," is "primarily" a "political" question. This is probably true in the sense that many questions of treaty construction do not come before the court, but in so far as they do the distinction between "public" and "private," taken, as we have seen, by the French courts, is not taken in our courts.

[186] Jordan *v.* Tashiro, 278 U. S. 123 (1928); Nielsen *v.* Johnson, 279 U. S. 47 (1929).

[187] United States *v.* Trumbull, 48 Fed. 94 (S. D. Calif. 1891) (consul exempt from subpoena *ad testificandum* under most favored nation clause).

[188] In re Ross, 140 U. S. 453 (1891).

matter directly concerning the rights and duties of the states themselves — the interpretation of extradition treaties.[189] Of greater significance are instances in which the courts have refused to follow the official executive view and have accepted the contention of the other nation. In 1876 a controversy arose between the United States and England over the Extradition Treaty of 1842.[190] The United States maintained that the receiving country might try an extradited person for any crime in addition to the one out of which extradition arose. This was denied by Great Britain. The point arose in *United States* v. *Watts*,[191] and the Court after examining the diplomatic correspondence between the United States and Great Britain adopted the contention of the latter. The Supreme Court in 1886 arrived at the same conclusion.[192] The case is not one in which the treaty is construed merely as a source of private right. The petitioner who sues out habeas corpus is not released because of any right of his own. If he had been kidnapped from Great Britain and carried into the United States he could not escape trial.[193] The prisoner is released in fulfilment of the obligation of the United States to Great Britain under the treaty; what is more, the Court here works a specific performance of the obligation, since it denies to the executive the power of bringing the man to trial.

The President, by authority of Congress, executed an agreement with France providing for reciprocally favorable tariffs. The question arose whether Algerian imports were entitled to the rate for French imports. The Department of State claimed that Algiers was a colony of France and not part of France proper, so that it was not understood from the word "France" in the treaty. Over the dual objection that the executive's opinion as to the political status of territory and as to the interpretation of a treaty bound the Court, the latter upheld the French interpretation, and directed the application of the favorable rate. Here again the Court acted directly on the Government in requiring it to fulfill treaty obligations.[194] What,

[189] In re Taylor, 118 Fed. 196 (D. Mass. 1902); United States *v.* Rauscher, 119 U. S. 407 (1886).

[190] Moore, *Digest*, IV, 306.

[191] 8 Sawyer 370 (D. Cal. 1882).

[192] United States *v.* Rauscher, 119 U.S. 407 (1886).

[193] Ker *v.* Illinois, 119 U. S. 436 (1886).

[194] Tartar Chemical Co. *v.* United States, 116 Fed. 726 (C. C. S. D. N. Y. 1902). The decision was appealed. In the interim the two countries agreed that Algiers should be included, and that the Amendatory Agreement should take effect thereafter. The Appellate Court held that this was equivalent to an

then, is the theory of this judicial independence? In *United States* v. *Watts* the Court said:

> It results as a necessary consequence of the duty imposed on the courts to respect and obey the stipulations of a treaty as the supreme law of the land that they are also charged with the duty of determining its meaning and effect; and this duty they must conscientiously and firmly perform, even though the construction they feel compelled to give to it should differ from that given to it by the political branch of the government.[195]

This is an inadequate reason, and proves far too much. The guarantee of republican government is part of the Constitution itself, and yet the courts refuse to have anything to do with it.

In *Decatur* v. *Paulding*[196] the Supreme Court held that the interpretation of a pension act by the Secretary of the Navy was binding upon a claimant and the Court could not by a mandamus to the Secretary review his decision. Mr. Chief Justice Taney said:

> If a suit should come before this Court, which involved the construction of any of these laws, the Court certainly would not be bound to adopt the construction given by the head of a department. And if they supposed his decision to be wrong, they would, of course, so pronounce their judgment. But their judgment upon the construction of a law must be given in a case in which they have jurisdiction, and in which it is their duty to interpret the act of Congress, in order to ascertain the rights of the parties in the cause before them. The Court could not entertain an appeal from the decision of one of the Secretaries, nor revise his judgment in any case where the law authorized him to exercise discretion, or judgment.[197]

---

understanding that Algiers was not within the original agreement and reversed the lower court (*sed qu.*). 127 Fed. 944 (C. C. A. 2nd, 1903).

[195] 8 Sawyer 370, 372 (D. Cal. 1882).

[196] 14 Peters 497 (1840). Also cf. Work *v.* Rives, 267 U. S. 175 (1925).

[197] *Id.* at 515 (1840). Cf. Viscount Finlay in Duff *v.* Kelantan, [1924] A. C. 797, 815: "There is no ground for saying that because the question involves considerations of law these must be determined by the Courts. The answer of the King, through the appropriate department, settles the matter whether it depends on fact or on law."

Dickinson, *Administrative Justice and the Supremacy of Law* (1927), p. 287, takes the position that when the court allows the executive determination to be final it is in effect deciding that no "question of law" is involved, for "what are questions of law is properly a matter of policy for the courts to determine, depending on the desirability or feasibility of establishing fixed rules of permanent and universal application." This is the idea, of course, that "rules of law" are entities that inhere in the decisions of courts and of courts alone; that the decisions are manifestations of fixed rules of "permanent and universal application," conceived of as underlying realities.

Thurman Arnold in a recent article takes the position that rules of law (or

It is quite clear, of course, that the court must apply a *law* of later date than a treaty, though it defeats obligations of the treaty. A treaty is on no higher plane than a law, and as between laws the later in time governs.[198] By the same token, a law which expressly or by implication interprets a treaty is conclusive. Such was the case of *Foster* v. *Neilson*, discussed above. In that case, however, there was more than an interpretation. Congress had exercised jurisdiction over the disputed territory. Suppose that this had been done by the executive rather than by Congress? Such a situation is neatly presented by a French case in which the French Government, purporting to act under the Treaty of Versailles, occupied the Ruhr and established martial law. The petitioner challenged the jurisdiction on the ground that the treaty did not justify the occupation in this instance. The French Court,[199] of course, refused to review the executive interpretation, but our court would no doubt have made the same decision.

The matter may be put in two ways. In certain types of cases the executive's interpretation is conclusive; or (in another way of putting it) the Court must forego its power of interpretation where the executive has created a situation as to which interference, contradiction, even the suggestion of doubt may be dangerous or impolitic. The latter, the writer believes, is the preferable statement. It avoids the difficult and deceptive distinction that dubs some problems of treaty interpretation as "legal" and others as "political," which, under the American cases at least, is an impossible dichotomy. Furthermore, it places the thrust on the nature of the political action which will foreclose judicial interpretation rather than on the nature of the treaty.

In the French case it would make no difference whether the Government purported to occupy the Ruhr under the treaty or in spite of it. If the President of the United States had claimed the dis-

more specifically "substantive" rules of law) are ritualistic pronouncements made by courts, lawyers, and teachers to create an atmosphere of reverence for the operations of courts. *The Rôle of Substantive Law and Procedure in the Legal Process*, 45 Harv. L. Rev. 617 (1932).

Both of these views are extreme. To say, as Dickinson does, that an interpretation of a statute when made by an administrative officer is not a determination of "law" unless and only so far as a court passes on it, is to "explain" a difficulty involved in the conception of the "rule of law" by the ingenious device of giving the word "law" a new and different meaning.

[198] Head Money Cases, 112 U. S. 580 (1884).

[199] Affaire Thyssen, 50 J. D. I. 847 (Cour de Cass. 1923) (1923).

puted portion of Louisiana by divine right rather than under the Louisiana Purchase and The Treaty of Ildefonso, the Court would have been bound. Thus, whether it is a constitution, a treaty, a statute, or a rule of common law, its effect may be modified, its force suspended, because an executive act, itself a source of law, has intervened. An assumption of territorial sovereignty is such an act. On the other hand, we have seen cases in which a claim of right against another nation asserted by the executive to arise from or despite a given treaty is not such an act. This was so even where coupled with an "act of state" such as the collection of a custom duty or the prosecution of a man, both of which were invalidated. Contrast with these *Williams* v. *Suffolk*,[200] in which the executive's denial of Buenos Ayres' jurisdiction over the Falkland fisheries was held binding in a suit between two of our citizens on an insurance policy.

The treaty cases demonstrate that the courts do not feel obliged to back up every claim made for the United States just because at the moment it seems to offer the United States some advantage, or because they will otherwise "embarrass" the executive. The courts speak for the nation just as do its other organs.

But, it is often argued, the executive may have had special reasons for interpreting the treaty as he did, of which the Court cannot be aware, of which it is in no position to judge. Asked what such reasons may be, a usual reply is that their nature is immaterial, that they inhere in the diplomatic process, about which no nine men sitting in a court can hope to know anything. This is part and parcel of the exaggerated conception of the "delicacy" and the esoteric quality of any and every international question, willy-nilly, coupled with the assumption that it is impossible for any mere non-diplomatic layman to say when a problem is and when it is not "delicate," even where, as in a court, every presumption is indulged in favor of judicial "hands off." When pressed further the apologists for this position state more frankly that the special reason may be that the executive is involved upon a negotiation in which it may serve his ends — assumed, of course, to be the nation's ends — to give a treaty a particular interpretation. Without arguing in detail the large question which this — to us — perverse suggestion raises, let us quote in reply some words of Mr. Justice Johnson spoken over one hundred years ago in *The Amiable Isabella*.[201]

[200] 13 Peters 415 (1839).

[201] 6 Wheat. 1 (1820).

Where no coercive power exists for compelling the observance of contracts [i. e. treaties] but the force of arms, honour and liberality are the only bonds of union between the contracting parties, and all minor considerations are to be sacrificed to the great interests of mankind. . . .[202] It is a melancholy truth, that nations and their Courts are too often inclined to restrict or enlarge construction under a temporizing policy suggested by the pressure or allurement of present circumstances. . . .[203] The execution of one treaty in a spirit of liberality and good faith, is a higher interest than all the predatory claims of a fleet of privateers.[204]

With respect to treaties the courts feel that they are peculiarly fitted to speak. It is par excellence a matter of international right. The parties have assumed to treat the matter as one of rights and duties, and to set them down in a formal document. The sources of law are clear and self-contained. It is not to be presumed that in treaty disputes the parties want more than they are entitled to. It is interesting to remember that Washington wished to have the opinion of the judges on the construction of the early French treaties, but the courts refused to give such advisory opinions. If in an actual litigation the court gives an opinion contrary to the executive's, the latter may be quite willing to accept it, and at least will have before him a well-considered opinion.

Even here, the court will strive to agree rather than differ with the executive.

[202] *Id.* at 85.

[203] *Id.* at 88.

[204] *Id.* at 91. The question at issue was whether under a treaty between Spain and the United States the United States Government was entitled to certain goods as prize.

The Supreme Court has adopted the view that treaties are to be given a "liberal" construction. In Neilsen *v.* Johnson, 279 U. S. 47, 52 (1929), the Court said: "When a treaty provision fairly admits of two constructions, one restricting, the other enlarging, rights which may be claimed under it, the more liberal interpretation is to be preferred." (In this case the rule was applied in favor of an alien against the effect of a state law.) But it is probable that an international tribunal would adopt the interpretation which requires the least onerous performance by the obligated state.

"If the wording of a treaty provision is not clear, in choosing between several admissible interpretations, the one which involves the minimum of obligations for the Parties should be adopted." Advisory Opinion, Turkey-Iraq Frontier (Permanent Court, 1925), Ser. B, No. 12, p. 25. But this rule will be applied only where "ordinary methods of interpretation have failed." Advisory Opinion, Polish Postal Service (Permanent Court, 1925), Ser. B, No. 11, p. 39.

Thus, in the great majority of cases it is doubtful that the mere "rule" of "liberal" construction would lead to very different results than the "rule" in international tribunals.

While the question of the construction of treaties is judicial in nature, and *courts when called upon to act should be careful to see that international engagements are faithfully kept and observed,* the construction placed upon the treaty before us and consistently adhered to by the Executive Department of the Government, charged with the supervision of our foreign relations, should be given much weight.[205] (Italics mine.)

In *Williams* v. *Suffolk*[206] this deference, as we saw, became an absolute. There are obvious differences. In the absence of a treaty to construe,[207] the court is relegated to the application of customary rules of international law, often vague and uncertain; the facts are likely to be complex and, particularly in a suit between private parties, may be inadequately presented. Furthermore, these suggestions proceed on the assumption that the claim is based on law, whereas it may be motivated by "power" politics. World organization is still largely political; to some extent there is an absence of law regulating important interests, and in others the law is not sufficiently powerful to maintain itself against the age-old arrogance of political pretension. In this latter field, the courts tread charily. In the absence of positive political action, our courts, bold and independent by tradition, impregnated by the doctrine of the

[205] Sullivan *v.* Kidd, 254 U. S. 433, 442 (1921). In Castro *v.* De Uriarte, 16 Fed. 93, 98 (S. D. N. Y. 1883), the Court states that the executive construction of treaties should be adopted when it is not "repugnant either to their letter or obvious intent."

[206] 13 Peters 415 (1839).

[207] There are many questions connected even with treaties which have been held "political." Doe *v.* Braden, 16 How. 635 (1853) (court will not question power of foreign nation or its representative to make treaty). Terlinden *v.* Ames, 184 U. S. 270 (1902) ("whether power remains in a foreign State to carry out its treaty obligations is in its nature political and not judicial," *id.* at 288). Charlton *v.* Kelly, 229 U. S. 447 (1913) (whether treaty terminated by breach of other party is a question for executive). However, in the amazing case of Karnuth *v.* United States, 279 U. S. 231 (1929), the Court decided that a certain clause in the Jay Treaty was terminated by the War of 1812, on the ground not that war terminated all treaties but that it did terminate those having a "political character," the object of which is "to promote relations of harmony between nation and nation." The decision, of course, at least in the absence of executive declaration, leaves it to the Court to determine which treaties fall within the "rule," if such an impossible criterion can be dignified by that name. A recent case decides that a treaty of commerce providing for reciprocal advantages is not a treaty of a "political nature," and so was not terminated by the World War. The Sophie Rickmers, 45 F (2d) 413 (S. D. N. Y. 1930). See *supra*, Introduction, note 1.

See generally Dickinson, *International Political Questions in the National Courts*, 19 A. J. 157 (1925).

supremacy of the law, will go far to uphold the international legal order as they conceive it. In a few instances, as with treaties and the prize law, they will apply well-established rules even in the face of adverse political action by the executive. This they do cautiously, fearful of jeopardizing legitimate national interests not always clear and explicit in the smooth surfaces of diplomacy, aware also of the limitations of deciding issues the materials of which cannot readily be reduced to the fortuitous mold of a lawsuit.[208]

Yet our judges will not swerve decision-making from paths already travelled or paths promising something for the future because standing in the way is some chance of diplomatic "embarrassment" which may never materialize, or may be ephemeral. Judge Learned Hand has suggested that if a decision may cause embarrassment, it is open to the Department of State to advise the Court to that effect. This should not mean that the court must follow such advice, but that without it the court should not prostrate itself before the fancied needs of diplomacy and foreign policy. The claim of policy should be made concrete in the particular instance. Only so may its weight, its content, and its value be appreciated. The claims of diplomacy are not absolute; to question their compulsion is not treason.

[208] Cf. Dickinson, *Administrative Justice and the Supremacy of Law* (1927), p. 306: "Apart from the obstacles which such interference would throw in the path of political action, these matters are not properly cognizable by a judicial tribunal because each case is so essentially unique, and the critical factors never repeat themselves so as to give any place or opportunity for the application or development of general rules to govern them. The questions involved are questions of pure policy, and whether or not it will ultimately become possible to win over a portion of this field of policy for the rule of law will depend on a much deeper canalization of international contacts by international courts and arbitrations than has ever yet been effected."

CHAPTER II

THE THEORY AND PRACTICE OF RECOGNITION

BEFORE a court can value a given course of political action, it must interpret that action and understand its significance. There is reason to believe that too often the courts in recognition cases have not only shown undue deference to the executive, but have taken too simple a view of the significance of non-recognition, with the result of exaggerating the difficulties and unfortunate effects flowing from the concept of judicial self-limitation. There is an idea abroad that a state or a government which has not been recognized has, at least for the court, no existence whatsoever (with the possible exception that its action will be taken account of as a *force majeure* as is a flood, or a band of robbers) or, as it is sometimes said, that recognition is a *sine qua non* of "international personality." This is the so-called constitutive or creative theory of recognition, a theory which, we believe, is out of touch with reality and should be consigned to limbo. Because of the havoc wrought in the cases by the uncritical reception of these ideas, and because an understanding of the theory and practice of recognition are necessary to a proper interpretation of political action, we propose a brief consideration of the subject.

THE THEORY OF RECOGNITION

Theorists of the last century, representative of the most diverse schools of thought, erected recognition of statehood into the "major premise" of the international system. The prestige of the so-called positivist school was, of course, predominant. Central in its thesis is the absolute, unconditioned independence of the state. The constitution of the international community and the rules applicable to it receive their character, both in fact and in law, from the consent of the subject states. No state need have any relation in law to another unless it has accepted that other into the community of nations; nor must it abide by any rule to which it has not given its consent. There is double recognition "of the imperative rules which regulate the relations of these States; of the capacity of recognized States of accomplishing acts with juridical effect as against all, or recognition of the personality of the State. This is indeed the major premise of positive international law." [1] This premise is put forth as the purest induction from the existing international order. Thus the majestic fiction of auto-limitation by the several states stands transmuted into fact.

The rival and much-scorned school of natural law arrived at conclusions not so very different:

> The fundamental doctrine of recognition, as the doctrine of international existence *de facto*, or of State life for international purposes, corresponds to that fundamental doctrine of natural law which teaches that all rights and duties have their origin in, and are limited by, the facts of natural life. As the doctrine which carries it back to nature, the general doctrine of recognition is thus the fundamental doctrine of the Science of International Law — the doctrine in virtue of which it is a science.[2]

In nature all moral entities are entitled to exist in freedom, in independence; this freedom, however, must be exercised consistently with the freedom of all other entities. These are the precepts of the law of nature, to which all moral entities are subject. But there is no super-national body to determine the proper application of this law; there is no authority to pronounce definitively whether a given group is, indeed, a moral entity, — in this context a state, — or whether, in the circumstances, a duty of action exists. Thus, consistently with the law of independence — at least from other units — a state is free to make these determinations for itself. In so doing, it is an agent of the natural, the moral, order which is the life-blood of its being. The ideal, the God-given form, is filled in, is materialized, is made positive. "Recognition, in its various phases," says Lorimer, the eminent Scotch Thomist, "constitutes the major premise of the positive law of nations, when stated as a logical system." [3]

These two schools start off on very different roads, one of which would seem to exclude the other; yet but a little way, and they converge. Consider the legal status of the world as the positivist sees it

[1] "C'est la double reconnaissance: 1° des règles impératives qui régissent les rapports de ces États entre eux; 2° de la capacité, pour les États reconnus, d'accomplir des actes avec effets juridiques à l'égard de tous ou reconnaissance de la personnalité de l'État. C'est bien la majeure du droit international positif." Le Normand, p. 32.

[2] Lorimer, I, 4.

[3] *Ibid.*, p. 103. And he adds: "To the communities which it subsumes, international rights and duties result from it logically, and consequently jurally. . . ."

prior to recognition. It is a chaos of formless, unconditioned space, in which absolute states drift crazily about. A few unfortunate collisions induce these majestic bodies to create a cosmos. Recognition — mutual consenting — is the tool. Recognition brings to pass the international order, international personality, international law. Very different is the universal picture of the natural lawyer. From the very beginning there has been a divine ordering of all entities which partake of the Godlike attribute of will. The state is such an entity. It has rights and duties — international personality — by reason of its very nature. Thus far, these positions could hardly be more squarely contradictory. But the school of natural law now executes a casuistical manoeuvre. Because the international order is faulty in its organization, because there is no super-national body, natural law does not possess, in any given case, automatic positivity. Recognition — consent — concretizes the viscous natural law. Lo! the high-thinking natural lawyer finds himself arm in arm with the denying positivist.

In truth there is nothing strange in this result. The most significant fact in modern history is the rise of the independent state. The most powerful theoretical conception in the field of political thinking is the dogma of sovereignty. Recently we have become conscious of the nearly unquestioned allegiance which both thinking and unthinking men have given, and still give, to it. It is not at all surprising that the exponents of natural law, while attacking and seeking to temper its formal absoluteness, have been seduced by its substance. Today there is a "pragmatic revolt" against the hegemony of this dogma. Publicists — Laski, Brierly, Verdross, John Fischer Williams — posit reformation of both intra-national and international law and politics in terms of the rejection or drastic modification of the theory of sovereignty. The argument that sovereignty exists as a stubborn, irresistible fact these men seek to dissolve in the dynamic of history. The whole controversy is important to us.

The classic theories of recognition are, as we have seen, inextricably tied into the very roots of thinking about international law. The rise and growth of the dogma of sovereignty, and — let us hope — its decline, have written the history of international law; the theory of recognition must be studied as one of the many responses to its influence.

"The sovereignty of the state," says Harold Laski, "is an *historical condition* which arises from the breakdown of the medieval *respublica christiana* of the Middle Ages. Broadly speaking, before the Reformation the will of the state lacked any sovereign character. It was regarded as inherently limited by the law of God and the law of nature; any enactment of the state contrary to their principles was inherently void of effect."[4] (Italics mine.) The feudal polity, throughout its intricate hierarchy, was one of limited powers. The relation between man and overlord was conceived as rooted in agreement. "These were the golden days of 'free' if formal contract," say Pollock and Maitland.[5] "The central idea of Feudalism was the subjection of the ruling body (grants of land, it must be remembered, always carried with them grants of jurisdiction) equally with the ruled to law."[6] Western Europe was a single Christian brotherhood; men, not states, were the essential units. Rulers and ruled found themselves somewhere in a pyramid, the apex of which pierced into heaven. Immediately below, the Pope claimed universal agency of Divine authority on earth, which the Emperor, his eyes cast backward on the Roman Principate, disputed. In this conception an ideal universal authority prevails over all men. The *jus gentium* is, as it was at Rome, a local law for deciding between diverse peoples. A law to reconcile equal, coexisting, independent authorities was not felt to be needed.

This grand ideal was, however, in time little more than a nostalgia, a memory of the ancient Roman Empire. Rome was a great organization before it was an ideal. Neither the later pretender-Empire nor the much more potent Papacy was equal to the task of universal government. Without such a cement, the atoms of feudal authority dashed themselves against each other in senseless and destructive anarchy. Power is not a laggard. The feudal kings seized upon the opportunity to effect the needed reorganization of Europe.

In fact, the transformation of Europe into a system of states was not at all a simple process. The nobility opposed it; the Pope anathematized it. But the accumulation of wealth, the rise of the commercial classes, the paramount desire among them and the peasantry for peace and order, favored the growth of ordered, self-contained units of proportions more modest than universal empires, more amenable to human resourcefulness. The thing was done with arms and money and personalities, but also with ideas. It was im-

[4] *Introduction to Politics* (1931), p. 93.

[5] *History of English Law* (2nd ed. 1898), II, 232–233.

[6] Ghose, *Comparative Administrative Law* (1919), p. 17.

portant to break down the dogma of universal authority, to clear the ground for the new monarchical pretensions. The material process was, of course, long under way before it was possible to give it the dignity of a political theory. It is said that it was Bodin who in 1556 first gave consistent form to the doctrine of sovereignty. The state, or (as it ordinarily was then) the Royal Person, was the source of law, was itself above law. Bodin, it is true, combined the theory with the supremacy of the older natural or divine law, and so, in place of one Pope, there were many.[7] But Hobbes, whose authority has been immense, rejected even this check on the power of Leviathan. By an ironic twist, Hobbes transformed natural law into a rule or right of self-preservation at all costs, a war of all against all. This was the condition of mankind in "nature" which was terminated as unbearable by an agreement among individuals, merging all power in the state. The states, with relation to each other, were still in a state of unbridled "nature." [8]

It is a mistake to regard the system of Hobbes as pure scientific induction. As Maine has said of him, "When, with a keenness of intuition and lucidity of statement which have never been rivalled, he has made out a case for the universal theoretical existence of Sovereignty, it becomes clear that he has, to say the least, a strong preference for monarchies over aristocracies and democracies. . . ."[9] And, undoubtedly, he had also a preference for order over confusion. The horrors of dynastic and religious wars inspired him to

[7] Verdross, *Fondement du Droit International*, I Recueil des Cours, Académie de Droit International, 313 (1927), quotes Bodin as follows: "Tout ainsi que les contrats et testaments des particuliers ne peuvent déroger aux ordonnances des magistrats, ny les édits des magistrats aux coutûmes, ny les coutûmes aux lois générales d'un prince souverain; aussi les lois des princes souverains ne peuvent altérer, ny changer les lois de Dieu et de nature." Verdross, of course, carries his own idea of the supremacy of international law into Bodin, Grotius, *et al.* when he says (*op. cit.*, p. 312): "Leur souveraineté n'est pas une souveraineté absolue, elle n'est qu'une *compétence* donnée aux États par le droit naturel et le droit des gens positif."

J. L. Brierly says of Bodin: "Ces qualifications sont incompatibles avec une théorie de la souveraineté rigoureusement logique, mais elles faisaient corps avec la méthode inductive et historique de Bodin, méthode qui fut malheureusement délaissée par la philosophie politique des siècles suivants. L'œuvre de la philosophie fut d'accomplir une réforme de la doctrine de Bodin comme si c'était une déduction de prémisses *a priori* découvrables." *Force Obligatoire de Droit International*, III Recueil des Cours, Académie de Droit International, 492 (1928).

[8] See Brierly, *op. cit.*, pp. 495–498, 504–505.

[9] Maine, *Early History of Institutions* (1874), p. 355.

passionate protest, as they did Grotius. Men were seeking for a force to rescue them from the hideous war of all against all. Hobbes seized upon the dominant fact of the growth of state power usually found in its historic association with the rise of a monarchical dynasty. He erected this fact into the brilliant generalization of sovereignty. He freed his conception from the hampering, irritating restrictions of natural law; he presented Europe with a central dogma for a new religion.

We should not forget that the dogma was called to a useful service, which, though in lessened degree, it still performs. But, as Professor Brierly says,

> The implications of such a theory in a world in which different states have to live in relations with one another were full of portent, for it led logically to the assertion of the complete separateness and irresponsibility of every state. It gave the death-blow to the lingering notion that Christendom, in spite of all its quarrels, was in some sense still a unity, and left the relations between states not only uncontrolled in fact, as they had often been before, but uninspired by any unifying ideal. For the first time, the state seemed to have become the final goal of unity.[10]

It is customary to take 1648, the date of the Treaty of Westphalia, as the time when the new system came into its own. The independence of Switzerland and the Netherlands, the virtual independence of the petty German kingdoms, were duly acknowledged. Protestant states were given equal standing with Catholic. The dismemberment of the universal hierarchy was complete. There they were, a whole brood of states, great and small, but all equally, in the a-legal, a-moral state of nature according to Hobbes. To be sure, no such situation, no sovereignty quite so absolute, ever did exist, but the Thirty Years War was a pretty fair approximation of "the war of all against all." Yet among the peoples of Europe there were common religious and intellectual sympathies, searing memories of the dreadful havoc of the religious wars, a ramifying network of commercial intercourse. Even as the doctrine of sovereignty found more and more complete expression in the agglomeration of powers in the state, these factors worked against it toward international organization, toward a way of adjustment between states, which has since come to be international law. But the nature and practice of this "law" were conditioned by the powerful doctrine of sovereignty, and still bear the stigmata. This "law" was the self-imposed morality of sovereigns dealing with each other, if,

[10] Brierly, *op. cit.* (*supra*, note 7), p. 7.

when, and in the manner they chose. The family of nations, as constituted and self-chartered by the Treaty of Westphalia, was an exclusive club, international law its by-laws. In this context it is not difficult to appreciate the basic significance of the concept of recognition.

Undoubtedly these were not the views of international law held by the great school of natural lawyers, the Spanish Jesuits, who blocked out the lines of the system, and Grotius, who sought to give it content. The Jesuits held to the medieval ideal of a unified, universal moral order. Only its constitution had now changed. "The human species, although divided into peoples and into various kingdoms, is not less a unity, not only specifically, but, it may be said, politically and morally. . . . That is why a sovereign State, republic or kingdom, although complete in itself and firmly established, is yet at the same time, in a certain way, a member of this great universe, in so far as it is concerned with the human species." [11] The moral law is, of course, supreme. But the Jesuits, and more particularly Grotius, distinguished between natural law and positive law, the latter the expression of the will of the international community, ultimately based on the consent of each state. "Grotius supplied, then," says Professor Brierly, "not a system of law, but a philosophy of inter-state relations which could be set against Machiavelli's brutal description of those relations as they often were. . . ." [12]

Vattel perverted the idea of natural law very much after the example of Hobbes. He identified it with the conditions prevailing in a "state of nature" in which the chief legal datum was the freedom and equality of states. This independence carried with it the sole right of a state to judge its own conduct in the light of the law of nature. It has been said that "this exaggerated emphasis on the independence of states had the effect in Vattel's system of reducing the natural law, which Grotius had used as a juridical barrier against absolute conceptions of sovereignty, to little more than an aspiration after better relations between states. . . ." [13] Yet it seems to the writer that it merely brings into uncomfortable prominence the weakness inherent in Grotius and most of the writers of the natural law school. The scope of natural law suffered a fearful shrinkage when treated, as the exponents of the system themselves

[11] Suarez, *De Legibus ac Deo legislatore*, quoted by Verdross, *op. cit.* (*supra*, note 7), p. 254.

[12] Brierly, p. 26.

[13] *Ibid.*, p. 31.

admitted it must be, in the acid bath of positivity. To be sure, it is only a weakness as seen through the eyes of today, in the light of the needs of today and the possibilities of tomorrow. We should not attack as a weakness their failure to underpin the international system with a structure which would have found little warrant in reality and not much more in hope. To have projected a structure too far ahead of the time would have made the discrepancy too obvious. The natural law systems were broken to the last of the doctrine of sovereignty, and so did they continue even after the growth of favoring circumstances had prepared the soil for a revival of the more forthright and seminal doctrines of the natural law.

It is an unfortunate quirk of the human mind that it undertakes to glorify an idea, to draw it out to its ultimate consequence just as it begins to decline in utility. The dogma of sovereignty was given apotheosis in the nineteenth century. Hegel presented the great pageant of history as a Gargantuan logical process in which the coexisting antinomies of liberty and authority were merged in the developing idea of freedom which had, until then, found its ultimate realization in the absolute state. Hegel's logic is dynamic, and Verdross [14] suggests that the state should in its turn provoke into being an antinomy which, with the state, would be resolved in the higher unity of the international community. However that may be (and Hegel's philosophy is convenient to prove many things), the nineteenth century did not draw that moral. An age supremely conscious of the history of the past, it forgot that the present and the future are, and will be, history.

Since 1648, then, the international community has regarded itself as an exclusively constituted club, at first of sovereign persons and finally of self-sufficient states.[15] The dominant principle of ad-

[14] Verdross, *op. cit.* (*supra*, note 7), p. 265: "Dans notre ordre d'idées, la 'thèse' est la souveraineté absolue de l'État. Mais à la souveraineté de l'un s'oppose en 'antithèse' la souveraineté absolue des autres États. De là naquit nécessairement une lutte entre les États, car chacun cherche à soumettre les autres à sa volonté. Pourtant aussi cette 'thèse' et cette 'antithèse' seront finalement surmontées d'une 'synthèse' qui ne peut être autre chose que la *communauté internationale*."

Verdross admits that Hegel did not draw this conclusion. He finds it quite remarkable that Hegel's thoughts, devised to vindicate the absolute will of the state and to deny an international superstate, should lead "necessarily" [!] to the sovereignty of the international community.

[15] "L'État qui reconnaît prend conscience, constate l'existence de l'État à reconnaître et son entrée dans la communauté internationale et *il manifeste la*

mission into a club is to let in only the "right people." Napoleon convinced the kingly powers of Europe of the divinely inspired validity of this principle. After 1815 the Concert of Europe solemnly resolved that only states with legitimist rulers were proper objects of the rule of international law. Revolutionary states were particularly obnoxious. This was the supreme — and rather absurd — expression of the idea that international law constituted the articles of a voluntary association known as the Family of Nations. Never had it been completely true. Indeed, into the original charmed circle of 1648 had been admitted the United Netherlands and Switzerland, both flagrant offenders against the principles of the Holy Alliance.

The United States, as befitted its recent revolutionary origins, set its face squarely against the doctrine of legitimacy. Jefferson wrote to Morris, our minister at Paris during the French Revolution: "It accords with our principles to acknowledge any government to be rightful which is formed by the will of the nation substantially declared. . . ." [16]

This is said "to mark the beginning of the *de facto* principle of recognition for which the United States has usually stood." [17] That contention will be discussed later. It is important here to note that the American policy did not purport to modify the prevailing conception of the structure of international relations. It was content to broaden the basis of recognition, to liberalize the entrance requirements. Thus, in 1861, Seward said that "to recognize the independence of a new state, and so favor, possibly determine, its admission into the family of nations, is the highest possible exercise of sovereign power." [18] This is a very clear statement of the idea that membership in the family of nations depends on the will of those already admitted.

The positivists do not contend that the state is created by recognition. The state necessarily exists prior to recognition, but is without international personality. Oppenheim says, "International Law does not say that a State is not in existence as long as it is not recognized, but it takes no notice of it before its recognition.

volonté de respecter ses droits et d'entrer en rapports avec lui comme membre de cette communauté juridique. C'est ainsi que l'État nouveau est admis dans la société des États." Le Normand, p. 37.

[16] Jefferson, *Works* (Ford ed. 1892–1899), IV, 131. Quoted and discussed in Goebel, p. 102.

[17] Goebel, p. 111.

[18] 1861 Dip. Cor. 63.

Through recognition only and exclusively a State becomes an International Person and a subject of International Law. . . ." [19]

Most of the positivist thinking was a reaction to the theories of the naturalists, and must be studied as the irritated response to them. The modern mind prides itself on its realism. The natural-law system is particularly vulnerable to its scorn because it practically concedes that its "theory" of international law does not prevail in "practice." The Grotian distinction between natural and positive law persists under varying guises. Fiore, for example, rejects the notion that recognition is a condition of international personality. "All peoples who by virtue of their will and freedom constitute a state assume thus, *jure proprio*, the character of persons in the *magna civitas*. In effect, as soon as politically constituted, it has the power to request of all other states the respect of its own rights." [20] In the word "power" there lurks a disturbing ambiguity, and confusion is further increased by the proposition that "the admittance of the new state into international society and the normal and effective exercise of all its international rights must be considered as conditioned upon its entrance into relations with other states which occurs when each of these powers recognizes it." [21]

An international personality which yet must wait upon other states to be admitted into the international society, which is fully

[19] Oppenheim, *International Law* (4th ed. McNair 1928), I, 144; this view is set forth in great detail in Le Normand, *La Reconnaissance Internationale* (1899). Le Normand says (p. 17): "Il n'y a pas de droit international sans une reconnaissance de la personnalité de l'État." On p. 50 he says: "La reconnaissance est constitutive de la souveraineté de droit, ou mieux des droits de souveraineté. L'État se pose comme personne et demande à être reconnu comme tel, c'est-à-dire, qu'au moyen de son auto-détermination qu'il possède par nature, il dirige son activité sur des points déterminés de la vie commune."

See Bonfils, *Manuel de Droit International Public* (7th ed. 1914), § 199: "En *fait*, un État peut exister sans avoir été reconnu par les autres. . . . En *droit* et dans la pratique internationale, la reconnaissance du nouvel État est indispensable pour qu'il puisse user des prérogatives et des droits inhérents au titre de membre de la société des États." (Italics mine.) Fauchille, editor of the 8th edition (1922), retains this language, but adds that recognition is simply "déclarative" and not "constitutive, créatrice ou attributive." It is doubtful, however, that this view is consistent with the quoted portion.

See also Pillet, *Des Personnes Morales en Droit International Privé* (1914), p. 310: "Qu'un État, pour posséder la personnalité civile et pouvoir exercer les droits y attachés, ait besoin d'être reconnu, cela va sans dire. *Un État qui n'est pas reconnu n'est pas une personne du droit international.*" (Italics mine.)

[20] Fiore, § 58, note.

[21] *Ibid.*, § 168.

clothed with rights and duties [22] and yet cannot exercise them, is likely to strike many minds as an anomalous and fruitless conception. In any case, it was the object of withering attack.[23] The natural lawyers, it is said, confuse individuality and its moral claim to justice on one hand with personality on the other. Personality is the capacity to enjoy and exercise rights, to be liable to duty. When a human creature is born, he is *ipso facto* a person, not because of God-given right, nor by reason of his individuality, but because the state, the juridical organization to which he and his fellows are amenable, gives him rights against those fellows.[24] But "in international law," says Le Normand, "there is not above States a subject of superior claims (*droit superieur*), toward which isolated States have obligations or against which they have rights." [25] "The autonomy of States, that is to say, the absence of

[22] "Every state politically constituted must be considered *ipso jure ipso que facto* as possessed of all the rights which ought to be considered as its rational rights, and of the ability to assume international obligations in its relations with other states." *Ibid.*, § 61.

"Every state which is considered as politically constituted is entitled to assume *jure suo* the status of a person independently of the formality of recognition and may require [?] in its relations with other states the application of international law." *Ibid.*, § 60.

In view of the foregoing, it is rather difficult to follow Goebel, p. 55: "Nor am I inclined to go as far as those writers who, basing their views upon theories of natural law, seek to give recognition a constitutive force, an institution by which the State is raised from a condition of pure lawlessness into one of legality." Among such he classes Fiore.

Fiore's rules as the effect to be given to the acts of unrecognized states are in characteristic confusion:

"Every state may freely exercise its rights of sovereignty within its own territory independently of recognition, and foreign officials and courts cannot ignore the entirely legal authority of the sovereign acts thus undertaken." *Ibid.*, § 181. With which compare: "The acts of government of a new state, so far as their operative effect in international relations is concerned, may be deemed as of no value in a state which has not recognized it. Consequently, the courts and political authorities of the latter country may consider the former conditions as still existing, until their government recognizes the new state." *Ibid.*, § 182.

[23] Le Normand's book, *La Reconnaissance Internationale* (1899), is in its entirety an attack on the natural-law position.

[24] "C'est l'erreur de la doctrine du droit naturel. Fiore attribue a l'individu une capacité juridique naturelle qu'il n'attribue pas avec raison à la nation. La verité est que, dans les deux cas, cette capacité juridique ne peut résulter que d'une organization juridique." *Ibid.*, p. 60.

[25] "En droit international, il n'y a pas au-dessus des États un sujet de droit supérieur, envers lequel les États isolés aient des obligations ou contre lequel ils aient des droits." *Ibid.*, p. 31. Cf. Goebel, p. 56: "It is important to note that

all superior authority which can impose law, makes it precisely necessary that the personality of States be born from a reciprocal recognition." [26]

Assuming for the moment the basic premise of this argument, namely that consent is the foundation of the international order of rights and duties, it does not follow by ineluctable logic that one state cannot be an object of international law without the consent of other states. It is sufficient to the argument (and nearer to the reality) that consent is given to international law as a system rather than to each and every relationship contained in it; and, in the final analysis, the position of an unrecognized state would be determined by whatever rules are given by international law with respect to the capacity of states.[27]

But the basic premise itself is under attack by a group of brilliant writers. It is said that it does not supply a sound basis for the obligatory force of international law. It is condemned as not in fact a reality of international life. Addressing himself to the first point, Verdross has recently said:

> The modern theory of auto-limitation sustains the thesis that international law finds its foundation in the will of the *isolated* State, but remains in spite of everything obligatory, because the state is capable of binding itself. It adopts, then, the same point of departure as Spinoza and Hegel, but it has not the courage to draw from it the same logical consequences, that is to say that an international law based solely on the will of the State

---

this law [international law] is self-imposed and that it is only by this self-sanctioning process that it is binding. This is the tribute which international law pays to the doctrine of sovereignty." But Goebel (p. 58) rejects the constitutive theory of recognition.

[26] Le Normand, p. 43: "L'autonomie des États, c'est-à-dire, l'absence de toute autorité supérieure qui puisse imposer des loi, exige précisément que la personnalité des États naisse d'une reconnaissance réciproque." Cf. Anzilotti (1929), I, 161: "La reconnaissance donc n'est autre chose qu'un pacte conclu sur la base de la règle *pacta sunt servanda*: la personnalité internationale, rendue possible par cette norme, devient effective et concrète par la reconnaissance. La reconnaissance, selon nous, est purement et simplement l'accord initial auquel se rattache la naissance de normes juridiques pour des sujets donnés et par suite leur personnalité l'un à l'égard de l'autre; de par sa conception même elle est réciproque et constitutive."

[27] In reply to the argument in the text that, even under the consent theory, international law might attribute personality to a state as soon as it came into being, Anzilotti (I, 163–166) replies that (*a*) it would impose personality upon the new state without consulting its will, and so be inconsistent with the idea that international law is based on agreement; (*b*) that no sufficient demonstration has been made that there is in fact such a rule.

ceases to be obligatory through a simple change of this will. This doctrine attempts to conciliate two irreconcilable theses: the absolute sovereignty of the State on the one hand, and the obligation of States under international law on the other. But these efforts are vain, for every obligation imposed on a will implies . . . the existence of a *rule superior to* this will.[28]

The writer confesses that, despite the vigor and clarity of its statement, he is not overly impressed with the argument that consent cannot be the basis of the obligation of law because, as it is said, obligation implies the existence of a superior rule. This is a modernized, continental version of the Austinian dogma, with a superior rule taking the place of the Austinian sovereign will. Verdross finds the superior rule to be the principles of justice which exist "in an ideal sphere, in the manner of mathematical truths which, in the same way, are absolutely independent of the fact of their comprehension or recognition by man." [29] This is to resolve the diffi-

[28] Verdross, *op. cit.* (*supra*, note 7), p. 266: "La théorie moderne de l'autolimitation soutient la thèse d'après laquelle le droit international trouve son fondement dans la volonté de l'État *isolé*, mais reste malgré tout obligatoire, parce que l'État est capable de se lier lui-même. Elle adopte, donc, le même point de départ que Spinoza et Hegel, mais elle n'a pas le courage d'en tirer les mêmes conséquences logiques, à savoir qu'un droit international basé uniquement sur la volonté de l'État cesse d'être obligatoire par un simple changement de cette volonté. Cette doctrine veut ainsi concilier deux thèses inconciliables: la souveraineté absolue de l'État d'une part et l'obligation des États par le droit des gens d'autre part. Mais ces efforts sont vains, car toute obligation d'une volonté suppose, comme nous le développerons plus tard, l'existence d'une *règle supérieure* a cette volonté."

Brierly (p. 36) makes the same point: "The positivist doctrine rightly looks to the practice of states and not to *a priori* deductions for the rules of international law, but it generally also attempts to explain the binding force of those rules as arising from the supposed fact that states have consented to be bound by them, and this latter part of the doctrine is both untrue in its assumptions and inadequate as an explanation. Law by its very nature is imperative, there must exist an *obligation* to obey it, however we may explain the origin of that sentiment. But to say that a man or state is *obliged* only by what he consents to is meaningless; no obligation can arise in such a case. If we say, as of course most positivist writers imply, that consent once given can not be retracted, we are deserting our premises and calling to our aid an unacknowledged source of obligation, which, whatever it may be, is certainly not the consent of the state, for that may have ceased to exist."

[29] *Op. cit.* (*supra*, note 7), p. 284: "Ces principes existent dans une sphère idéale, comme les vérités mathématiques qui de même sont absolument indépendantes du fait de leur connaissance ou reconnaissance par les hommes."

Anzilotti also derives the obligatory character of international law — in fact, all law — from an abstract, supreme norm. But whereas Verdross presents his

culty which Verdross raises as to the consent theory with a few vague and useless words. The consent theory itself probably has implicit in it an idea that consent is morally obligatory. And, as Triepel has said, "One must always arrive at a point where a juridical explanation of the obligatory character of law itself becomes impossible. The foundation of the validity of law is outside of law." [30] The nature of obligation lies in the field of metaphysic, and this line of attack on the positivist school does not substantially advance the cause. It is valuable, however, in so far as it points out that it is very difficult to reconcile the dogma of absolute sovereignty with the admission that international law is binding.

It will be more fruitful to inquire whether consent is in fact an ingredient of every international legal relationship. This is the crucial test of the positivist doctrine, purporting, as it does, to rest on observation. To minimize the large part played by consent in this field would be stupid. But it seems that the positivists have made a partial explanation into the whole explanation. No doubt they did so because it was immensely useful in preserving intact the form of absolute sovereignty, if not its substance. And, as with most generalizations based upon observation, a good deal of the originally motivating hypothesis adheres to it, whether or not it has been completely transmuted into observed fact. Indeed it is very difficult to find anything like a universal consent to the so-called customary rules of international law which have grown slowly through the years, unless resort is had to the solving formula that acquiescence is consent.

Undoubtedly there was and still is considerable force in the idea that the international community is an exclusive association of sovereigns who on occasion would graciously, if condescendingly, receive a new member. But we have no reason to suppose that such an organization is the final word. The positivists, with their passion for crystallization, for seizing upon some dominant trait and torturing everything into its mold, have based their whole structure

supreme norm as an ideal truth, Anzilotti, with Kelsen, posits the supreme norm as an hypothesis. For Anzilotti, this norm is *pacta sunt servanda* (pacts are to be obeyed). Stating his theory of recognition in terms of this concept, he says (p. 161): "Cet accord [recognition] . . . tire sa valeur juridique de la norme-hypothèse *pacta sunt servanda.* Une fois constatée l'existence d'un accord dans le sens du droit international, le caractère obligatoire juridique de cet accord dérive non de la volonté des entités qui l'ont appelé à l'existence, mais de la norme qui attache ces effets déterminés à ces manifestations de volonté."

[30] Quoted by Brierly, *op. cit.* (*supra,* note 7), p. 485.

on an assumption of the free association of sovereign, absolute, irresponsible states. Clearly international law is not an immutable system. To ignore its constant growth, and the slow subtle shifts in its very foundation, is to reckon without its vital principle.

Today, the international order is a world order, and all the world is subject to international law. We are beginning to find a contradiction in the admission on one hand that a State can exist *ex proprio vigore*, but on the other that it is without international personality prior to recognition. To quote Professor Brierly, who is here criticizing generally the concept of absolute sovereignty as held by both the natural law and the positivist schools:

> Both are involved in unrealities because they assume as a starting-point a false idea of the State as a personality with a life and a will of its own, living in a "state of nature" in the phraseology of the naturalists in contrast with the *political* state in which individual men live together in a State. . . .[31]
>
> They exist not in a political vacuum but in continuous political relations with one another.[32]

This reasoning is applicable to unrecognized, as to recognized, states. Today there is little likelihood of an "isolated" state; the

[31] Brierly, p. 62. Brierly (p. 78), for all his realistic and in general enlightened approach, in a few words devoted to recognition sets down all the old clichés.

Cf. Pitt-Cobbett, *International Law* (5th ed. 1931), § 17: "Strictly, perhaps, international law should be regarded as applying equally to all communities that answer to the description of States. But in fact, owing to the circumstances of its development, its actual scope . . . is probably somewhat narrower. It was in its commencement the outcome of conditions and of a civilisation exclusively European; and many of its rules still bear the impress of their origin." (P. 46.)

"At the same time it can scarcely be said that States, such as China, etc. . . . are altogether outside the pale of international law." (P. 47.)

"So long as a political community possesses in fact the requisites of statehood formal recognition would not appear to be a condition precedent to the acquisition of the ordinary rights and obligations incident thereto." (P. 48.)

And see Goebel, pp. 51–52. See Sir John Fischer Williams, "Recognition," *Trans. Grotius Society*, xv (1929), 53, 60: "Indeed, the conception of 'civilized society' as a community of nations or states distinct from the rest of the world no longer corresponds with the main facts of contemporary life."

[32] Brierly, p. 63. Cf. Goebel, p. 55: "We assume as fundamental to our discussion the necessity of international relationships. Long ago the theory of the isolated state fell into disrepute, and today even those writers who are most susceptible to the influence of natural law cannot admit that a state may exist apart from surrounding political bodies."

very definition of a state as a defined territory ordinarily supposes that, at the limits of this territory, it impinges on other organized territories, constituted as it is and for the same ends. Le Normand has put the idea well, only, however, to criticize it: "One could say that these limitations which States impose on each other through mutual recognition are only those which result from the natural equilibrium of their respective forces." But to this he replies categorically that "their juridically obligatory character can find no explanation from that source." [33]

Here we have the clear line which the "formal" jurist draws between content and form, source and sanction, becoming and being. Facts, as we are well aware, have "normative" force. The constant repetition, with but non-significant variations, of a patterned event-sequence, the mere persistence of a condition, tends to create a conviction of its "sanctity" — not necessarily, of course: there are "bad" as well as "good" habits. Nor is the quality of "sanctity" always the same; it may be religious, social, political. Must this process result in a statute, a judicial decision, or a treaty, for example, before it has normative significance? The analytic jurist answers categorically "Yes." The historical jurist replies emphatically "No." To him law is growth and decay; even statute law, formally static, is not immune from the process, as witness for example the Volstead Act. In the field of international law and politics, if nowhere else, we cannot accept the all-or-none analytic conception. It seems to us that "the natural equilibrium" of social and economic forces existing between two states may create a relationship which, even if not complete until regularized or formalized in consent, is nevertheless not devoid of legal significance.[34]

It is the task of international law to promote order throughout the world. It finds this task imposed upon it because the unifying

[33] Le Normand (p. 43): "On pourrait dire que ces limitations que s'imposent les États en se reconnaissant ne sont autres que celles qui résultent d'un équilibre naturel le leurs forces respectives. . . . Mais le caractère juridiquement obligatoire ne se trouve pas expliqué par la."

[34] See Goebel, p. 47; following Jellinck, he says: "There are two constituent factors in the formation of all law. One is the normative force which is contained in the purely factual, the other the exact reverse, the tendency of conviction in abstract norms to be realized in concrete form. As regards the first conception, law is to every people that which is in fact practiced as law. Continuous practice produces the conviction in its normative character until the point is reached where the norm which is produced is looked upon as the authoritative command of the community."

forces of commerce, of free, easy, and quick communication, and the growing sentiment of universal humanity have created a network of relations requiring the regulation of law. The chief instrument of organizing this order is the state, which, though not the only person known to international law, is the most significant for its needs. There can be no doubt that a state prior to recognition fills some of the needs of the international order and performs the functions normally performed by states. By organizing order in a given portion of the globe, it brings under the force of law a portion of the world population, not only its citizens but all those who may find themselves within the territory at the time, or who may have cause to go there. Anarchy by definition is not localized; it is a threat to the entire international order. And by the same token a state organization is a safeguard of that order. A state, whether recognized or not, protects surrounding states from the anarchic pressures of unorganized humanity. The international function of the unrecognized state finds expression in a statement of Earl Russell. In it he answers the protest of the United States to the relations between England and the Confederacy.

Her Majesty's Government holds it to be an undoubted principle of international law, that when the persons or the property of the subjects or citizens of a state are injured by a *de facto* government, the state so aggrieved has *a right to claim* from the *de facto* government redress and reparation; and also that in cases of apprehended losses or injury to their subjects states may lawfully enter into communication with *de facto* governments to provide for the temporary security of the persons and property of their subjects. . . . (Italics mine.)

It may be necessary in future, for the protection of the interests of Her Majesty's subjects in the vast extent of country which resists the authority of the United States, to have further communication both with the central authority at Richmond and with the governors of the separate States, and in such cases such communications will continue to be made, but such communications will not imply any acknowledgment of the Confederacy as an independent State.[35]

[35] Moore, *Digest*, I, 209. Cf. Letter of Secretary Cass to Mr. Clay, Minister to Peru, *ibid.*, p. 183: "Mr. Osma insists, however, that a civil war in one country can not be known to the people of another but through their own government; that the existence or non-existence of civil war is a question not of fact, but of law, which no private person has a right to decide for himself; that foreigners must regard the former state of things as still existing, unless their respective governments have *recognized* the change. But I am very clearly of the opinion that an American citizen who goes to southern Peru may safely act upon the evidence of his own senses. If he sees that the former government has been expelled or overturned by a civil revolution, and a new one set up and

It may be replied that this quotation is not apt, that the Confederacy was in fact a recognized belligerent, and not an unrecognized state; that furthermore the two are unrelated. Lord Russell's statement, however, is quite general, and the reasons given make it applicable to either. Furthermore, there is a relation between the two. When a recognized belligerent becomes completely successful and war has ceased, does it by reason of ceasing to be a belligerent become nothing? Where, before a prize decree would be respected, would a different reception now be given to a decree confiscating a ship for violating the revenue laws? To answer that the rebel group is still a recognized belligerent is to cover the problem with a phrase. It is more real to say that recognized statehood is but the completion of a process wherein fact is informed by law, and where at any particular stage it may be difficult to say whether a thing is so because it is the fact or because it is the law. No doubt this view is obnoxious to those who like clarity even at the sacrifice of truth. "There is no middle ground. Either it is a member of the international community and it has the capacity (*le jouissance*) and the exercise [i. e. immediately effective enforcement] of rights and prerogatives or it is not, and it possesses no juridical aptitude." [36]

This statement attacks the distinction dear to the hearts of the natural-law writers between the capacity (*le jouissance*) or possession of rights and the enjoyment or exercise of them. These writers argue, as we have seen, that states have rights prior to recognition, but that to enjoy them, to make them enforceable against any other country, there must be recognition by that country.[37] To this the positivist says cynically, "In other words, you admit that in fact

maintained in its place, he can not be molested or even blamed for regulating his behavior by the laws thus established. Nay, he has no choice; the government *de facto* will compel his obedience. It will not give him leave to ignore the matter of fact while he waits for the solution of a legal problem at home."

[36] Le Normand, p. 40: "Et remarquez qu'il n'y a pas de milieu. Ou il est membre de la communauté internationale et il a la jouissance et l'exercice des droits et prérogatives comme tel, ou il ne l'est pas et il ne possède aucune aptitude juridique."

[37] Thus Fiore, § 165: "Recognition of a state is the solemn act necessary to establish diplomatic relations between states as well as the reciprocal enjoyment and exercise of international rights."

And Pradier-Fodéré, *Droit International Public* (1885), I, § 136: ". . . la jouissance, la possession de la souveraineté extérieure appartient à l'État nouveau dès le moment où il s'est formé, par le fait même de son existence, mais l'exercice de cette souveraineté, sa mise en action au dehors, sont, par la force des choses, subordonnés à la reconnaissance par les autres États."

there are no rights before recognition, but it pleases your fancy to say that there are." The controversy is reminiscent of the famous case of *The Western Maid*.[38] Here it was held, contrary to intimations in *The Siren*,[39] that because the United States does not consent to be sued in tort, no lien can attach to one of its ships involved in collision, and a purchaser from the government takes the ship free from such lien. Said Mr. Justice Holmes: "Legal obligations that exist but cannot be enforced are ghosts that are seen in the law but that are elusive to the grasp." [40]

Lawyers, familiar with many instances of rights enforceable conditionally or contingently, and with the demi-monde of rights barred for some purposes and not for others, barred in some places and not in others by the Statute of Limitations or the Statute of Frauds, may feel that this statement is an over-simplification.

Even assuming that prior to recognition rights are not enforceable, it is nevertheless not without meaning to posit their existence. Let us suppose that state *A*, at war with *B*, seizes as prize a ship of state *C*, a state which *A* does not recognize; and that there is illegality in the condemnation procedure. If, after recognition, *C* could claim damages from *A* for this wrong, it would look very much as if a right—or something like it—existed before recognition.[41] And if,

It is rather surprising to see Brierly (p. 78) adopt these same well-worn phrases: "Theoretically a state might exist without being recognized by other states, though in that case it would be unable to act as a state in the international community." See comment on Brierly's views on recognition (*supra*, note 31).

[38] 257 U. S. 419 (1922). [39] 7 Wall. 152 (1869).

[40] The Western Maid, 257 U. S. 419, 433 (1922).

[41] This raises the problem of the "retroactivity" of recognition, about which something is said below. Generally, it may be said that once a new *government* is recognized, its acts within its own territory will be given full effect in the recognized country though done prior to the recognition. But the writer knows of no cases in which the doctrine of retroactivity arose in connection with an unrecognized state. Furthermore, the point raised in the text is not the effect to be given to acts done by it, but whether it is the subject of rights prior to its recognition, and, also, of duties. In The Tinoco Arbitration, 18 A. J. 147 (1923), Taft, Arbitrator, held that the Government of Costa Rica was responsible to Great Britain for the acts of the prior Tinoco Government, though Great Britain had not recognized the Tinoco Government. Much discussion has been had on the question whether the United States (*inter alia*) is liable to the U. S. S. R. for its participation in the expedition against the Soviets in 1920, when, as now, that government was unrecognized by us. See Schuman, "Soviet Russia's Claims Against the United States," *Cur. Hist.*, XXXII (1930), 911; reprinted in Buehler *et al.*, *Recognition of Soviet Russia* (1931), p. 307.

as Lord Russell says, a state has a right to claim damages against a *de facto* government for injury to its nationals, it would seem that the *de facto* government has equivalent rights. Surely to treat the *de facto* state as an outlaw, to consider the relationship between two unrecognizant states (of course, the elder state does not usually consider itself as "unrecognized") as completely anarchical does not express either the reality or the needs of the world order.[42]

It will be said that we are confusing what ought to be with what is. But we trust that no one claims in these days to be able to isolate the pure element "what is." We have already seen that both sovereignty and auto-limitation, put forth as pure fact, were equally credos pressed into the cause of utility. And now, as then, it is our business to marshal as many of the facts as possible into desirable categories.

Furthermore, it does not seem entirely true that these rights are completely unenforceable before recognition. Retorsion,[43] reprisals, and war are admittedly modes of enforcing international rights. Does a state have to be recognized by another before it can fight a war with the other? It may be said that we are assuming that resort to arms is necessarily war. There is force in this criticism. If the conflict, however, is carried on under the rules of war, we should have a basis for characterizing the conflict as war. The practice in civil conflicts is to abide by the rules of war where, as in our Civil War, the combatants present temporarily the situation of nation against nation. And it is highly probable that in a war between unrecognized states the practice would be the same.[44]

But it seems to us superficial to test the existence of a legal relationship between states by the sole query of the enforceability of

[42] Cf. Goebel, p. 60: "A protracted period without law in the international sense would mean what outlawry means in private law, that the new political entity might be subjected to violence at the hands of other states and in general be treated as beyond the pale, without such treatment being in any way a violation of the international obligation of the third state."

[43] Fiore (§ 174) records that when Germany refused to recognize the new Italian Kingdom, Cavour withdrew the exequaturs of German consuls; this brought Germany around.

[44] But cf. Anzilotti (p. 164): "Il y a sans doute certaines exigences élementaires d'humanité qui sont difficilement mises de côté même au regard d'un État non encore reconnu; mais la question est précisément de savoir si de telles exigences ne valent pas alors simplement comme exigences morales. La réponse dépend de la manière de concevoir les normes juridiques internationales et la distinction de ces normes d'avec les normes morales; si nous partons de la distinction qui est adoptée ici, il ne semble pas qu'elle puisse être douteuse."

claims arising from breaches of right; it is, of course, this final perfectability of a right, its realization in a coerced remedy, which is to some the very hallmark of law. Admittedly, international law even between recognized states is weak in this respect; and we admit that between unrecognized states it is still weaker. In fact it is a commonplace to say that, because of this lack of enforcement by a superior body, international law is not law at all; that it may be a form of social control, but that not all social control is law. To this latter we can agree: the rules of a game, the decrees of churches, the standards of social intercourse are all forms of social control. The difference between all of them and law, as we commonly use the term, is in the nature of the organization which evolves and applies the rules. In the case of law it is the state, society politically organized, which evolves and applies the rules. It is usually said, also, that only the state can make effective its rules by the use of force. This means that, in addition to forms of pressure available to the other organizations, the state alone can inflict imprisonment and corporal punishment. Judged by these standards, international law bears significant resemblances to law. It is evolved by the states acting internationally; the states consider themselves the subjects of these rules, even when they have had no hand in making them; and behind them is the sanction of authorized force to be applied by the states, which are the instruments of the international order. No one, of course, denies that there are important differences between international and municipal law; in the former, the institution of sanction is more rudimentary. In our opinion the difference between the law as applied between recognizant states and unrecognizant states is a difference in the same scale of values.

Until recently, at least, most writers have agreed that a state has no right to recognition. Even some of the natural lawyers agree to this. Fiore says: "Recognition is in its nature a political act. It is the privilege of every government to determine with perfect freedom and independence whether conditions render desirable or opportune the recognition of a new state. . . ." [45]

[45] Fiore, § 169. But Fiore (§ 174) says: "The unjustifiable refusal to recognize as an autonomous and independent state one constituted *de facto*, must be considered as contrary to international law and may justify acts of retorsion."

And see Lorimer, p. 104: "Any doctrine of recognition which stops short of asserting recognition as a right on the one hand, and accepting it as a duty on the other — which professes to regard it as an act of courtesy, comity, or the like, the exercise of which may be jurally withheld — deprives international

Recently, however, Sir John Fischer Williams has ventured to make a confession of faith (and hope):

> One who believes, as I do, that International Law has in it an element which does not depend on the express or even implied consent of States — as distinct from the general opinion of civilised mankind — will have a tendency to answer this question [i.e. is there a right to recognition?] as Bluntschli answered it, in the affirmative. If we do not let ourselves be hypnotized by the contemplation of States alone, but recognize that the State is only one form of human organization, it seems impossible to affirm as a legal proposition that it lies within the power of even a majority of states to deny to human beings, not their subjects, fulfilling the necessary conditions of civilized government, the right to enter international society.[46]

With the aspirations of this we are in accord; but Sir John seeks, by positing a right of recognition, the same end as does the writer in denying the need of recognition at all, at least as a condition of membership in international society.

law of a permanent basis in nature, and fails to bring it within the sphere of jurisprudence."

To this Le Normand (p. 55) objects strenuously. The act of recognition, he maintains, is free, and it is subjective. 1st, there can be no right to recognition, since no juridical relation exists prior thereto from which a right could arise. 2nd, the act is subjective: it is the judgment of one free-willing organization that another organization exists. To the same effect is Anzilotti, p. 167.

Goebel (p. 55) is not entirely clear on the point: "I do not think that we can relegate the recognition process to the category of a mere formality, a consecration of what it [the state] already possesses. *It is neither a right of the new state nor a free act* on the part of the state which grants it." (Italics mine.) However, at p. 64 he says: "In the sense that the declaration by the third state is itself an imposed obligation of will, *it must be a formally free act on its part.* This does not affect the *de facto* relationships which are carried on before this act takes place. Just as there is a certain international necessity which compels the new state to bind its will, so this same compulsion operates upon third states." (Italics mine.)

It is Goebel's thesis that the creation of the international relationship is a slow "becoming," is the growth of fact into norm; the process is crowned by recognition. He believes, however, that the legal sanction of the status proceeds from free self-limitation on both sides; he rejects the idea of super-imposed law based on the inevitability of "social forces." (P. 56, n. 3; p. 59, n. 1.) But it seems to us that Goebel lays too much stress on the self-imposed quality of international relations. He admits that in fact international relations may exist irrespective of the will of states, but says that that compulsion cannot be the source of their quality as *legal* relationships. But why not? In the above quotations on the right of recognition, he himself does not seem able to keep the two as distinct as he claims they are. Cf. note 74, *infra.*

[46] *Loc. cit.* (*supra*, note 31), p. 61.

Oppenheim objects to this conclusion because, as he says, rather naively, "It can . . . not be seen what the function of recognition could be if a state entered at its birth really of right to the Family of Nations."[47] But must recognition have a function? To be sure, as a conception for organizing thought about international law, there is nothing to restrain a writer from weaving it into his system and assigning it a function. But avowedly the positivists are concerned with the practice of recognition, and so are we, since it is the conduct of the Department of State which our courts are called upon to interpret. However, the word "recognition" may be used in either sense: to describe a systematic conception, or to indicate a practice in international politics. Because of this, considerable confusion has arisen recently in discussion of the question. The Department of State maintains, for example, that the United States has not recognized Soviet Russia. John Bassett Moore replies that our conduct "amounts" to recognition. His reasoning is based on the orthodox conception of what recognition is supposed to be, rather than on the practices which states today choose to call recognition. The institution has changed; the word remains the same. We must be on our guard against this. Even if the Department of State were misusing words, it would be immaterial in the context of this study. The very purpose of our inquiry is to search out the meaning and the function of recognition as practiced by foreign offices, and by the Department of State in particular. It is this practice which is involved in the litigation which comes before the courts; it is this practice, its significance and its logical implications, which the courts should understand and to which, in the administration of justice, they should assign its relative value. The question then is, does recognition in practice have a function, and, if so, what is it? To give answers to these questions, a hasty survey of some significant recognition practices is essential. In our opinion, these will demonstrate that the orthodox dogmas of recognition are untenable, and that, furthermore, the practice is growing so diverse, so heterodox, that it is hardly possible to give any very clear or systematic exposition of the function of recognition.

Before proceeding to this survey, it will be convenient to consider for a moment the views of the learned on the recognition of new governments in states already recognized. Though theoretically a much simpler and less controversial question than recognition of state existence, it bulks far larger in practice, and causes today far

[47] *Op. cit.* (*supra*, note 19), p. 144.

greater difficulty in the world of law and politics. Most writers draw a sharp distinction between recognition of a state and of a government. A state does not lose its identity by reason of a change of government, even a revolutionary change.[48] It retains its right to have relations with other states; and since these relations can be effected only through its government, it is said, "A recognized state has a *right* to exact the recognition of the will of its organ as its own will." [49] Goebel proclaims that "the recognition of governments is purely a formality, and attempts to make it something different are born of a misconception of the relations between the state and government." [50]

He says further, in a naive statement which more nearly destroys than enforces his conclusion:

> Because recognition of governments, through a mere formality, is generally considered to be a necessity, foreign powers by making recognition of new governments conditional, frequently extort from new de facto organizations concessions which they otherwise would not obtain. This policy gives to an almost meaningless process a constitutive force which it does not and should not possess, and which is inconsistent with the facts of international existence.[51]

[48] Rougier, *Les Guerres Civiles et le Droit des Gens* (1903), § 130: "L'existence d'un État souverain, sa personalité juridique, sont en effet, comme nous l'avons vu, absolument indépendants des changements gouvernementaux internes et de la reconnaissance de ces gouvernements par les tiers. Napoléon a résumé cette idée en signant le traité de Campo-Formio, dans un mot célèbre: 'La République française n'a pas besoin d'une reconnaissance tout comme le soleil n'a pas besoin d'être reconnu.' "

Hyde, *International Law* (1922), I, § 43; The Sapphire, 11 Wall. 164 (1871); Russian Government (later, State of Russia) *v.* Lehigh Valley Railway Co., 293 Fed. 133 and 135 (S. D. N. Y. 1919 and 1923); affirmed 21 F (2d) 396 (C. C. A. 2nd, 1927).

[49] Borchard has recently stated very forcefully that a refusal to recognize a new government is contrary to international law, a hostile and unfriendly act, and a *casus belli*. *The Unrecognized Government in American Courts*, 26 A. J. 261 (1932).

Le Normand, p. 184: "C'est . . . un droit pour l'État reconnu que d'exiger la reconnaissance de la volonté de son organe comme la sienne propre.

"Après avoir reconnu un État, et tant que cette reconnaissance de l'État n'est pas retirée, on reconnaît forcement le gouvernement qui est à la tête de l'État, et qui est indispensable de l'existence de celui-ci."

Rougier, *op. cit.* (*supra*, note 48), § 127: "Les Puissances doivent reconnaître le gouvernement existant, quel qu'il soit, dès l'instant qu'il est régulièrement organisé et accepté par la nation."

[50] Goebel, p. 65.

[51] *Ibid.*, p. 67.

These over-simplified assertions proceed on the basis of easy (and convenient) assumptions that once a state always a state, and always the same state. In 1889, when Legitime and Hyppolite divided Hayti into two warring camps, the United States recognized no government at all in Hayti, in fact it recognized neither faction even as belligerents.[52] It is a large question whether Hayti at that time was the same state with which we had relations under the deposed regime of Salomon. It is more nearly true that at that time there was no state of Hayti at all.

By definition, a state must have a government. Revolution, civil war, incipient anarchy may for a time dissolve the state.[53] It would be pedantic to maintain that, when order is once more reconstituted, it is always a case of "The King is dead; long live the King." Yet for other states the problem of recognizing the new government raises a number of the same considerations involved in recognizing a new state. True, there is no question of offending a parent state as where a new state is formed by secession from an old. But whether the new government can maintain order, and whether it is capable of performing its international functions, are in both cases of like concern.[54] Not every change of government involves a violent disruption of the internal polity, and a mortal sickness of the state. Because of the variety of situations that may arise, Goebel's statement is a dogmatic over-simplification which, as is quite apparent on the face of it, does not represent the current practice of states that would itself seem to be part of "the facts of international existence."

The Practice of Recognition

The policy to be pursued in recognizing new states first became acute in modern history in connection with the revolt of Spain's

[52] Moore, *Digest*, I, 201. In The Conserva, 38 Fed. 431 (E. D. N. Y. 1889), it was held that neither faction was "a prince, state, colony, district, or people" within our neutrality laws forbidding the outfitting of ships, etc., to aid one such entity against another in the course of war or civil conflict.

[53] Baty, *So-called de Facto Recognition*, 31 Yale L. J. 469, 481 (1921): "Much current popular talk proceeds on the footing that a state endures always and for ever, whether it has a settled government or not. . . . If a nation ceases to have a government, it ceases *ipso facto* to be a state."

[54] Cf. Funck-Brentano et Sorel, *Précis du Droit des Gens* (3rd ed. 1900), p. 209, who assimilate the recognition of governments to the recognition of states.

South American colonies, beginning in 1805.[55] The revolt was originally devoted to the exiled Ferdinand; it gave notice to Napoleon that to the colonies Joseph Bonaparte was *persona non grata.* But by 1810 the goal of most of South America was independence. By 1818 the colonies were almost entirely successful, and Spanish rule was non-existent. Within South America, at least three communities were organized as states: "Buenos Ayres," Chili, and Colombia. Since 1805 England and the United States had done a thriving trade with South America, and in England particularly the merchant class was eager for recognition. Yet it was 1822 before the United States recognized any of the South American republics, and 1826 before England joined the United States in this action.

The recognition of revolted territories as new states is a delicate matter. Recognition before assured independence or before it is clear that the parent state is without reasonable hope of success is an unfriendly act, even an act of war, toward the parent state. John Quincy Adams was well aware of this. In the face of Henry Clay's insistent demands for recognition of the South American republics, he quietly bided the time when the United States might act with a clear conscience. In the year 1818 [56] the occasion was ripe, but at this time we were treating with Spain over the purchase of Florida. The Spanish Government seemed reluctant to ratify the treaty; better, perhaps, to secure ratification before irritating Spain by recognizing her colonies. We waited three years. England's position was even more difficult. In a vague way she was committed to the dogma of legitimacy; at least she had, as a hangover from the anti-Napoleonic combination, bonds with the Holy Alliance. The Tory Cabinet looked askance at revolution; the hope was that Spain would first recognize the colonies, and so relieve England and the neutral powers of their embarrassment. For a time (1821–1822) there was a suggestion of armed European intervention in behalf of Spain, but England frowned on it, and no one took it seriously. All the while the English merchantry pressed for recognition; but it was not until 1826 that Canning, even then in the face of his reluctant ministry, the disapproval of Europe, and the excited protests of the Spanish Ambassador, recognized "Buenos Ayres."

[55] See Paxson, p. 20. The "recognition" of the American Colonies by Louis XVI was really a declaration of war on Great Britain rather than an authentic recognition. See *infra*, p. 106. The account here of the recognition of the South American republics is based on this book.

[56] *Ibid.*, p. 160.

The South American experience shows that recognition of undoubted states may be withheld for a considerable time; the reasons do not arise necessarily from antipathy toward the unrecognized state, or from a desire to coerce the grant of concessions, or from a hope that non-recognition will kill it. The United States, in fact, was from the first friendly toward the new sister republics. The United States was represented in South America by agents from 1810 on. In 1810 Joel Poinsett was given the non-committal title of "Agent for Seamen and Commerce in the Port of Buenos Ayres." [57] But in 1811 he was commissioned Consul-general, and a consul was appointed under him. No trace has been found of an exequatur issued to any of these agents, but they speak in their dispatches of being formally received. No one treated these relations, though undoubtedly typical of relations between states and more or less presupposing the existence of states, as equivalent to recognition. John Quincy Adams, Secretary of State, refused exequaturs to South American agents until 1822.[58]

Interesting are the cases of Hayti and Santo Domingo. After the French betrayed Toussaint L'Ouverture, the negro population in 1803 expelled the French from the island, and except for Spanish rule of Santo Domingo from 1806 to 1821, and the voluntary submission to the same rule again between 1861 and 1864, the island has been independent. Revolutions have been frequent; and until 1843 the two parts of the island were sometimes under one govern-

[57] *Ibid.*, p. 109. There has been some difference of opinion as to the effect of sending or receiving consuls on the relations between the sending and receiving powers. Oppenheim, *op. cit.* (*supra*, note 19), § 428, maintains that though a state does not recognize a *de facto* government by authorizing its consul to function in the territory controlled by such government, application for a formal exequatur does constitute recognition. Cf. Hall, *International Law* (8th ed. 1924), § 26*; *Research in International Law, Harvard Law School, Drafts of Conventions Prepared for the Codification of International Law* (1932), "Legal Position and Functions of Consuls," Art. 6 (*a*): "A sending state shall not be presumed to have recognized that the authority in actual control of a territory is entitled to such control, because it has appointed a person or has permitted a person previously appointed to exercise consular functions within such territory, nor because such person has applied to that authority for permission to exercise consular functions."

[58] It is generally recognized that a receiving state by granting an exequatur recognizes the sending government. Moore, *Digest*, I, 79. Authorities cited in comment to Art. 6 of draft mentioned in above note. Art. 6 (*b*) of that draft provides: "A state shall not be presumed to have recognized a government because it has raised no objection to the exercise of consular functions within its territory by a person appointed for that purpose by such government."

ment, sometimes independent of each other. However, General Boyer ruled the entire island in peace from 1822 to 1843, and since then, with intermittent revolution, governments have functioned regularly. Yet the United States did not recognize Hayti until 1862, nor the Dominican Republic until 1866.[59] As in the South American republics, we had our commercial agents stationed at the principal ports.

On the other hand, premature recognition to secure political advantage is not unknown in our national career. France, in 1777, recognized our independence long before it was assured. Louis XVI's motive, as told to Charles III of Spain, was "to prevent their [the colonies'] reunion with the mother country." Blandly the French ambassador communicated the news to the Court of St. James, stating that "the King is firmly persuaded, that it [the English Court] will find in it fresh proofs of His Majesty's constant and sincere Dispositions for Peace";[60] His Britannic Majesty found in it an act of war. Roosevelt recognized the Republic of Panama within four days after its revolt from Colombia.[61] On September 2, 1918, the United States recognized the Czechoslovak[62] National Council, an organization with headquarters in Washington, as a *de facto* belligerent government "clothed with proper authority to direct the military and political affairs of the Czecho-Slovaks." At this time Czechoslovakia was a state without a country, a pious hope.

Even greater variety of practice has been displayed in the recognition of new governments. In this matter the United States was

[59] Moore, *Digest*, I, 107.

[60] Paxson, pp. 25–26.

[61] 1903 For. Rel. 225, 230, 231. The revolt occurred on November 3. On the same day Hay instructed the U. S. S. *Nashville* to prevent the landing of Colombian troops in Panama "in the interests of peace" (p. 231). On November 6 our consul in Panama was instructed to recognize a "de facto government republican in form" if and when formed in "the State of Panama" (p. 233). On the same day our Colombian minister was informed by Hay that we had "entered into relations" with the people of Panama, who have "resumed" their independence (p. 225).

[62] *Recognition of the Czechoslovak Nation*, Am. Pol. Sci. Rev., XII (1918), 715. At the time of the "recognition" the population and territories claimed by the National Council were parts of Austria-Hungary. In a number of cases the question has arisen whether these peoples ceased to be alien enemies from the moment of recognition, so as to remove the bar to their suing in the United States and so as to set the Statute of Limitations running. See *infra*, p. 226, for a discussion of the cases.

the pioneer of so-called "de factoism." The legitimist dogma was unpalatable to a state of revolutionary origin; but Jefferson's formula for recognizing governments which represent "the will of the nation, substantially declared," has been found capable of "interpretation" so as, in its turn, to take on a tinge of legitimism. Under Seward, and again under Wilson, legitimacy masqueraded as "legality" or constitutionalism.

Jefferson wrote:

> It accords with our principles to acknowledge any government to be rightful which is formed by the will of the nation substantially declared. . . . With such a government every kind of business may be done. But there are some matters which I conceive might be transacted with a government de facto; such, for instance, as the reforming the unfriendly restrictions on our commerce and navigation.[63]

Of Jefferson's ideas Goebel has said that they "mark the beginning of the de facto principle of recognition for which the United States has usually stood." [64]

But clearly Jefferson's statement is not pure "de factoism." On its face, a distinction is made between "*de facto*" governments with which some sorts of business can be done, and "rightful" governments formed by "the will of the nation substantially declared." It is true that during Jefferson's time and, indeed, until the time of Seward, a government if obeyed was held to represent "the will of the nation substantially declared." In a much-quoted letter Buchanan stated:

> In its intercourse with foreign nations the Government of the United States has, from its origin, always recognized *de facto* governments. We recognize the right of all nations to create and reform their political institutions according to their own will and pleasure. . . . It is sufficient for us to know that a government exists *capable of maintaining itself*; and then its recognition on our part inevitably follows.[65] (Italics mine.)

But not so Seward. In 1868, refusing to recognize a revolutionary government of Peru, he wrote: "What we wait for in this case

[63] Jefferson, *Works* (Ford ed.), IV, 131. Quoted and discussed in Goebel, p. 102.
[64] Goebel, p. 111.

[65] Moore, *Digest*, I, 124. Letter of Buchanan to Rush, Minister at Paris, advising recognition of the Republic of 1848. In his letter of January 12, 1852, Webster, advising Rives to recognize the Napoleonic coup d'état, said: "While we deeply regret the overthrow of popular institutions, yet our ancient ally has still our good wishes for her prosperity and happiness, and we are bound to leave to her the choice of means for the promotion of those ends." Moore, *Digest*, I, 126.

is the *legal* evidence that the existing administration has been *deliberately* accepted by the people of Peru. When a *republican* form of government is *constitutionally* established, we hasten to recognize the administration. . . ." [66] (Italics mine.)

Yet undoubtedly both of these expressions are possible interpretations of Jefferson's "will of the nation substantially declared," for that phrase has no such clear and single meaning as is sometimes assumed.[67] After Seward, the United States abandoned his policy and reverted to its original practice. Its revival under Wilson is a well-known story. It finds its most extravagant expression in the Treaty of Washington (1923), to which the United States was not a party but to the principle of which it announced its adherence. The Latin American states agreed "not to recognize any other government which may come into power in any of the Republics through a coup d'état or a revolution against a recognized government, so long as the freely elected representatives of the people thereof have not constitutionally reorganized the country." [68]

[66] 1868 Dip. Cor. Part II, 863. Goebel traces Seward's policy to a distaste for revolution growing out of the Civil War experience. Curiously enough, Goebel considers that our objections to other states recognizing the Confederacy in 1861 was a reversal of our traditional policy of de factoism. But to recognize a rebellious organization as a new state is very different from recognizing a new government. It probably is true, however, that Seward's later policy toward *de facto* governments was colored by his Civil War experience. See Goebel, pp. 172, 193, 200–201.

[67] Goebel assumes that the phrase is an apt and single-meaninged expression of pure de factoism. But it is evident that the phrase "will of the people substantially declared" is capable of infinite interpretation. Lorimer gives the phrase an exegesis unlike anything known before or since. Thus, he classes states according to their "value." This "value" depends on the extent to which they express the will of the nation. Thus, a state ruled over by an absolute monarch has nearly no value at all, and need not be recognized: "According to the strict principles of international law [!] France would have had no *casus belli* against any State which declined to receive the Emperor's [Napoleon III] Ambassador, if the declinature had been put expressly on the ground that he was not the ambassador of France." Lorimer, I, 164.

A milder form of this doctrine is found in Funck-Brentano et Sorel, *op. cit.* (*supra*, note 54), pp. 209–210, and Hyde, *International Law* (1922), vol. I, § 43, who place it on the danger of dictatorships, revolutionary governments, etc., to international peace.

[68] This was a treaty of peace and amity between Guatemala, El Salvador, Honduras, Nicaragua, and Costa Rica, signed at Washington, February 7, 1923. To be found in Hudson, *International Legislation* (1931), II, 901. See *The Central-American Policy of Non-Recognition*, 19 A. J. 164 (1925). Of the pre-

And the crowning feature of the system is that even where the government has been so reorganized, recognition is not to be given in certain cases where the *elected* officials of the new government were involved in the revolution or related to such persons, or were in high military command during the election or within six months of the revolution.

What a dilemma if revolutionary governments were to appear in all the republics at the same time! However laudable the desire of discouraging excessive governmental turnover through revolution (though we are apt to forget that the coup d'état may be a legitimate and normal instrument of politics), it is doubtful that such treaties can stop it. The treaty adds to the international confusion incident to revolution, retarding the healing of breaches in the body politic.

Seward's defense of constitutionalism was that "the adoption of a different principle in regard to foreign states would necessarily tend to impair the constitutional vigor of our own government, and thus favor disorganization, disintegration, and anarchy throughout the American continent." [69]

And Hyde puts the justification on broader ground:

> *If in the interest of the society of nations* the members thereof should habitually manifest extreme reluctance in recognizing as a new government one which acquires power in the teeth of popular opposition and by inhuman methods, evidence both of popular support and of abstinence from arbitrary procedure would be commonly if not invariably offered by a party demanding recognition, as a necessary means of preventing indefinite delay.[70] (Italics mine.)

Potter pronounces our new attitude "courageous." The real meaning of the Jeffersonian policy was "to make the world safe for republics." The policy promotes "greater individual and national liberty." [71]

The whole world went off the *de facto* standard in its policy toward Soviet Russia. Our Government, still maintaining the

vious treaty of 1907 from which the treaty of Washington derives S. Séfériadès says: "C'est là tout simplement refuser toute reconnaissance internationale à des gouvernements de fait. C'est-à-dire vouloir ignorer les faits et remplir de pages blanches une grande partie de l'histoire de l'Univers." *Droit de la Paix*, IV Recueil des Cours, Académie de Droit International, 340 (1930).

[69] 1868 Dip. Cor. Part II, 863 *et seq.*

[70] Hyde, *International Law*, vol. I, § 43.

[71] Potter, *The Nature of American Foreign Policy*, 21 A. J. 53, 55, n. 6 (1927).

Wilsonian thesis, said on August 10, 1920, through Secretary of State Colby: [72]

> We are unwilling that while it is helpless in the grip of a non-representative government whose only sanction is brutal force, Russia shall be weakened still further by a policy of dismemberment. . . . The Bolsheviki, although in number an inconsiderable minority of the people, by force and cunning seized the powers and machinery of government. . . . It is not possible for the government of the United States to recognize the present rulers of Russia. . . .

But there were further reasons which, rather than the above, explain the policy of the European powers. Mr. Colby continues:

> The existing regime in Russia is based upon the negation of every principle of honor and good faith, and every usage and convention, underlying the whole structure of international law, the negation, in short, of every principle upon which it is possible to base harmonious and trustful relations, whether of nations or of individuals.

If this is true some theorists might argue that Russia had ceased to be an international state. Surely if she became entirely incapable of fulfilling international functions this would be true; and it is often stated that the disposition as well as the ability to fulfill obligations is a condition of international personality; it would be said that a state, unwilling to perform international functions, in effect declared itself unwilling "to enter the family of nations" — which was its own concern.[73]

But we believe that the day is past when membership in the "family of nations" depends on the concept of "free-willing" states. So far we have argued that membership does not depend on the will of those already in, that any group fulfilling the requirements is *ipso facto* an international personality. But we feel that it is equally true that membership in the international community does not depend on the inclination or desire of the state whose membership is in question, though most writers assume or assert the contrary.[74] No individual can withdraw himself from the sway

[72] Quoted in Russian Socialist, etc. Republic *v.* Cibrario, 235 N. Y. 255, 264; 139 N. E. 259, 262 (1923).

[73] Séfériadès, *loc. cit.* (*supra*, note 68) at 295, makes it part of the definition of a state that it accept the principles of international law. And cf. *id.* at 341.

[74] Thus Goebel (p. 56) says: "It is possible that civilized states may exist in a community of uninterrupted continuity, as history has shown to be the case, and we may argue that for this reason the international system is as independent of the wills of the single members as a state is independent of the conscious

of social control. His personality and responsibility depend not on his willingness to perform, but on his capacity as an individual. And it is questionable whether any state today would be suffered to declare that it does not acknowledge the empire of international law, that it withdraws from the international community, or, if a new state, that it is not minded to accede. In such a case, non-recognition should be considered not as a denial of international personality, but as a sanction, as a mode of compelling an international personality to perform its duties. Non-recognition thus becomes one of the weapons along with war and retaliation for bringing delinquent nations to book.[75] Whether such a dynamic use of the recognition process is legitimate it is not our business to say. Clearly it is very different from the Wilsonian doctrine with which it is too often jumbled together. The Wilsonian doctrine has been nearly universally condemned, as lending itself to the dictation and interference by large powers in the domestic matters of minor ones.[76] However, with the worth of neither of these doctrines are we

will of the individual, but this explains only the historical phase, and does not answer the legal problem of the extent to which the will of the participants is to be taken into account. It is exactly this dilemma, the inevitability of the international system, *the right of the state to adopt this order as an act of free will*, which makes the international position of the newly created state so difficult to comprehend." (Italics mine.)

Of Huber, he says (p. 59, note): "The only compulsions which Huber recognizes are the so-called social forces which contribute to the formation of international law. These, he thinks, are of sufficient force to override completely the subjective nature of participation in international law. . . . His great error rests in making the nature of international relationships social rather than political or legal. . . .

"The social forces furnish the base upon which the subjective rule is conditioned."

Of Goebel's point we would say (1) that the sharp conceptual distinctions between "legal" and "social" are conceived too absolutely, but (2) admitting the distinction, there seems a failure to perceive that the social force may d termine the "type" of the legal system. Why is Huber not correct in saying that the social force may override "the subjective nature of participation"? This involves no confusion of "social" and "legal." It merely means that because of the strength of social forces the legal system is founded not upon consent but upon compulsion; such a legal system is no anomaly; it is, in fact, the normal type.

[75] Thus Litvinov, speaking for the U. S. S. R. on the occasion of the Peace Pact, considered non-recognition as a non-pacific sanction which should be outlawed along with war. See the statement set forth in the text *infra*, p. 147. Quoted in Buehler *et al.*, *Recognition of Soviet Russia* (1931), p. 160. Cf. Borchard, *loc. cit.* (*supra*, note 49).

[76] References to some of the literature pro and con have already been made

primarily concerned. Rather we wish to show that the granting or withholding of recognition is today an instrument of international policy; that, as such, there is no warrant for making a sharp distinction between recognition of states and recognition of governments, and for insisting that the latter is "purely a formality, and attempts to make it something different are born of a misconception of the relations between the state and the government." In short, non-recognition may be, and is, used as a political weapon against a state without denying either its statehood or the capacity of its government.

Our experience with unrecognized powers is a demonstration of this assertion. We have already seen that for years we had commercial intercourse before recognition with the states of South America and of Hayti and Santo Domingo. This intercourse was fostered and protected by agents appointed by our Government to communicate and treat with the unrecognized states. And with unrecognized governments we have had the same non-official, what the French call "officious," relations. Seward, though he decided that this government "does not find itself at liberty to make a formal recognition" of the new government in Salvador (1864), nevertheless provided for "unofficial" communications with the minister accredited to our Government, and refused to receive the president of the ousted government, though it still had forces in the field.[77] Though in 1913 Wilson refused recognition to Huerta's gov-

in notes 45, 49, 67–71, *supra*. See also Lécharny, *La Validité des Actes Internes* (1929), pp. 12–15, for an elaborate comparison between Wilson's declaration with respect to Mexico and the declaration and practice on legitimacy of the Holy Alliance; cf. Goebel, p. 220.

Secretary of State Stimson, in an address of February 6, 1931, states that the Wilsonian doctrine has been abandoned. He points to our ready recognition of recent revolutionary governments in Bolivia, Peru, Argentina, Brazil, and Panama. Speech set forth in Lippmann and Scroggs, *The United States in World Affairs, 1931* (1932).

And in Baty, *op. cit.* (*supra*, note 53), pp. 474–475, we see a violent reaction to the fundamental assumptions of the Wilsonian creed: "It [the Wilsonian doctrine] was an assumption that Astraea is a child of the Boss and the Caucus. . . . But it is perfectly possible that the real opinion of a country may be better represented by the authors of a coup d'état than by the notoriously untrustworthy verdict of a plebiscite.

"Besides, does international law forbid a nation to organize itself without reference to the voice of its ill-instructed, crowd-emotional, less civilized members?"

[77] Moore, *Digest*, I, 237. Baty, *loc. cit.* (*supra*, note 53), p. 478, criticizes

ernment, the ordinary business between the two governments continued to be done for Mexico by ambassador and consuls, as representatives of the existing government.[78]

It will be said that these are merely facts of a social and political type, that they are not conceived by the parties as implying the existence of a legal relation, of the norms of right and duty. We have already addressed ourselves to this distinction. We shall let it pass, and go on to a situation in which it cannot be taken.

What of the making of a bilateral treaty? Does it necessarily imply recognition? Clearly it presupposes international capacity and mutual admission of statehood. Lorimer says that the Barbary States were never recognized, because a band of robbers cannot be a state.[79] But in 1801 Sir William Scott gave credit to a confiscation decree of the Dey of Algiers.[80] In reply to the argument that Algiers was not a state but a mere pirate gang, he said that "they have long acquired the character of established governments, with whom we have regular treaties, acknowledging and confirming to them the relations of legal states."

In fact the year before this decision (1800) a treaty between Great Britain and Algiers had been concluded.[81] It was entitled "Articles of Peace and Commerce between His Most Excellent Majesty, George the Third, etc., and the Most Illustrious Lord Mustapha, Dey, Bashaw and Governor of the most famous and warlike City and *Kingdom of Algiers.*" The treaty "agreed and concluded that there shall be a lasting peace and friendship" between the parties. This treaty is but one of a series stretching back more than 100 years to 1682.[82] All are entitled "Articles of Peace and Commerce" or simply "Articles of Peace." It is worthy of note that nowhere in his opinion does Sir William Scott use the word "recognition"; he argues, simply: Algiers has been treated by

Seward for refusing to receive the ousted president as long as he had forces in the field and we refused to recognize any other government.

[78] See United States of America on behalf of Hopkins *v.* United Mexican States, 21 A. J. 160 (1926).

[79] Lorimer, I, 160–161. The Barbary states were infected with "criminality" which argues the absence of "rational will"; being the expression of a low form of will or none at all, these groups had no "value" as states. *Ibid.*, pp. 182 *et seq.* See *supra*, note 67.

[80] The Helena, 4 Robinson Ad. 3 (1801).

[81] Hertslet, *Commercial Treaties, Great Britain* (1820), I, 83.

[82] *Ibid.*, pp. 58–83.

Great Britain as a state; it has therefore the powers of government incidental to statehood.[83]

During the years 1919 and 1920 the Russian Soviet Republics (R.S.F.S.R) made a number of agreements for the mutual exchange and repatriation of war prisoners and nationals.[84] Such agreements were made with countries with whom the R.S.F.S.R. had never had diplomatic relations. They are strictly limited to the subject at hand, and contain no indication of the general relations between the parties. Subsequently treaties were made with the same states setting up diplomatic and commercial relations. Usually these treaties contain no specific reference to recognition.[85] Thus, they do not of themselves exclude the possibility that the earlier treaty was intended to or did operate as a recognition. We do know, however, that it was not so regarded either by the Foreign Office or the courts of Great Britain. A repatriation agreement was concluded between the R.S.F.S.R. and Great Britain in 1920.[86] In 1921 a British divi-

[83] In 1928 the United States concluded a treaty with the Republic of China for tariff regulation (signed at Peiping, July 25, 1928. 45 Stat. 2742). In the preamble the plenipotentiary for China is stated to be "N. V. Soong, Minister of Finance of the Nationalist Government of the Republic of China," named by "the Government Council of the Nationalist Government of the Republic of China." Of this treaty a Federal court has said: "While this treaty has not as yet been ratified by the Senate, it contains a clear recognition by the Executive Department of this government of both the National Government of the Republic of China and of its accredited representative. This recognition by the Executive Department would seem to satisfy the requirements of the law." Republic of China *v.* Merchants' Fire Assurance, 30 F (2d) 278 (C. C. A. 9th, 1929).

Hudson, though considering that a treaty of amity, providing for diplomatic relations, would be tantamount to recognition, says: "But it would be going too far to say that two governments might not regulate urgent matters by treaty without the consequence of a recognition which at least one of them did not desire." *Recognition and Multipartite Treaties*, 23 A. J. 126, 128 (1929).

[84] With Denmark December 18, 1919 (Russian text in *Sbornik Deistvuiushchikh Dogorov* [Collection of Treaties in Force Concluded by the R. S. F. S. R. with Foreign States], I, 139); with Belgium April 20, 1920 (*ibid.*, p. 119); with France April 20, 1920 (*ibid.*, pp. 156–162); with Great Britain September 7, 1920 (*League of Nations Treaty Series*, I, 264).

See Fischer, *The Soviets in World Affairs* (1930), p. 250, for a list of the countries with which such agreements were made.

[85] The general trade and diplomatic agreement with Denmark of April 23, 1923, specifically excludes *de jure* recognition as an effect of the treaty, but the treaty does not purport to be or involve in terms a *de facto* or any other kind of recognition. Martens, *Nouveau Recueil Général* (3rd Série), XIV, 411.

[86] *Supra*, note 84.

sional court decided on the basis of a letter from the Foreign Office that there had been no recognition.[87] The agreement does not seem to have been considered. Pending appeal from this decision a general commercial treaty was concluded,[88] from which the Court of Appeal deduced recognition.[89]

It seems to be the conception of all governments, including the Soviet, that these limited agreements do not involve recognition. Thus, Belgium made a repatriation agreement in 1920,[90] and it is the common understanding that there has not been, even now, recognition.[91] In 1920 France signed an agreement with the R.S.F.S.R. providing not only for repatriation, but containing a clause that "the Government of France again formally promises that it will not intervene in the internal affairs of Russia, and that it will not cooperate in any aggressive measures against the Soviet Republics." [92] Yet despite the extensive and important nature of this obligation, it was not considered, apparently, as having any bearing on recognition. Until 1924 [93] both the government and the courts of France treated the Soviet and its acts as legally non-existent or worse.[94]

The United States has signed a number of multipartite treaties to which the Union of Socialist Soviet Russia is a party. These include the Universal Postal Convention (1924), the International Sanitary Convention (1926), and the General Pact for the Renunciation of War (1928). In the Sanitary Convention, the United

[87] Luther *v.* Sagor, [1921] 1 K. B. 456.

[88] Agreement of March 16, 1921. *League of Nations Treaty Series*, IV, 128.

[89] Luther *v.* Sagor, [1921] 3 K. B. 532.

[90] *Supra*, note 84.

[91] See Fischer, *op. cit.* (*supra*, note 84), p. 499.

[92] *Ibid.*, pp. 250–251. The author adds: "Before long, on July 28, 1920, Litvinov was able to call the attention of M. Puech, of the French Legation in Copenhagen, to the fact that the Paris authorities had broken an international pledge by granting military aid to Poland." This is an interesting example of intercourse between non-recognizant states to enforce an international obligation.

[93] By a telegram of October 8, 1924, the French Government informed the Soviet that "it recognizes *de jure* from the day of this communication the Government of the U. S. S. R. as the Government of the territory of the former Russian Empire where its authority is recognized by the population and as a successor of previous Russian Governments therein." *Sbornik Deistvuiushchikh Dogorov* (Collection of Treaties in Force Concluded by the U. S. S. R. with Foreign States), II, 25.

[94] Consult Lagarde, *La Reconnaissance du Gouvernement des Soviets* (1924), chap. v, and discussion, *infra*, pp. 165, 176.

States thought fit to enter the following declaration in the protocol of signature: [95]

> The plenipotentiaries of the United States of America formally declare that their signing the International Sanitary Convention of this date is not to be construed to mean that the United States of America recognizes a régime or entity acting as government of a signatory or adhering Power when that régime or entity is not recognized by the United States as the Government of that Power. They further declare that the participation of the United States of America in the international Sanitary Convention of this date *does not involve any contractual obligation* on the part of the United States to a signatory or adhering Power [96] represented by a régime or entity which the United States does not recognize as representing the Government of that Power until it is represented by a Government recognized by the United States. (Italics mine.)

To the other two conventions the United States attached no provisos of this type. One of these was prior and the other was subsequent to the Sanitary Convention.

Of particular significance is the Universal Postal Union Convention: [97]

> ARTICLE I. COMPOSITION OF THE UNION
>
> The countries between which the present Convention is concluded form, under the denomination of Universal Postal Union, a single postal territory for the reciprocal exchange of correspondence. The purpose of the Postal Union is also to assure the organization and perfection of the various international postal services.[98]
>
> ARTICLE 10. ARBITRATION
>
> 1. In case of disagreement between two or more members of the Union as to the interpretation of the Convention and Agreement or as to the responsibility imposed upon an Administration by the application of those Acts, the question in dispute is decided by arbitration.[99]

Article 20 provides for modification of certain provisions of the Convention by a two-thirds vote, and for official interpretations by absolute majority, except in cases in which provision is made for arbitration.[100]

95 45 Stat. 2605. And substantially the same provision is incorporated in the procès-verbal of the deposit of ratification. 45 Stat. 2612.

96 This clause has an interesting bearing on the alleged distinction between non-recognition of governments and non-recognition of states. It is said that we continue to recognize "Russia" (*sic*), but in this treaty it is clear that the outlawing of the government carries with it the outlawry of the state.

97 44 Stat. 2221.

98 *Id.* at 2222.

99 *Id.* at 2226.

100 *Id.* at 2230.

ARTICLE 25. LIBERTY OF TRANSIT

1. Liberty of transit is guaranteed throughout the entire territory of the Union.[101]

Articles 50–57 impose "the obligation of paying indemnity" upon administrations responsible for certain losses.[102]

There is a special provision relating to the gathering of statistics by the Soviet to serve as the basis for transit charges.[103]

Here, then, is an international community of which both the United States and Soviet Russia are members. Each submits to the legislative power of the other (Article 20), gives and receives guarantees (Article 25), undertakes mutual obligation and liability (Articles 50–57), and caps the whole with agreements to arbitrate differences (Article 10). These facts cannot be explained away by the argument that though we do not recognize the government, we do recognize the state. A state is not a disembodied spirit; it is an organization expressing its will through a government, and it is the Soviet Government with which we join in forming "a single postal territory," with which we share its governance, to which we have granted rights. Thus, our recognition policy was not allowed to prevail over the compulsions of international need. Again we see that non-recognition does not preclude the existence of legal relations between state and state, government and government.

The Peace Pact [104] is of another breed. Primarily it is a solemn declaration of faith. The parties renounce war as "an instrument of national policy in their relations with one another"; they agree to the settlement of disputes by pacific means. The only positive duties expressly imposed [105] are incidental to the formalities of the treaty; the United States is required to furnish all governments adhering to the treaty with certified copies of it and with the instruments of ratification or adherence, and to notify such governments upon the deposit of ratifications or adherences. Whatever the effect of this treaty upon the relations between Russia and the United States, the latter, being one of the prime movers in this effort toward world peace, would have exposed itself to the just ridicule of the world if it had made any such factitious provisos to

[101] *Id.* at 2233.
[102] *Id.* at 2246.
[103] *Id.* at 2348.
[104] 46 Stat. 2343.
[105] Secretary of State Stimson has recently formulated the doctrine that the Peace Pact imposes, by implication, upon the signatories the duty of consulting with each other, should there be a threat that the treaty may be violated. See speech of Secretary Stimson in Pittsburgh, *New York Times*, October 27, 1932.

this treaty as it did to the Sanitary Convention.[106] And in 1929 the United States sent a note to the U.S.S.R. via the French ambassador in Moscow invoking the Kellogg Pact.[107] Recently we have had an even more forceful instance of the extent of intercourse possible between non-recognizant powers. On May 16, 1933, President Roosevelt communicated directly with the U.S.S.R. on the subject of the current Disarmament Conference, at which both the United States and Soviet Russia were represented.[108] The President told newspaper men that the note to Russia was not intended as "recognition," but that (in the words of the press dispatch) "it never occurred to the President to ignore the Soviet officials in their capacity as fellow-conferees with the United States delegates. . . . As at previous world gatherings, the American delegates will have the ordinary relations and communications with the Russian delegates which they maintain with delegates from other countries." [109] Thus, in conclusion, it may be said that the record shows how wide and how significant may be the range of international relations which can take place *infra* "recognition." [110]

The League of Nations provides for the admission of new states by a vote of two-thirds of its membership. Does admission of a new state constitute recognition by all the member states? By only those who vote in favor of admission? By none of them? Writers have been extremely cautious in venturing a positive opinion. They all join in pointing out that members of the League are obliged to protect the territorial integrity of any member. Not even recog-

[106] Secretary of State Kellogg was unwilling that the U. S. S. R. be one of the original signatories of the Pact, but consented to its adherence prior to final ratification. See Fischer, *Why Recognize Russia?* (1931), pp. 73 *et seq.*

[107] *Ibid.*, pp. 79 *et seq.*

[108] *New York Times*, May 17, 1933, p. 1. The communication was one of fifty-four identic notes sent to foreign states. This note was addressed to "President Mikhail Kalinin, All Union Central Executive Committee, Moscow, Russia." See Salimoff *v.* Standard Oil Co., 262 N. Y. 220 (1933) discussed in Appendix A in which the Court apparently refers to this communication.

[109] *New York Times*, May 17, 1933, p. 2.

[110] John Bassett Moore, in an address "Candor and Common Sense," delivered on December 4, 1930, before the Association of the Bar of the City of New York, maintains that we have recognized the U. S. S. R. We have already commented on the dubious device of maintaining that because the conduct of state is equivalent to what a certain person conceives to be recognition, therefore it is, though that state emphatically denies it. Perhaps the more modest procedure would be for the person to revise the conception to fit the facts.

nition imposes such an onerous obligation. Coucke asks: "How can it be admitted that there are no regular political relations between two States which exchange guarantees in the hour of danger, of their territorial integrity and political independence?" [111] But he hesitates to resolve the paradox, and so does De Visscher,[112] who concludes that no state can be forced to have individual relations with another against its will, but further than that says nothing.

But however free a state may be to grant recognition when and how it chooses, clearly it may qualify its power by treaty. The Central American states did this in the Treaty of Washington, and it is arguable that the members of the League have committed their power of recognition to the Assembly, in so far as the League has occasion to admit new members. It seems strange that so few [113] of the men who have considered this question indicate this possibility. These men are over-impressed with the dogma that recognition is a "free political act"; however much they may deprecate current recognition practice, they tend to adopt its assumptions and to think of free political action as necessarily involved in any and every recognition. A central agency pronouncing a single judgment would be a valuable substitute for the current confusion of the uncoördinated and capricious bilateral transactions that now go to make up the mass which is called "recognition."

Surely this dilemma and the unwillingness of these men to resolve it illustrates neatly the present uncertainty as to the meaning and function of recognition, at least as it is practiced. Undoubtedly, if recognition creates international personality, if without it there can be no relations between states or governments, admission to the League, mutual adherence to a treaty, presuppose recognition. But

[111] Coucke, *Admission dans la Société des Nations et Reconnaissance de Jure*, 2 Rev. de Droit Int. (3rd Série) 320 at 329 (1921): "Comment admettre qu'il n'y ait pas de relations politiques régulières entre deux États qui se portent réciproquement garants, à l'heure du danger, de leur intégrité territoriale et de leur indépendance politique?"

[112] De Visscher, *Les Gouvernements Étrangers en Justice*, 3 Rev. de Droit Int. (3rd Série) 149, 166–170 (1922). Hudson (*loc. cit.* [*supra*, note 83], p. 129) concludes that the members of the League recognize each other as "members of the League of Nations, but not otherwise," a solution which does not get much beyond a form of words. This seems to be the view of Anzilotti (p. 172).

[113] Fauchille, in his edition of Bonfils, *op. cit.* (*supra*, note 19), § 213,[4] adopts the view that admission of a state to the League is equivalent to recognition by *all* members of the League.

the nations seem to see the matter differently; undoubtedly recognition asserts both the facts of another nation's existence and the existence of relations with it, but non-recognition does not necessarily deny either.

But what, then, is recognition? It might be stated shortly that recognition is equivalent to a declaration of status in private law. A decree of filiation does not create or constitute the filiation, nor does it create the rights incident to that relation. It may or may not be a condition to their enforcement. There is no international tribunal or agency competent to extend recognitions binding the world. So each state must do it for itself.[114] But "recognition" is something more than this recognition of a fact. It is too easy — and unrealistic — to criticize current recognition practice by hugging the literal meaning of the word. For example, in this vein Baty says:

> Any entry into relations with the new state, *as a governing authority*, implies recognition of its statehood.[115] . . . Recognition cannot be conditional. It is impossible to recognize a fact conditionally. . . . The very essence of recognition is that the recognizing state thereby declares that it has satisfied itself that the recognized authority possesses the distinguishing marks of a state. . . . To say that one recognizes that it has them, subject to its conduct being satisfactory in other particulars, is sheer nonsense. It is like telling a pupil that her sum is right if she will promise to be a good girl.[116]

[114] Cf. Goebel, p. 61: "In a certain sense, therefore, the participation by third states in the complete legalization of the de facto community is not only an acknowledgment of the fact that the internal process of transformation is over and that the new state by its acceptance of the customary rules of international law is a legal equal, *but its definite juristic meaning is that in so far as a third state is concerned, it will recognize to be binding upon itself those obligations which the new state has assumed.*"

And Bonfils, *op. cit.* (*supra*, note 19), § 200, and Fauchille, § 203 in 8th ed.: "Dans l'organization internationale actuelle, il n'existe pas d'autorité centrale, supérieure à tous les États, d'où puisse émaner pour le nouvel État une reconnaissance générale, absolue, s'imposant à tous. La reconnaissance ne peut être que particulière et qu'individuelle, ne conférant au nouvel organisme les droits internationaux qu'à l'égard de ceux des États qui l'ont reconnu."

[115] Baty, *loc. cit.* (*supra*, note 53) at 469.

[116] *Id.* at 470. Goebel (p. 65) also maintains that recognition cannot be conditional: "Excluding the element of the independent expression of the will of the new state, it reduces the process to one of complete constitutive force, and makes of it an instrument for enforcing the demands of the recognizant state."

Le Normand (p. 56) maintains, of course, that recognition may be conditional. And so, too, does Anzilotti. His thesis (p. 173) is that recognition is "un accord constitutif de normes internationales, qui ne se distingue pas de

These remarks, however sensible they may sound, do not reflect current reality. Professor Baty plants himself foursquare on the solid ground of common sense; he defines the word "recognition" as the dictionary might, and says, "That's what recognition is, that's all there is to it." But granted that recognition does not create international personality, it nevertheless does create a special and particular relation between states; there may be limited relationships, necessarily implying the statehood of the parties, which do not rise to the dignity and completeness of the relation between recognizant states.[117] International law does not require a state to enter into such a relation; the parties are free to do as they wish; recognition is the formal process which signifies their will and intention.

It is not easy to say just what are the special qualities of the relation created by recognition which distinguish it from lesser relations. Some of the positivists have spoken of grades of recognition depending on the cultural condition of the nation to be recognized: "The more civilization progresses in a nation, the more its rights and duties are augmented until it achieves plenary recognition." [118] The distinction for which we are seeking might be conceived in some such quantitative fashion. Surely the right of legation, in so far as there is any, does not exist unless there is recognition. One

tout autre accord du même genre, sinon parce qu'il marque le commencement des relations juridiques entre les parties et par suite qu'il en manifeste la personnalité dans l'ordre juridique international." Because recognition is a voluntary pact there may be "stipulations accessories: des conditions, des termes, des modes. La nature juridique, la valeur, les effets de ces stipulations accessoires doivent être appréciés espèce par espèce, parce qu'il s'agît toujours d'interprétation de volontés." *Ibid.*, p. 175.

[117] Cf. Hudson, *loc. cit.* (*supra*, note 83) at 127: "The Government of the United States has not recognized the Government of the Union of Socialist Soviet Republics. This does not mean that in the view of the Government of the United States, the Government of the Union of Socialist Soviet Republics does not exist. Nor does it mean, necessarily, that the two governments can have no relations with each other. It means, rather, that their relations are not those which members of the international community ordinarily have, and are not conducted according to established usages and the general principles of international law [*sed quaere*]."

See also Coucke, *loc. cit.* (*supra*, note 111) at 326: "La reconnaissance *de jure* ne crée que des liens spéciaux d'État à État, elle règle les relations particulières d'un gouvernement vis-à-vis d'un autre."

[118] Le Normand, p. 69: "Plus la civilisation progresse chez une nation, plus ses droits et devoirs positifs augmentent jusqu'à ce qu'elle arrive à la reconnaissance plénière." Also cf. Lorimer, I, 104.

might also have said that only so would there be channels for presentation of grievances and enforcement of rights. Yet in 1929 the United States through the French legation called the Kellogg Pact to the attention of the Soviet. In truth, recognition practice today is so diverse and of such uncertain implication, the structure of the international system itself is of a nature so shifting, that no dogmatic assertion of the exact legal effects of recognition should or could be made. Indeed, the writer inclines to the position that the bearing of recognition upon the international system is to a much larger extent political than legal. By this we mean that refusal to recognize is an expression of distaste or disapproval, a notice that one state will not manifest toward another the ordinary courtesies, the normal willingness to foster and stimulate customary international social and economic intercourse. The most important function of recognition is to put an end to this unpleasant situation.

It is not a crime to use a word in more than one sense, or to represent different truths with the same words. There is a danger, however, that because they are called the same thing the two truths will compete with each other for sole possession of the field. This has been true when problems relating to unrecognized states or governments have come before the courts. The failure or refusal of the political branch of the government to accord recognition has been held to demonstrate the international non-existence of the unrecognized state or government, thus equating the practice known to the states as "recognition" with the thoroughgoing creative or constitutive recognition of the positivists; ignoring the infinite gradation of relations which may and do exist *infra* recognition; and treating recognition as white and non-recognition as black and exiling the whole world of unresolved color.[119]

In our opinion, no consequences follow from non-recognition in

[119] It is not that the positivist ignores these gradations. To him the existence of any legal relation logically involves a recognition, but, as he says, "Les modes, l'étendue, le but même de cette coopération, sont, comme l'enseignent l'histoire et la pratique même des nations civilisées, infiniment variables." Le Normand, p. 69. And, as Anzilotti has said recently, "Since recognition depends on the will of the parties, nothing hinders from adding *accessory stipulations*, conditions, terms, modes." (For French text of this quotation, see *supra*, note 116).

But we have seen that there are relations between states to which current practice does not attach the term "recognition" at all. The danger is that such a state of "non-recognition" will be confused with the condition of legal vacuity which the positivist understands by non-recognition.

simple and quasi-logical fashion, as where with a statute for premise we appear, at least in some cases, to derive results by inevitable deduction. In practically all the cases which have arisen, the courts might, without violence to the logical implications of the fact of non-recognition, have applied the rules of law which, recognition aside, had been found good. Whether these rules should be modified or be held inoperative is properly a question of the extent to which the ordinary course of judgment should be deflected in the furtherance of the foreign policy of that government.

CHAPTER III

NON-RECOGNITION AND THE COURTS

History of Doctrine

The ideology still current in judicial utterances on recognition originated with Eldon and Marshall. The period of the cases was roughly between 1804 and 1826. It was a time when the political map of the world was kaleidoscopic: England could still remember the bitter business of 1776; Hayti between 1800 and 1806 was throwing out the French and the Spanish; in 1806 South America first stretched its limbs and discovered their strength; and by 1826 the last thought of Spanish dominion had flickered out. England was fighting and winning the grim struggle with Napoleon. By 1815 Europe was weary of turmoil and change. Peace and permanency were eagerly desired. The dogma of legitimacy flowered. England looked with little favor on colonial revolutions. Particularly was this true of the Government, rigidly Conservative in tone; even as late as 1826 Canning, recognizing the new South American republics, had to drag his reluctant cabinet with him.[1] Now from 1801 to 1826 (except for the year 1806–07) Eldon was on the woolsack. He had remarkable power in the Cabinet and in the Lords; he was the core of the Conservative resistance.[2]

In 1804 the *City of Berne* moved the Court of Chancery to restrain the Bank of England and the South Sea Company from permitting a transfer of, and the trustees from transferring, certain funds standing in their names under a purchase by the old government of Berne before the Revolution, which, at the time of the litigation, had been absorbed into the Swiss Confederation.

[1] Paxson, p. 244. This period is considered in some detail in Chapter II, p. 103, *supra*.

[2] Campbell, *Lives of the Lord Chancellors* (7th ed. 1878), Life of Eldon, chs. cc, ccvi, ccxiii. (There seems to be no standard pagination.) The following is a characteristic sample:

"The only Bills he ever brought into Parliament, or cordially supported, were for suspending the Habeas Corpus — putting down public meetings — rendering persons convicted a second time for a political libel subject to transportation beyond the seas — and extending the laws against high treason." Vol. ix, ch. ccxiii, p. 437.

It was objected that the existing "*Government of Switzerland*, not being acknowledged by the Government of this Country, could not be noticed by the Court." (Italics mine.) Eldon refused the order, observing:[3] "It was extremely difficult to say, a judicial Court can take notice of a Government, never authorized by the Government of the Country, in which that Court sits; and whether the Foreign Government is recognized or not, is a matter of public notoriety."

In the following year a motion was made, this time by "the plaintiffs, constituting the present Government of Switzerland," to require the trustees of the fund, involved in the previous case, to pay accrued dividends into court. A point was made that the old Swiss Government being defunct, the goods were *bona vacantia* and passed to the Crown. Lord Eldon did not agree to this, but thought that at least he should not grant the motion until the Attorney General was joined.[4] Of the opinion in the previous case he was apparently doubtful:

> Another, and a very considerable, question is, whether, if that subsequent Government was never acknowledged by the Government of this country, the Municipal Courts, merely administering the law of this country, can act upon it. Some perplexity arises from what we know and what we can only know judicially. I cannot affect to be ignorant of the fact, that the Revolutions in Switzerland have not been recognized by the Government of this country: *but as a Judge I cannot take notice of that.* (Italics mine.)

This is a curious reverse twist of the previous opinion. There he doubted whether he could "take notice of an unrecognized Government." Now, he doubts whether he should take notice of the fact that the revolutions have not been recognized. It may be that for the moment Eldon thought that the political considerations of the Council Chamber were not appropriate in the court. The point was made throughout these proceedings that either this fund was *bona vacantia*, or that at least passage of title to the new government depended on recognition. Neither of these contentions prevailed. Yet even denial of capacity to sue would have entailed serious interference with the property rights. There was at this time no consistent practice of recognition; Portugal and the Netherlands had waited decades before their independence of Spain and their statehood were recognized; and in 1804 the recognition of the new order in

[3] City of Berne in Switzerland *v.* The Bank of England, 9 Ves. Jr. 347, 348 (1804).

[4] Dolder *v.* Bank of England, 10 Ves. Jr. 352, 354 (1805).

Switzerland, then under the thumb of Napoleon, might be postponed for similar decades. So in these cases and the subsequent one of *Dolder* v. *Lord Huntingfield*,[5] involving a trial of the title to the funds, Lord Eldon might well have hesitated to tie up the funds of a foreign government because of the capricious mutations of diplomacy.

The eventual disposition of these cases is not of record,[6] and the results of them in terms of our problem are indecisive. In 1823 Eldon returned to the problem in *Jones* v. *Garcia Del Rio*.[7] This was a bill filed by subscribers to a loan to the unrecognized government of Peru. The defendants were the English bankers who floated the loan, and the prayer was for recission and restitution on grounds of fraud. The bill was dismissed for misjoinder, but Eldon remarked:

> I want to know, whether, supposing Peru to be so far absolved from the government of Spain that it never can be attached to it again, the King's Courts will interfere at all while the Peruvian government is not acknowledged by the government of this country. What right have I, as the King's Judge, to interfere upon the subject of a contract with a country which he does not recognize? [8]

He said further:

> Practically speaking great inconvenience may result from these transactions; for if at any future time the government of this country shall be disposed to say Peru shall continue annexed to Spain, these creditors will immediately come to the government and say, do not accede to the arrangement unless Spain will pay us what we have advanced to the colony.

In this case there is adumbrated the rather doubtful rule that private loans to the revolted colony of a friendly state are against public policy.[9] But there is more. We seem to hear the echoes of the arguments then going forward in the Council Chamber over the

[5] Dolder *v.* Lord Huntingfield, 11 Ves. Jr. 283 (1805).

[6] But by the Act of Congress of Vienna (1815), Art. 82, the title to the English funds was to continue in the City of Berne; the interest accumulated between 1798 and 1815 was to be applied to the payment of the Helvetic (Swiss) debt. See Feilchenfeld, *Public Debts and State Succession* (1931), p. 168. These were probably the same funds involved in the English cases.

[7] Jones *v.* Garcia del Rio et al., Turner and Russell 297 (1823).

[8] *Id.* at 299.

[9] In Kennett *v.* Chambers, 14 How. 38 (1852), Taney decided that a loan in aid of Texas in her fight against Mexico was void as violating our neutrality. As between two recognized belligerents it is not a violation of neutrality for a national of a neutral to loan to one of the belligerents. And we had recognized Texas as a belligerent. Moore, *Digest*, I, 176. Westlake states the rule that it is

recognition of these colonies. "What right have I, as the King's Judge, to interfere upon the subject of a contract with a country which he does not recognize?" This is the accent of a judge who is also an advisor to the King, and his servant.[10] The suggestion that the Government might "be disposed to say Peru shall continue annexed to Spain" is characteristic of the pretensions of the European Concert; it reveals the statesmanship behind these decisions.

Lord Eldon seems to have carried this point of view to extreme limits in the unreported case of *Biré* v. *Thompson.*[11] The defendant had secured a lease from the unrecognized state of Colombia. He had pledged it as security to the plaintiff. The plaintiff sought to enjoin the defendant from assigning the lease. Mr. Justice Shadwell, who held a brief in the case, says that Eldon refused the application "because he could not take notice of the Republic of Colombia." Here there is no question of an illegal contract. It was a lease of land in Colombia. The Republic was not seeking relief, so that there was not as in the *Berne* case a question of capacity, unless of capacity to make the contract, and it is absurd to suppose that Colombia's ability to make contracts should be held to turn on England's [12] recognition. Eldon seems to have finally adopted the formula that whatever the question or the issue, if the fact of the existence of Colombia was material to it the Court must shut its

an unfriendly act to allow a national to loan to an *unrecognized* insurgent. 2 Int. Law (2nd ed. 1913) 252.

[10] Cf. Bacon's letter to King James set out in the text, *supra*, p. 24: "Your Majesty knoweth your Chancellor is ever a principal councillor and instrument of monarchy, of immediate dependence on the King; and therefor like to be a safe and tender guardian of the regal rights."

[11] The case is stated and commented on by Shadwell, J., in Taylor *v.* Barclay, 2 Simons 213, 222 (1828). Lord Brougham strongly disapproved, but felt compelled to follow Biré *v.* Thompson in Taylor *v.* Barclay, 9 L. J. (O. S.) Ch. 215 (1831), affirming Shadwell's decision on appeal. See note 17, *infra*.

[12] Noël-Henry, however (p. 128) says:

"Un gouvernement non reconnu n'ayant l'exercise d'aucune personnalité juridique, ses contrats sont nuls."

". . . lorsqu'il s'agit de contrats passés avec les représentants d'un gouvernement insurgé en lutte contre un gouvernement reconnu, une seconde considération intervient. L'acte des particuliers qui traitent avec un tel gouvernement est contraire à l'ordre public territorial. . . ."

For this proposition Kennett *v.* Chambers, 14 How. 38 (1852), and the group of cases under consideration in the text were alone cited. All except Biré *v.* Thompson involved loans contracted in a "neutral" country for the benefit of an unrecognized insurgent. Biré *v.* Thompson was, however, based on a lease given by the insurgents in their own dominion.

ears. In *Taylor* v. *Barclay*,[13] a case much like *Jones* v. *Garcia del Rio*, Shadwell, following Eldon, said "It appears to me that sound policy requires that the Courts of the King should act in unison with the Government of the King," and said further that a person could not sue who founded his case on the representation that there was that existing as an independent government which was not acknowledged by the country to be such.[14]

But Chief Justice Best of the Common Pleas stated very different views in *Yrissari* v. *Clement*.[15] This was in 1826, just prior to Canning's recognition of the South American republics. For years English merchants had been dealing with these republics. Their independent existence was notorious. It is not surprising that Best, who was not sitting in the troubled councils of the Cabinet, should have differed with Eldon. The case was a libel action brought by the envoy and financial agent of the unrecognized state of Chile; the gist of the libel was that the plaintiff was defrauding the Chilean State. Commentators have pointed out that it would have been no less a libel, though Chile were no state at all. However, the statehood of Chile though not an essential fact was a material one, so that Best's remarks if not necessary were at least pertinent. At *nisi prius* Best said there were three sorts of foreign states:

> First, states that were merely acknowledged as sovereign independent states; secondly, states in connection, or such as were connected with us by existing treaties; thirdly, sovereign states neither in connection with us, nor acknowledged by our government, such as Japan, Siam. . . . The existence

[13] Taylor *v.* Barclay, 2 Simons 213 (1828) a companion case, Thompson *v.* Powles, 2 Simons 194 (1828) and Jones *v.* Garcia del Rio, Turner and Russell 297 (1823) were all suits by subscribers to loans on behalf of the South American insurgent states against London bankers for fraud, praying for recission and return of the subscription money. Relief in all these cases was denied on the grounds (*inter alia*) that the complaint alleged the existence of an independent government that His Majesty did not acknowledge to be such, and that the contract was illegal. Both grounds seem about as strained and far-fetched replies to the action of recission for fraud as can be imagined.

In Taylor *v.* Barclay there was an allegation that the insurgent had been recognized, which Shadwell easily found from the Foreign Office to be untrue. But there was no such allegation in Thompson *v.* Powles or Jones *v.* Garcia del Rio, though Shadwell says that those cases were founded on the proposition that one who founds his case "on the representation that there was that existing as an independent Government, acknowledged by this Country, which in fact was not so," cannot succeed. Taylor *v.* Barclay at 221.

[14] *Id.* at 221.

[15] 3 Bing. 432 (1826).

of unacknowledged states must be proved by evidence. . . . It makes no difference that the new state formed part of another acknowledged state; states may be legitimately divided.[16]

These views, however, may have been entirely *ad hoc*; it is simply common sense that when the question of a state's existence is a collateral issue — a fact of the case — non-recognition is immaterial. This was all that was strictly involved in this case. Yet even construed thus narrowly, the case is in contrast to the narrow word-formalism of Lord Eldon and Justice Shadwell. These men seemed to think that any suggestion in a pleading or in a judicial proceeding that an unrecognized state did in fact exist was *ipso facto* a kind of recognition, thus placing the court in a conflict with the executive. Eldon uses indiscriminately the words "take notice of," "acknowledge," and "recognize," and probably as far as he had any conception of the meaning of recognition it was a crude form of the literalist view which we have examined.[17] As already suggested, there was at this time no body of practice and hence of theory from which any clear idea could be gathered of the function and meaning of recognition. Eldon with his conservative caution was content simply to ignore any asserted changes in the *status quo*, particularly when they sprang from revolution. As he remarked in cavalier fashion, the English Government might at some future time be disposed to say that "Peru shall continue annexed to Spain."

In the United States, the courts were grappling with the same problem. In *Rose* v. *Himely*[18] the question arose whether Santo Domingo, which had rebelled against French rule and was largely

[16] *Id.* at 437.

[17] See Bushe-Fox, *The Court of Chancery and Recognition, 1804–31*, 12 British Yearbook of Int. Law 63, 74 (1931).

The case of Thompson *v.* Powles, 2 Simons 194 (1828) (*supra*, note 13), was affirmed on appeal by Lord Chancellor Brougham (*s. n.* Taylor *v.* Barclay, 9 L. J. (O. S.), Ch. 215 (1832). Lord Brougham, however, felt compelled to affirm on the authority of Lord Eldon's opinion in Biré *v.* Thompson (*supra*, note 11). That case he felt to be clearly wrong. At 272 he says: "Lord Eldon appears to have been led away by the idea that if he allowed anything to be said of the government at all, whether in the case of complaint of fraud committed in its name, or of a fraud sought to be committed by its agent upon another; if he gave relief at all when that government was named, that was a recognition of its existence. . . . I cannot help thinking, therefore, with the greatest submission, that the words 'recognition' and 'acknowledgement,' and the generalities of these expressions to a certain degree misled the judgment of Lord Eldon in that case."

[18] 4 Cranch 241 (1808).

rid of it, could in the absence of recognition be considered by the Court as independent. A French court in one of the few remaining French strongholds had condemned an American ship for trading with the rebels contrary to a French ordinance. Counsel maintained that Santo Domingo, being in fact independent, was entitled to trade with anyone, and that in the absence of an effective blockade by France, with whom it was, under this way of looking at it, at war, the condemnation decree was void. Marshall, speaking for the majority, repudiated this argument by a course of reasoning which constitutes for us the importance of the case; however, since he nevertheless held the decree void on another ground, it is said that the remarks are dictum.[19] For more than one reason that observation is trivial; who shall say what is dictum and what the grounds of decision? [20] If counsel's argument had been valid, if Santo Domingo were to be treated as independent, then the Court need not have found another ground for holding the French decree void; and since at the next term Marshall's other ground was repudiated by the Court and the actual decision in *Rose* v. *Himely*, holding such a decree void, was expressly overruled,[21] Marshall's so-called dictum became absolutely necessary to sustain the French decrees.

Marshall's remarks were these:

> It has been argued that the colony, having declared itself a sovereign state, and having thus far maintained its sovereignty by arms must be considered and treated by other nations as sovereign in fact, and as being entitled to maintain the same intercourse with the world that is maintained by other belligerent nations. . . . It is for governments to decide whether they will consider Santo Domingo as an independent nation; and until such decision shall be made, or France shall relinquish her claim, courts of justice must consider the ancient state of things as remaining unaltered, and the sovereign power of France over that colony as still subsisting.[22]

[19] Hervey, 29. A layman sometimes rides the lawyer's distinctions harder than the lawyer himself. See next note.

[20] See argument in Cohen, *The Ethical Basis of Legal Criticism*, 41 Yale L. J. 201, 216 (1931), that the holding of a case stands for what we think it ought to stand for, since to state the "material" facts in the case presupposes a selection of what facts ought to be considered material. Therefore, if the court gives certain reasons for its decision, that is an extremely authoritative determination of what the court considered material, and we should not be too astute to label it dictum, because we can find another way to arrive at the result.

[21] Hudson *v.* Guestier, 6 Cranch 281, 285 (1808).

[22] Rose *v.* Himely, 4 Cranch 241, 272 (1808).

It is vital to a proper understanding of these remarks to remember that they are directed towards the matter of recognizing a revolting colony. The recognition of a revolted colony is, as has been said, a procedure of the greatest delicacy. In the English cases which we have noticed and in the American cases of this period, the problem of recognition always concerned such cases, and in appraising their authority, in determining the limits of their validity, this fact should be kept in mind. Premature recognition may mean international bad feeling, liability for damages,[23] even war. In *Rose* v. *Himely* the rights of the parent state to govern her colony were directly involved, which is not ordinarily the case in a private litigation, and which made the political considerations unusually acute. There is in Marshall's remarks one phrase not noticed by commentators, which indicates pointedly that the Court was concerned primarily not to give offense to the parent country, France, rather than with the impropriety of trenching upon the executive. Thus, Marshall says that the Court cannot take note of Santo Domingo's independence until recognized by our government "or *France shall relinquish her claim*" [24] [italics mine], indicating that in the latter alternative recognition by the executive would not be necessary.

Tazewell *arguendo* in *The Santissima Trinidad* [25] makes clear the significance of these decisions:

> Now, to the belligerent sovereign, the effect is precisely the same, whether the interference with his rights be by the executive and legislative departments, or by the judiciary alone. In either case his rights are examined into and he may be deprived of them. . . . It is no answer to the reclamation of a foreign sovereign to say that he has been injured by the judiciary only. To him all the departments of the government make but one sovereignty.

The good sense of Marshall's ideas seems quite absent from the decision of Mr. Justice Washington in *Clark* v. *United States* [26] five years later. This was a forfeiture of goods under the Non-Inter-

[23] The United States paid Colombia $25,000,000 for its premature recognition of Panama. This was paid under the Thompson-Urritia Treaty signed April 6, 1914, but not proclaimed until March 30, 1922 (42 Stat. 2122). The purpose of the treaty was stated to be "to remove all the misunderstandings growing out of the political events in Panama in November, 1903." Naturally, the United States did not explicitly admit any fault.

[24] Story uses the same language in Gelston *v.* Hoyt, 3 Wheat. 246, 324 (1818).

[25] 7 Wheat. 283, 299 (1822).

[26] 3 Wash. C. C. 101, Fed. Cases No. 2,838 (C. C. 3rd, 1811).

course Act of March 1, 1809,[27] prohibiting the importation of goods into the United States from France or Great Britain, or the colonies of either. As in *Rose* v. *Himely*, the status of Santo Domingo was in question. The opinion relates that in July, 1809, the French Army surrendered and was entirely expelled from the island. The Court held that Santo Domingo must continue to be considered a French colony until declared otherwise by the executive or until France relinquished her claim. Much was made of the fact that Congress in 1806, at the behest of the French minister, had passed an act [28] forbidding commercial intercourse with the rebel ports of the island.

In 1806 there were still remnants of French authority on the island, and the friendly attitude toward France and her claims manifested in the Act of 1806 was proper enough. But in 1811 the situation was very different. The French rule had been extinguished completely for at least four years. As the Non-Intercourse Act shows, we were no longer excessively friendly toward Napoleonic France. To treat the Act of 1806 as a Congressional declaration of opinion appropriate in 1811 was absurd. The Non-Intercourse Act aimed against French commerce as a retaliation for the Paper Blockades could have no application to Santo Domingan trade. And as for giving France cause for offense by treating her erstwhile colony as independent — the motivating factor in *Rose* v. *Himely* — the Court's failure to apply our Non-Intercourse Act to the colony could hardly be offensive. In sum, *Rose* v. *Himely*, by which the Court felt bound, received a most unrealistic and wooden application.

Mr. Hervey,[29] in his book on recognition, supports the case. It is the thesis of his book that "in the absence of a definite attitude, either favorable or unfavorable, on the part of the political departments of the government" the courts may and should "evaluate the governmental competency as a matter of fact." Naturally, he is inclined to explain as many cases as he can by this thesis, and when possible he finds that there was an unfavorable "attitude" whenever the court refused to make an independent evaluation. Mr. Hervey's criterion is valuable, but such an application of it as we see in *Clark* v. *United States* reveals its defect. It has been conceived too absolutely; once given an unfavorable "attitude," the court is foreclosed from investigating the "governmental capacity"

[27] 2 Stat. 528.
[28] 2 Stat. 351.
[29] Hervey, pp. 156, 157.

of the unrecognized power regardless of the issue, of the relative values of the executive policy on one hand, and the interests at stake in the litigation on the other.

In 1819 Mr. Justice Johnson, in his characteristically trenchant and outspoken fashion, attempted to scotch the dogmatic distortion of the *Himely* case and its progeny. For at least a year Adams had been on the verge of extending recognition to the South American republics. It was quite clear that the light of Spain had burned out. But, as we have already remarked, there was as yet no internationally established practice of recognition. It was quite possible that the new South American states might wait year upon year in the antechamber for admission into the august councils of the nations. In the indefinite meanwhile were these states to be treated by the courts as non-existent? Eldon seemed to think so, and the thought did not bother him in the least. Mr. Justice Washington in *Clark* v. *United States* was somewhat troubled, but believed that *Rose* v. *Himely* settled the law. Johnson was clearly of a different opinion, and seized the first opportunity to give it expression.

Johnson's statement in *Consul of Spain* v. *La Conception*[30] was probably unnecessary to the decision. The question was the validity of a commission to capture Spanish shipping, issued by the unrecognized state of Buenos Ayres. Buenos Ayres had, however, been recognized by the United States as a belligerent, and it had already been decided [31] that such recognition was sufficient support for the commission. Johnson, however, took occasion to say:

> Much has been said and some cases and opinions cited to show that this court cannot recognize the independence of a revolted colony until that recognition shall have proceeded from our own government or the parent state. . . . The recognition of our own government, whatever be the state of fact, removes all question of doubt and our courts must consider the governments thus recognized as independent; and so the recognition of the parent state actually produces a state of independence. But courts exercising jurisdiction of international law may often be called upon to deduce the fact of national independence from history, evidence, or public notoriety where there has been no formal public recognition. The actual possession and long exercise of all the attributes of a state of independence may be legally resorted to without giving just cause of umbrage to a nation that does not possess the power to subjugate a revolted colony. *There exist many nations at this day which may claim of courts of international law all the*

[30] 2 Wheeler Cr. C. 597, Fed. Cases No. 3,137 (D. C. S. C. 1819). Reversed on additional findings of fact. 6 Wheat. 235 (1821).

[31] The Divina Pastora, 4 Wheat. 52 (1819).

rights of independent nations and may be judicially recognized as such, notwithstanding no act of government has acknowledged them in that capacity. (Italics mine.)

Johnson thus anticipated the realism of Best in *Yrissari* v. *Clement.*[32] But in Johnson's statement is far more than the bare idea that the existence of an unrecognized state may be proved by evidence.

Syllogistically Johnson's argument might be put thus: States which are in fact independent have all the rights, regardless of recognition, which international law gives to independent states; the courts are organs for the enforcement of international law; therefore not only may the existence of an unrecognized state be shown in a court, but its rights may be enforced. This reminds us of Lord Stowell's conception, if not his realization in practice, of the Prize Court. It contrasts forcibly with Eldon's position of the Chancery as a municipal court presided over by the "King's judge" administering municipal law. To Johnson, Marshall, and Story, steeped as were all their generation in natural law and its ideal embodiment in international law, the courts of justice were by their nature not only courts of the nation, but courts of the world.[33] And however far the truth may limp behind it is a fruitful ideal, one ready to hand when the bold judge would break new ground. Johnson's *major* premise is also, as we have seen,[34] highly controversial. It is flatly denied by the positivists (who flowered many years after Johnson) that a state has any rights prior to recognition.

A number of litigations concerning revolutionary states have arisen under our neutrality laws. These cases turn on statutory construction. These constructions, however, have been influenced

[32] 3 Bing. 432 (1826). See *supra*, note 15, and text.

[33] In a recent article (*Changing Concepts and the Doctrine of Incorporation*, 26 A. J. 239, 260 [1932]) Dickinson, writing on the relation between international and municipal law, contrasts the natural-law point of view held by Johnson and Story and the positivist point of view which later superseded it. He concludes: "The law of nations became a source, rather than an integral part, of the national system. . . . It means simply that the national law governing matters of international concern is to be derived, in the absence of a controlling statute, executive decision, or judicial precedent, from such relevant principles of the law of nations as can be shown to have received the nation's implied or express assent." See Chapter I, notes 98–101, and text. However, we have seen from our study in the previous chapter that the word "controlling" describes a result rather than something given.

[34] This was discussed under the theory of recognition in Chapter II, p. 86.

by the extreme views of judicial self-limitation which Johnson sought to combat. In *Gelston* v. *Hoyt*[35] the Supreme Court had occasion to interpret the Neutrality Act of 1794,[36] which made it a crime to fit out any ship "with intent that such ship or vessel shall be employed in the service of any foreign prince or state to cruise or commit hostilities upon the subjects, citizens, or property of another foreign prince or state with whom the United States are at peace. . . ."

In 1810, after the French had been driven from Santo Domingo, the native leaders Pétion and Christophe fell to fighting each other. The plaintiff fitted out a ship to aid Pétion. In a prior suit the defendants, United States customs officials, acting, as they alleged, upon the instructions of President Madison, seized the ship for violation of the neutrality laws and instituted forfeiture proceedings, which were decided in favor of the ship-owners. This was an action by the owners against the officers for trespass. Though the Court decided that the judgment in the original forfeiture suit was conclusive against the officers, Mr. Justice Story gave his opinion on the merits:

> No evidence was offered to prove that either of these governments was recognized by the government of the United States, or of France "as a foreign prince or state."
>
> No doctrine is better established than that it belongs exclusively to governments to recognize new states in the revolutions which may occur in the world; and until such recognition, either by our own government, or the government to which the new state belonged, courts of justice are bound to consider the ancient state of things as remaining unaltered.[37]

But the reasons for this doctrine were even less applicable here than in the non-intercourse case (*Clark* v. *United States*[38]). Of what possible concern could it be to France if we should enjoin upon our citizens neutrality in the civil war raging in an island which once belonged to her? Her rights would be in no way compromised or denied. Mr. Hervey supports the case in characteristic fashion:

> The Act of 1794 expressly stated that it should apply only where a "foreign prince or state" was involved. If the court had acknowledged either the Pétion Government or the Christophe Government as a "foreign prince or state" it would have put them at variance with Congress which anticipated that the Act of 1794 should apply only to recognized government.[39]

[35] 3 Wheat. 246 (1818). [36] 1 Stat. 381. [37] 3 Wheat. 246, 324 (1818).
[38] 3 Wash. C. C. 101, Fed. Cases No. 2,838 (C. C. 3rd, 1811).
[39] Hervey, p. 31. See criticism of Hervey, *supra*, p. 132.

There is absolutely nothing to show what Congress "anticipated." This much can be said: the Act of 1794 was intended to put teeth into our obligation of maintaining neutrality in conflicts between foreign powers. Mr. Hervey's statement is an explanation after the event. It is based on the assumption that toward an unrecognized power there can be in international law no duty. This assumption is one of the chief axioms of the positivist's doctrine of the late nineteenth century, and we have no reasons for supposing that it was known to Congress in 1794. Yet it does not follow that the actual decision in *Gelston* v. *Hoyt* was necessarily wrong. The organizations of neither Pétion nor Christophe were states in the international sense, and it may be doubted that there was any duty of neutrality.

Closely related, however, to the obligation of neutrality, but not so clearly defined, is that of non-intervention. Three situations should be distinguished. A revolution may take place within the territory of a state with whom we are at peace. Our nationals must not give aid to the rebels of the sort prohibited by the Neutrality Act, but they may give aid to the established government, nor will the established government be prohibited from buying munitions and fitting out ships in this country.[40] However, we may recognize the rebels as "belligerents." This is a device developed to a large extent by the United States during the revolt of the Spanish colonies in South America.[41] It is said to convert the insurgency from a mere internal dissension into war in the international sense, so far, at least, as third powers are concerned. Primarily,

[40] Opinion of Attorney-General Hoar in relation to the building of ships in America for Spain to be used against the Cuban insurgents. 13 Op. Attny. Gen'l 177 (1869).

[41] Noël-Henry (pp. 47–52) traces the rise and decline of the practice of recognizing "belligerency." It received its most complete application in our recognition of the belligerency of the South American republics between 1815 and 1822. These republics were held to have equally with Spain, the parent state, the rights of war. Thus, their ships preying on Spanish commerce were not piratical. United States *v.* Palmer, 3 Wheat. 610 (1818) (their captures will be recognized as valid prize). The Divina Pastora, 4 Wheat. 52 (1819) (the decrees of their prize courts will be given credit). The Nueva Anna and Liebre, 6 Wheat. 193 (1821). After 1822 this device was little used by us. We objected strenuously to its use by European powers in the Civil War. Not until 1918 do we find it again in the anomalous "recognitions" of the various minority nations in the Austro-Hungarian Empire, which purported to be recognitions of new states, but were war measures designed to hasten the disintegration of the Empire.

it brings into play the obligation of neutrality. Such recognition, rarely accorded in these later years, is given only where the insurgents have exclusive control over a defined territory, a responsible political organization, and a decent prospect of making good their claim to independence. It is accorded normally only when the war has extended on to the high seas and is threatening to place neutral commerce in an unprotected position. It may be that if such are the facts, international law will impose a duty of neutrality even in the absence of a recognition of belligerency. A third situation, of which *Gelston* v. *Hoyt* is an example, is where a civil conflict rages between two warring factions, neither of which is recognized and neither of which are states in the international sense. In such cases it is not clear that there is an international duty to either faction. Can it be said that we owe it to the people of the place to allow them to determine their government without outside interference? Whatever our international duty, the present Neutrality Act has eventually been interpreted to apply to this situation.

The narrow interpretation given to the Neutrality Act in *Gelston* v. *Hoyt* rendered that act inadequate for the enforcement of our duties of non-intervention and neutrality. It is a curious fact that in that case the attempt to enforce the act had been made at the request of the President himself. This might have been construed as a recognition of belligerency by the President, at least for the purposes of neutrality. Indeed, to use the very phrases of the Court, we might say that there was an indication that the Government no longer considered "the ancient state of things as remaining unaltered." But Story maintained that the act called for a "foreign prince or state," and that under the rule of *Rose* v. *Himely* the Court could not take notice of any power as a state until it was "recognized" as such by the executive. It is ironical that a rule intended to keep the court from clashing with the executive in his proper sphere, devised out of a fear of embarrassing the executive, should thus be used to hamstring the executive himself. It is a very pretty instance of the way that word-formulas have of growing on themselves, of inbreeding so as to rise superior to the realities for which, in their beginning, they were but forms of speech.

It was feared by many persons that under the decisions not even a recognition of belligerency was sufficient to call the act into play, either in favor of the parent state or of the recognized belligerent.

To meet the demands of Spain, the act was amended; [42] in its new form it forbade the fitting out of ships, etc., with the "intent that such vessel shall be employed in the service of any foreign prince or state, or of any colony, district, or people to cruise or commit hostilities against the subjects, citizens, or property of any foreign prince or state, or of any colony, district, or people with whom the United States are at peace."

There was a time when the influence of *Gelston* v. *Hoyt* threatened to emasculate this act also. The executive sought to apply the act to prevent the fitting out of ships in aid of the unrecognized insurgents of Cuba against Spain. Our duty to Spain was clear. Yet a lower Federal court held that the act was applicable only as between political groups, both of which were recognized. This decision was reversed by the Supreme Court in *The Three Friends.*[43] Finally, in the *Lucy H* [44] the lower Federal court decided that the act was applicable when neither group was recognized; the policy of the law was to prevent intermeddling in the political affairs of other countries, whether there was or was not in the specific case a strict duty of neutrality or non-intervention. Thus, at last, was the problem of interpreting these statutes divorced from the extraneous issue of recognition.

A formula, once let loose from the mooring post of its reasons, is apt to reach strange shores. This, we have seen, is what happened in the non-intercourse and neutrality cases. But strangest of all is the famous case of *The Ambrose Light.*[45] This was a libel to forfeit a ship for piracy. At the time of its seizure by an American war vessel, it was being used by an insurgent group of Colombians to blockade the port of Cartagena. A vessel which destroys and preys upon shipping is, argued the Court, a pirate unless authorized (quoting Hall) by a "politically organized society." And a court cannot decide whether a society is politically organized.

[42] Act of March 3, 1817, ch. 58, 3 Stat. 370; Act of April 20, 1818, ch. 88, 3 Stat. 447.

[43] 166 U. S. 1 (1897), reversing district court.

[44] 235 Fed. 610 (N. D. Fla. 1916), refusing to follow the earlier cases of The Carondelet, 37 Fed. 799 (S. D. N. Y. 1889), and The Conserva, 38 Fed. 431 (E. D. N. Y. 1889), in both of which the Court held that the Neutrality Act had no application where neither of the foreign groups was recognized by us. It was stated that an unrecognized group could not be "a colony, district or people with whom the United States are at peace." Peace implied mutual relations of a friendly nature.

[45] 25 Fed. 408 (S. D. N. Y. 1885).

"The error [of holding otherwise] lies in not observing the limitations of the judicial function, which preclude the courts from recognizing any new authority in foreign nations until the political or executive department has done so." [46]

From this it follows that men and ships the world over which engage in political rebellion are pirates unless the foreign office of the forum chooses to "recognize" them as a "politically organized society." Having arrived at this amazing conclusion, the Court talked of "tacit recognition of belligerency" [47] and ended up by deciding, *despite a statement by the executive to the contrary*, that the Colombian insurgents had been recognized as belligerents — a most curious conclusion for an argument which started from "the limitations of the judicial function."

It is the early decisions of Eldon, of Marshall, of Story which laid the basis of the law. It was a time when the political face of the world was being made over; when the bonds of allegiance were being broken; when the pride of parent states was high and touchy; when recognition of the rebellious offspring was a gingerly and dangerous performance. It might mean strained and difficult foreign relations; it might as in the case of Texas cast grave reflections on our national honor; in some cases it might hatch a war. In this light these decisions should be valued and their limits fixed. Eldon, and after him Shadwell, reduced the formula to an absurd nominalism. Eldon seemed to believe that any mention of a state unrecognized by his King was in derogation of duty. Both in England and America it came to be very broadly held that the court must not for any purpose take account of the existence of an unrecognized political organization, though the litigation in no way threatened either the political rights of a parent state or the stability of our international relations. Johnson alone fought this extreme and unfounded generalization. He went far in the other direction. In cases of long-standing independence and undoubted statehood he believed that the courts, being organs of international law, should enforce the rights of unrecognized states.

During the last fifty years the courts have had little to do with the problems of unrecognized states, but a great deal to do with unrecognized governments, though often the decisions manifest slight realization of the differences involved and treat all cases of "non-recognition" alike. To be sure, there is no hard and fast line between the recognition of states and that of governments. By and

[46] *Id.* at 437–438. [47] *Id.* at 420.

large it is true that a state does not lose its identity merely because of a change of government.[48] But a protracted period of anarchy may dissolve the state; when order is restored it is difficult to say whether we have the old state, or a successor to it. Furthermore, during the process the territory may be broken into a number of autonomous parts and raise puzzling questions of identity. Yet the problem of policy in such a case is that involved in recognizing governments, rather than in recognizing new states formed through rebellion. In these cases the courts, except in questions of succession to state funds, should find little occasion to distinguish between new states and new governments.

The Unrecognized Power [49] as Plaintiff

At the very heart of our inquiry is the question: can an unrecognized state or a state with an unrecognized government sue or be represented in our courts? The earliest cases seem to be those involving the controversy over the Swiss funds.[50] Lord Eldon's views in these cases have been set forth above. At first he doubted that he could "take notice" of a government not "acknowledged" by His Majesty. The following year he doubted that he could take notice that it had not been acknowledged. Certainly he was not clear on the point, and in two of the stages of the litigation, one a motion for discovery,[51] certain parties purporting to represent the Government of Switzerland were allowed to argue to the Court. It is not possible to say categorically whether this was a case of an unrecognized state or merely an unrecognized government. When the city of Berne invested the disputed funds, it was one member of a loose confederation of Swiss communities. In 1798 Switzerland came under the unified control of the Helvetic Republic. In 1803

[48] This matter is discussed in Chapter II, p. 101.

[49] The ambiguous word "power" is used advisedly to cover shortly both unrecognized states and recognized states with unrecognized governments. When the distinction is material it is indicated in the text.

[50] City of Berne *v.* Bank of England, 9 Ves. Jr. 347 (1804); Dolder *v.* Bank of England, 10 Ves. Jr. 352 (1805); Dolder *v.* Lord Huntingfield, 11 Ves. Jr. 283 (1805).

Borchard, *The Unrecognized Government in American Courts*, 26 A. J. 261, 265 (1932), says of the Berne case: "The decision is inadequately reported, occupies three lines, is unsupported by reasons, and does not, it is believed, deserve the weight that has been attributed to it." With this we agree.

[51] Dolder *v.* Lord Huntingfield, *supra*, note 50.

the Republic gave way to a federal form of government existing at the time of the litigation.

In *The Hornet*,[52] a proceeding against a vessel for violation of the neutrality laws, an agent of the so-called Republic of Cuba applied to be allowed to intervene and contest the suit. The Cuban insurgents had not been recognized, even as belligerents. Intervention was denied.[53] Counsel argued very broadly, and the Court accepted the proposition "that a power or government must necessarily be recognized to have existence before they can be admitted as claimants to defend or be in any way heard in the court." [54] The Court was well aware [55] that the case before it involved the status of a group rebelling against a friendly power, though it did not limit its language to that situation.

In 1891 the courts of France and England had before them suits instituted by an unrecognized government of a recognized state. In France it was the famous case of *The Chilean Ships*.[56] The Government of Chile, headed by Balmaceda, contracted with a French firm for some ships. In 1891 the authority of Balmaceda was disputed by the Congress, whose prerogatives he sought to suppress. The parties resorted to arms. The Congressists brought a suit in the French courts to prevent the shipbuilders from turning the ships over to Balmaceda. The Chilean minister accredited to Paris intervened on behalf of Balmaceda. The Court ruled that the Congressional agents had no standing, because they had been unable to prove that their government was in fact in power and because only Balmaceda was recognized by France. Implicit was the idea that if France recognized no other government the Congressional government might be allowed to sue provided it was supreme in fact.

On July 4, 1891, five days before the French decision, Kekewich,

[52] 2 Abb. 35; Fed. Cases 6,705 (D. N. C. 1870).

[53] It seems that there would be nothing to prevent the owners of the ship, even though insurgents, from intervening, but intervention here was in the name of the Republic.

[54] *Supra*, note 52, 2 Abb. 37. The Court places its limitations on the ground of an absence of "power" to recognize. "If the courts, before the political departments had spoken, have the right to take one step in this direction, I do not see any limit to their power, short of declaring perfect freedom and independence." (*Id.* at 41.)

[55] *Id.* at 41 (pointing out the danger of involving the country in war through a premature recognition).

[56] Matte et Ross *c.* Société des Forges et Chantiers de la Méditerrannée (Cour d'appel Paris, 1891), 18 J. D. I. 868, 880 (1891).

in the unreported case of *Republic of Chile* v. *Rothschild*,[57] had denied the Congressional agents an injunction to restrain the defendants from releasing Chilean funds to the agents of Balmaceda. By August 28, 1891, the Congressional group were in unchallenged control of the Government. On September 2nd and again on the 9th Collins, J., on the motion of the Congressional agents granted temporary orders restraining the release of funds held to the credit of the Republic of Chile. The cases are unreported.[58] It does not appear whether the objection was taken that the petitioner had no recognized government. Even Avocat Sarrut, who appeared in the French suit for the shipowners and against the Congressional agents, warmly rejected the idea that an unrecognized government could not sue. Otherwise "reason and right (*le droit*) would be equally shocked. What! A *de facto* government whose authority extends throughout the territory [of the State] . . . has not sufficient personality to ask justice in the name of the Government of France. That would be absurd!" [59]

A contemporary commentator says, "As all living and organized beings, it has the right to the distribution of justice." Significantly he adds, "It cannot, from the fact of the slowness of diplomatic formalities, be put outside the law for an indefinite time. . . . These diplomatic baptisms involve 'pourparlers' and 'procedures' which, for divers motives, chancellories do not like to hasten." [60]

This French writer is unwilling to allow the usual course of justice to be diverted by the, to him, whimsical and uncertain devices of diplomacy. To understand his easy assurance it is necessary to remember that during this era the granting of recognition was not

[57] Reported in the *Times*, July 4, 1891, and referred to in 91 L. T. 225 (July 25, 1891). (The reference here is to the *Law Times Magazine*, not the Reports.)

[58] Republic of Chili *v.* City Bank, 91 L. T. 325 (September 5, 1891); Republic of Chili *v.* Royal Mail Steam Packet, 91 L. T. 341 (September 12, 1891).

[59] *Supra*, note 56, 18 J. D. I. 875: "La raison et le droit seraient également choqués. Comment! un gouvernement de fait dont l'autorité s'étend sur tout le territoire . . . n'aurait pas une personnalité suffisante pour parler en justice au nom du Gouvernement de la France! Ce serait absurde." And he adds: "Donc il est impossible de poser en thèse que la reconnaissance officielle d'un gouvernement est la condition *sine que non* de la recevabilité des actions qu'il intente en justice."

[60] *Id.* at 886: "Comme tout être vivant et organisé, il a droit à la distribution de la justice. Il ne saurait, du fait de la lenteur des formalités diplomatiques, être mis hors la loi pendant un temps indéfini."

"Ces baptêmes diplomatiques entraînent des pourparlers et des procédures que, pour des motifs divers, les Chancelleries n'aiment pas à précipiter."

being used as a conscious instrument of policy. Wilson's device of using recognition as a means of reforming our neighbor's house was still in the future. Diplomatic delays were simply part of the deliberation dear to the diplomat's heart. In the days of personal sovereignty, the recognition of a new sovereign was a denial of the claims of the old; premature recognitions carried a threat of dynastic and international war. There was consequently a real need for diplomatic caution, as there is still today in recognizing the independence of rebel states. But the recognition of a new government which has effectively annihilated the old does not present this diplomatic dilemma. When, then, delays in recognition are more or less perfunctory and without vital significance there should be no hesitation in allowing a recognized state with an unrecognized government to sue. We should not be troubled in reaching this result by tenuous structures of thought positing recognition as a logically necessary condition of personality. In any case proponents of the constitutive theory of recognition are solely concerned with the proposition that an unrecognized *state* has no international personality.[61] They are the first to insist that a state once recognized does not lose its personality solely because its government is unrec-

[61] It is quite arguable, too, that the constitutive theory does not stand in the way of even an unrecognized *state* being a party plaintiff. The constitutive theory denies it *international* personality, but not existence as an organism. When a state sues in a foreign court, it sues as a private suitor, not as a sovereign state. It is much in the same position as a foreign corporation, which, of course, has no international personality. It is true that a foreign corporation has been created by law at the domicile and so been given personality. It is arguable that a state, under current conceptions, has no comparable personality within its own system, since it is the source of law rather than a creation of law. Under this line of reasoning its only possible personality would be *international*, and so under the constitutive theory it could not sue. In Russian Socialist Federated Soviet Republic *v.* Cibrario, 235 N. Y. 255, 258; 139 N. E., 259, 260 (1923), the Court, speaking of the right of a state to sue, said of the state: "Neither a natural person nor a corporation, ordinarily we would not recognize it as a proper party plaintiff. . . . We permit it to appear . . . as a body analogous to one possessing corporate rights, but solely because of comity." Cf. Le Normand, p. 283.

Even if the state is considered to have private personality, as is the case in many countries, a further difficulty may arise from the theory of conflict of laws (prevalent on the Continent) that the application of the law of another state is *pro tanto* an extension of that state's authority across its boundaries, and so an indicia of its international personality. (See *infra*, p. 166, for a discussion.) Thus, adopting the constitutive theory, no creature of an unrecognized state — either a private corporation or the personalized state itself — could sue.

ognized. It is simply a question of who in fact represents that state, what is the organ through which its powers are exercised.[62] If such a state cannot sue by its *de facto* government, it is because of policy rather than because of any logic inhering in the concept of recognition.[63]

Quincy Wright has given us an account [64] of a case in a Massachusetts trial court in 1923 in which the "Government of Mexico" sought to restrain the removal of assets of the Mexican State from a safe-deposit vault. This government was unrecognized.

> This fact, however, [said the Court] does not affect the recognition of the Mexican state itself, which for years has been recognized by the United States as an "international person" as that term is understood in international practice. The existing situation simply is that there is no official intercourse between the two states.[65]

After hearing evidence of the effective control of Mexico by this Government, of the maintenance of commercial agents in the United States, though lacking exequaturs, the Court adverted to current negotiations looking toward recognition which, under principles of international law, could retroact to a time prior to the initiation of this case.[66]

Obregon's government had been established since 1921. Was it simply diplomatic *pourparlers* that had held up recognition for two years? Not at all. There has in recent years been a significant development of recognition practice along two distinct lines.

We have already pointed out [67] that from Seward on, American recognition policy swung back and forth between the "*de facto*" and the "legality" principles. Seward said: "What we do require,

[62] Thus Le Normand (p. 284), a leading exponent of the constitutive theory, believes that a recognized state with unrecognized government should be permitted to sue.

[63] We do not lose sight of the fact that, given the personality of a foreign organism, whether it can be a party plaintiff depends on the law of the forum. Recognition, though not a *sine qua non* of personality, may be a *sine qua non* of the right to be a party plaintiff. We are here discussing the former question.

[64] Wright, *Suits Brought by Foreign States with Unrecognized Governments*, 17 A. J. 742 (1923).

[65] *Id.* at 743.

[66] In State of Yucatan *v.* Argumendo, 92 Misc. 547; 157 N. Y. Supp. 219 (1915), it was held that recognition validated a suit commenced prior to recognition by the unrecognized government. Criticisms of this application of the retroactivity doctrine will be discussed *infra* (p. 220).

[67] *Supra*, p. 106.

and all that we do require, is when a change of administration has been made, not by peaceful constitutional processes, but by force, that then the new administration shall be sanctioned by the formal acquiescence and acceptance of the people." [68]

What is behind this policy? Seward gave his reasons thus: "We insist upon this because the adoption of a different principle in regard to foreign states would necessarily tend to impair the constitutional vigor of our own government, and thus favor disorganization, disintegration, and anarchy throughout the American continent." [69]

Latter-day apologists have given even broader reasons. One writer says [70] that it "make[s] for greater individual and national liberty" and that its aim is to encourage "the establishment and maintenance of republican institutions."

Professor Hyde says:

> The United States now appears to take the stand that normally a government, which by force has won the ascendancy in opposition to the will of the people and with contempt for rights created under a local constitution, is *internationally* a menace because its very supremacy sows seeds of discord bound to ripen into a conflict which, however localized, may fairly be deemed hurtful to the maintenance of the general peace.[71] (Italics mine.)

These rationalizations probably far overstate the case. If such large gains were to be had from the policy, it is hard to account for our spasmodic adherence to it. With Wilson, it may have been his distaste for "mere military despotism" that led him to his view. In his statements refusing to recognize the Huerta government in Mexico in 1903 and 1914 the tone is more that of the political moralist than the statesman or politician.[72] By and large, the practice [73]

[68] 2 Dip. Cor. (1868) 863 *et seq.* [69] *Id.*

[70] Potter, *The Nature of American Foreign Policy*, 21 A. J. 53, 55 (1927).

[71] 1 Int. Law 73.

[72] In his annual message of December 2, 1913, Wilson says, speaking of Huerta's government in Mexico, that "such pretended governments will not be countenanced or dealt with by the Government of the United States. . . . Even if the usurper had succeeded in his purposes, in despite of the constitution of the Republic and the rights of its people, he would have set up nothing but a precarious and hateful power, which could have lasted but a little while. . . ."

[73] Recently Secretary of State Stimson has repudiated the Wilsonian policy, and states that we no longer practice it. In 1930 we recognized the revolutionary governments of Bolivia, Peru, Argentina, Panama, and Brazil as soon as they were in control.

See Lippmann and Scroggs, *The United States in World Affairs, 1931* (1932),

was an effect of our hegemony in the Americas, and for the most part limited to them. Undoubtedly in Mexico and Central America, at least, we should welcome a modicum of stability; our recognition policy does point that way, but has not yet laid claim to quite the philosophic breadth which some theorists find in it.

Nor was it a merely passive policy of "We don't like you, so we will let each other be." Secretary of State Bryan stated that the President deemed it to be "his immediate duty to require Huerta's retirement from the Mexican Government, and that the Government of the United States must now proceed to employ such means as may be necessary to secure this result." [74] We have gone further: we have placed [75] embargoes on shipments of arms to revolutionary governments, and in Nicaragua have intervened to protect governments, and to make sure that acceptable governments are put in power.[76]

There has emerged within the last few years a second and far more significant development in recognition policy. The Soviet Government, whatever its real intentions, led the nations to believe that it would not pay Russian debts contracted by previous governments. The United States was not alone in refusing recognition, and is still not alone.[77] Our reasons are mixed. In part they are based on an extension of the policy discussed above. We declared [78] that the Government was a vicious tyranny of a minority; that it boasted that it would repudiate international obligations at pleasure; that it sought through propaganda to undermine our institutions; in short, that to recognize it was repugnant to our moral sense and dangerous to our institutions. But we furthermore refused recognition until Russia should promise to pay the debts of previous governments, and to compensate expropriated Americans. On this ground other nations refused recognition. Thus, refusal of

for the address of Secretary Stimson on February 6, 1931, on our current recognition policy.

[74] 1913, For. Rel. 856. And note the remarks of Secretary Stimson (*supra*, note 73) that Wilson used the "influence and pressure of his great office to force it [Huerta's government] from power . . . against the desire of the authorities and people of Mexico."

[75] 37 Stat. 630, 1733 (1912).

[76] See Potter, *loc. cit.* (*supra*, note 70) at 55.

[77] E.g. Belgium, Egypt, Switzerland.

[78] The remarks of Secretary Colby on this score are very well known, and have been much quoted. See Hyde, *International Law*, § 45; also Russian Socialist, etc. Republic *v.* Cibrario, 235 N. Y. 255, 264; 139 N. E. 259, 262 (1923).

recognition is being used as a sanction for the enforcement of international obligations.[79] It is of the class of negative sanctions such as the breaking off of diplomatic relations, the embargo on commercial intercourse. Of late its character as a sanction is becoming very clear. M. Litvinov, on the occasion of the Peace Pact said:

> The Soviet government believes that there should also be put among the non-pacific means that are forbidden by the covenant such means as a refusal to resume normal pacific relations between nations or breaking such relations, for acts of that character, by setting aside the pacific means which might decide differences, aggravate relations and contribute in creating an atmosphere that is conducive to the unleashing of wars.[80]

It is probably in pursuance of this policy of using non-recognition as a lever that we refused to recognize Obregon. His government had passed certain anti-foreign legislation which the United States considered inimicable to its citizens.[81] In this case, however, our use of it smacked more of "power" politics than of the application of a sanction to coerce the performance of something to which we were entitled.

A remarkable application of this policy is adumbrated in Secretary Stimson's note of January 7, 1932,[82] to China and Japan, in which it is declared that the United States will not recognize any agreement "which may impair the treaty rights of the United States . . . in China, including those which relate to the sovereignty, the independence, or the territorial and administrative integrity of the Republic of China." The reference is to the new Manchurian State, Manchukuo, which, inspired and sustained by Japan, has declared its independence of China. This refusal to recognize is directed not so much at the new state as at Japan for its alleged breach of treaty; it is a curious form of sanction.

The first of these recognition policies has been nearly universally

[79] The idea of non-recognition as a sanction is discussed *supra*, p. 111. On the other hand, "it has been asserted that Great Britain seems to have considered that it could better deal with the Soviet régime upon questions of international obligations and revolutionary propaganda *after* recognition than before." Buehler et al., *Recognition of Soviet Russia* (1931), p. 139. France took the same course of conduct (*id.* at 140): "The government of the Republic believes in the possibility of a general agreement between our two countries of which the resumption of diplomatic relations is a preface."

[80] *Ibid.*, p. 160. Note addressed to M. Herbette, French ambassador in Moscow, August 31, 1928.

[81] See Note (1923), 17 A. J. 758.

[82] *New York Times*, January 8, 1932.

condemned by writers [83] as an interference with the domestic concerns of other states, as officious intermeddling, as a weapon in the hands of the strong to coerce the weak. And, indeed, in the few examples of its use by the United States, it has been directed solely against weak American powers, nor has it been of any particular value in securing stability; embodied by the Central American powers in the Treaty of 1923,[84] there are signs that already they are seeking to do away with it.[85] The second is more debatable. If enough nations cooperate it may have a telling effect. Like the economic blockade, it might prove a substitute for war, although, as suggested by Litvinov, it might just as easily lead to war, or to armed intervention, as when in 1920 the Allies gave comfort to the civil foes of the Soviet. Practiced by isolated nations, as by the United States against the Soviets, it is not much more than a source of mutual irritation and petty backbiting. Apparently in no case of non-recognition have we sought to back up our policy by placing an embargo on commercial intercourse. The Department of State has discouraged bankers from extending long-term credits to the Soviets, but it has not directly interfered with the large body of Russo-American trade, all of which, of course, is conducted by the Soviet itself, which operates in this country through a government-owned corporation. In some instances non-recognition as practiced today differs very little from the breaking off of diplomatic relations, and it may be largely a matter of chance which will be used, depending on whether it is a new or an old government which displeases us. Non-recognition of the new Obregon Government of 1921 gave us merely a new way in which to object to Mexican legislation which since 1917 had displeased us.

Now with the merits of either of these recognition policies, or any other, the courts are not directly concerned. Surely the court will not question the *wisdom* of the practice, either generally or in its specific applications. On the other hand, it may and should take account of its *function* and "value." This distinction, though fine, is a real one. It is argued, of course, that with the "value" of non-recognition the court has no concern. The foreign office has decided to use it to achieve certain national ends; the court must do nothing which in the slightest degree might render the policy less

[83] See Chapter II, note 76.

[84] See Chapter II, note 68.

[85] See *Projects for the Codification of American International Law,* 21 A. J. 306, 312 (1927).

effective. And so an unrecognized power should not be allowed to sue, and in particular to recover funds useful to its maintenance. But this line of argument proves far too much. Why would it not apply every time we protest against the conduct of another state? France refuses to pay her debt to us; we sever diplomatic relations. Napoleon harasses our commerce; we decree non-intercourse. Is France barred from our courts? In time of war not only is the enemy state barred, but its citizens as well. Is it to be the same in the cases of severence of relations, non-intercourse, non-recognition? The banks of an unrecognized power seek to recover their deposits and place them at the service of the unrecognized government. Is the court to take its cue from the foreign office and deny relief?

In other words, unless the court is to be a mere weathercock of foreign policy, it must value the various types of international relations and sanctions, and their bearing on the administration of justice. War presents the clearest case. Intercourse of every sort is interdicted.[86] To give comfort to the enemy is treason. Very probably the economic blockade, with its avowed object of isolating the assailed state, would be assimilated to war. Suits by either the state or its citizens would be denied. On the other hand, non-recognition and severance of relations have not ordinarily been accompanied with the suppression of commercial intercourse, which carries a suggestion that the quarrel is one to be left to the devices of diplomacy and state action, and that the ordinary currents of international intercourse may flow on as well as they may.

Is the administration of justice, the righting of wrongs, the delivery of property to its owners part of this ordinary current? In *Russian Socialist Federated Soviet Republics* v. *Cibrario* [87] the New York Court implied that the grant of judicial relief to foreign states is exceptional.

> Neither a natural person nor a corporation, *ordinarily* we would not recognize it [a foreign state] as a proper party plaintiff. It represents, however, the general interests of the nation over which it has authority. We permit it to appear and protect those interests as a body analogous to one possessing corporate rights, but solely because of comity.
>
> Comity may be defined as that reciprocal courtesy which one member of

[86] However, an alien enemy is allowed to appear in a prize court to protect a ship in which he claims an interest from condemnation. Garner, *Prize Law During the World War* (1927), §§ 78, 79.

[87] 235 N. Y. 255; 139 N. E. 259 (1923).

the family of nations owes to the others. It presupposes friendship. It assumes the prevalence of equity and justice.

The use of the word "comity" as expressing the basis of jurisdiction has been criticized. It is, however, a mere question of definition. The principles lying behind the word are recognized. Whether or not we sum them up by one expression or another, the truth remains that jurisdiction depends upon the law of the forum, and this law in turn depends upon the public policy disclosed by the acts and declarations of the political departments of the government.[88]

Here we are concerned with a great question of starting points. The New York Court begins with the proposition that the enforcement of the rights of a foreign state by judicial process is abnormal. Jurisdiction depends on the law of the forum, which in turn depends on the favorable attitude of the Department of State. Very different is the starting point of Mr. Justice Johnson in the *Consul of Spain* [89] case, discussed above, in which it is said that the court is an organ of international law and should enforce the rights of a nation, whether recognized or not.

In the *Cibrario* case the Russian Soviet sought to compel an accounting by one of its buying agents in the United States. Fraud and misappropriation of funds were alleged. The nub of the decision, once given the premises already set forth, is as follows:

We are the more ready to reach this conclusion because to hold otherwise might tend to nullify the rule that public policy must always prevail over comity.[90] More than once during the last 70 years our relations with one or another existing but unrecognized government have been of so critical a character that to permit it to recover in our courts funds which might strengthen it or which might even be used against our interests would be unwise. We should do nothing to thwart the policy which the United States has adopted.[91]

There is surely a grave question whether the Court has started off on the right foot. We need not talk in this case of the court as an organ of international law. The right here asserted arose under our own law. And this would also be true of a deposit of funds. This country has not forbidden its nationals to have relations with the Soviet Government. International intercourse does exist, and de-

[88] *Id.*, N. Y. at 258; N. E. at 260.

[89] *Supra*, note 30.

[90] This language would imply that even where "comity" does exist it must still give way to "public policy." This means that the right, even of a recognized state, to appear as party plaintiff depends on how that state "stands in" with the foreign office.

[91] *Supra*, note 87, N. Y. at 263; N. E. at 262.

mands the regulation of law. Whether or not our courts are organs of international law, it still remains that they are ministers to the maintenance of international order in a given segment of the world. This is so whether the law they apply is municipal or international. This function is of universal value, and for that very reason, if no other, is valuable to this country. Call this "comity" if you will, but it seems something more significant than the chameleon described by the Court; it is a value to be weighed against the value of any given policy of state.

A word of warning is necessary. Today, it may be proper for a court to refuse to ascribe certain consequences to the fact of non-recognition, but we do not believe that such a determination has eternal validity. We have been at some pains to analyze the content and the significance of current recognition practices. We have seen how vague and how various this content may be; and it is in the light of this data that we have arrived at the views here suggested as to the relative weight of the opposed (the extent of this opposition has been exaggerated) executive and judicial functions. But it is not at all unlikely that recognition policy may in the future take on an entirely new significance. Already this is adumbrated in our refusal — and the refusal of most of the nations of the world — to recognize Manchukuo, because, as it is claimed, it was established and continues to be supported by Japan in violation of its treaty obligations.

That particular situation is likely to be of rare occurrence; but the practice of non-recognition may come to have an established application in the enforcement of international obligations. In that case the terms of our problem would be changed, and a reexamination would be in order. In sketching the history of our courts, we sought to make the point that the ends of government may be accomplished by a variety of means. The relative usefulness of the different organs of government is affected by changing circumstance. In the territories of governmental activity, the boundaries between "political" and "legal" action sway back and forth. Executive administration of a recognition formula may at some future time have a defined value in promoting the ends of national and international organization of such consequence as to overbalance any contribution that a court by adopting an independent course might make toward those same ends. It is quite possible for a court to be of the opinion that that day has arrived. If a court were to reach its results on the basis of that assumption, it would not be easy to quarrel with it. We might attack the truth of the assumption, but not the theory of decision. But the present technique denies in large measure the competence of the courts to make any valuation whatever.

At this point we may take account of some distinctions that have been made with respect to suit by an unrecognized power. There is our Massachusetts case,[92] in which the Obregon Government applied for an injunction to prevent the removal from a bank of certain funds. The application was only to conserve the assets and maintain the *status quo*. Such also was the case of the *City of Berne*,[93] in which Lord Eldon rejected the application and as to which he subsequently may have had doubts. Such was the case of *The Chilean Ships*,[94] but there relief was denied, because France recognized another government and because the applicant failed to show that his government was in control. A few months later Justice Collins gave a series of injunctions maintaining the *status quo* on the application of the unrecognized Chilean Government.[95] And so did the Massachusetts Court in the Obregon case.[96] All commentators agree with these cases. Even Noel-Henry, who believes that an unrecognized government has no capacity [97] to be a plaintiff, descends from his high plane and gives practical reasons in favor of allowing such relief [98] without so much as a nod to his general thesis. It protects the property of the state, which presumably we still recognize, without directly aiding the unrecognized government. The decision of the Massachusetts Court appears to have been based on special facts. It took account of the fact that negotiations looking toward recognition were under way. This is in line with Hervey's idea that the court should base its action on whether the "attitude" of the foreign office is favorable or adverse — a view which ostensibly assumes the primacy of the foreign office but tempers it toward judicial competency whenever there has been no adverse talk by our diplomats.

The *Cibrario* case was an action to recover damages. The funds if recovered would be released to the Soviet. Of course the Court could have allowed recovery and then held the funds in its custody

[92] *Supra*, note 64.

[93] *Supra*, notes 3, 4, 5.

[94] *Supra*, note 56.

[95] *Supra*, note 58.

[96] *Supra*, note 64.

[97] Noël-Henry, p. 125: "La capacité du gouvernement non reconnu est nulle pour le juge tiers. Ce gouvernement n'a l'exercice ni de la personnalité juridique, ni de la souveraineté de l'État qu'il prétend représenter."

[98] *Ibid.*, p. 127.

or appointed a trustee. Surely this would have been preferable to letting Cibrario go scot-free, a shocking result. Where the defendant is a bank, the court might give a judgment declaring the plaintiff to be entitled but ordering the bank to hold the funds.[99]

In fact in the *Cibrario* case a receiver and an injunction to preserve the funds *pendente lite* was asked for,[100] but the entire action was thrown out on the ground that the plaintiff had no capacity to sue. This seems contrary to the Massachusetts case, and is illustrative of the all-or-none jurisprudence which so often prevails in our courts of law.

The *Cibrario* case has been harshly criticized by some writers.[101] Professor Borchard [102] says that where a *de facto* government claims as legal owner of property in its own right recognition is immaterial; where it claims as successor of the prior government, recognition is necessary. In the *Cibrario* case, the Government was

[99] In the case of Russia, the Secretary of State had taken steps to protect state property by recognizing a diplomatic appointee of the Kerensky government as custodian of Russian property. The whole matter and its relation to protection by the courts is discussed in Chapter IV, pp. 212–219.

[100] Indeed, the case came up on an exception to the order of the trial court appointing a receiver *pendente lite* and an injunction restraining transfer of funds by the defendant. This appears more clearly in the report of the case in the Appellate Division. Russian Socialist, etc. Republic *v.* Cibrario, 198 App. Div. 869; 191 N. Y. Supp. 543 (1931).

[101] Dickinson, *The Unrecognized Government or State in English and American Law*, 22 Mich. L. Rev. 29, 118, at 123 (1923): "Must it be said, then, that the funds of an unrecognized government are free plunder for anyone who has a mind to help himself? . . . the courts may be impressed with the disadvantage to society in permitting foreign states to own valuable property without assurance that there shall always be someone legally capable of looking after it. They may be impressed with the danger of serious international complications when such property becomes a unique sort of *res nullius* in the absence of any agent recognized as capable of asserting the owner's rights. . . . Unless the courts can find a way to do this [allow suit without recognition] or at least a way to protect such property by some kind of temporary receivership pending recognition it may become necessary to create a federal custodian who will look after the property of foreign states in cases in which recognition is withheld."

It is just this (appointing a receiver) which in an oblique way the Secretary of State seems to have done in the case of Russia, and this may to some extent account for decisions like the Cibrario case. See Chapter IV, pp. 212–219, for a discussion.

[102] Borchard, *Can An Unrecognized Government Sue*, 31 Yale L.J. 534 (1922). Borchard has recently abandoned this distinction, and believes suit should be allowed in all cases. *The Unrecognized Government in American Courts*, 26 A. J. 261, 266 (1923).

claiming "in its own right." This seems to have been the view of the trial court.

> Whether the government be a *de facto* government or a society, colony, district of people or a voluntary association capable of owning and disposing of money and property is not inherently germane to its rights to succession to the former sovereignty of Russia . . . or the possession of other indicia of sovereign power.[103]

This idea seems hopelessly muddled; a national government is not a personality; it owns no property; it succeeds to no rights. It is the organ of the state. Does an improperly elected board of directors "own" the property bought by the corporation under its regime, but not that of previous regimes? It owns neither, of course.

The funds held by *Cibrario* belonged to the R.S.F.S.R. Now, it may well be that the R.S.F.S.R. is not identical with the old Empire of Russia and with the subsequent U.S.S.R., a federation of which it became and still is a member; it may be a new and unrecognized state. The Court of Appeals speaks of it [104] indiscriminately as an unrecognized "power" and as an unrecognized "government." If this is true, problems of state succession might arise; it is also true, and this is what may have prompted Borchard's idea, that in the *Cibrario* case there could be no problem of *state* succession because the funds in question were the property of the R.S.F.S.R. But where the identity of the state persists and the government changes, no succession is involved. All funds, whether or not raised by the new government, belong to the state which it purports to represent. Professor Borchard's distinction might be justified, however, on less formulistic grounds. Assuming that we allow the new unrecognized government to trade here, to place its funds here, to have relations with our citizens, it may be that the more pressing demands of international good order will be met if legal protection is given *qua* those transactions. On this ground, the reducing to possession of rights accrued prior to the advent of the new government might be denied. Personally, we are inclined to doubt the validity of this limitation.

First there is the question of preserving the funds. In the *Cibrario* case this was totally ignored. Professor Dickinson says: "Must it be said, then, that the funds of an unrecognized government are free plunder for anyone who has a mind to help himself?" [105] To be

[103] Unreported decision quoted in Hervey, p. 63 n.

[104] Cibrario case (*supra*, note 87), N. Y. at 260, 263; N. E. at 261, 262.

[105] *Loc. cit.* (*supra*, note 101).

sure, in practice this applies primarily to chattels and actions in tort or contract. Funds in banks and financial institutions are reasonably safe, though even here there should be someone to protect the funds from losses through insolvency and failing investments. It has been suggested that if the courts will not allow recovery, they should at least appoint a receiver to hold and preserve the assets, or that a Federal custodian might be created by statute.[106] The unrecognized government might be allowed to sue, and the proceeds of the suit held in trust or in the custody of the court.

Though protection may be thus provided, it still seems reprehensible to withhold funds from a foreign state placed in this country in the ordinary course of business. It is one thing to deny a state favors because we do not like its government; it is quite another to hold up its own funds. To make its rights turn on the "attitude" of the foreign office is a dangerous principle. The arguments which make it applicable to non-recognition make it applicable to severance of diplomatic relations,[107] to any case in which our foreign policy negatives the facts of "comity." There is nothing in the statutes, nothing in the nature of recognition as a process, which compels the result. It proceeds from an idea that where a case has a bearing on foreign affairs, the court must subordinate its ordinary procedures and adjust its decision to the supposed needs of the foreign office. It seems to us that the relation between the two departments should be one of *mutual* respect. To allow suit contra-

[106] *Ibid.*

[107] Cf. The "Gul Djemal," 264 U. S. 90 (1924). It was stipulated that the ship, libelled for supplies furnished, was owned by the Turkish Government; that relations between the United States and Turkey had been severed, but that the two countries were at peace. The master of the ship asserted a claim of immunity, which under the peculiar rule of Ex parte Muir, 254 U. S. 522 (1921), was held insufficient to properly invoke immunity. See Chapter I, note 133. In the Supreme Court the decision was put squarely on the rule in Ex parte Muir. But Knox, D. J., in an unreported opinion, said (*Transcript of Record on Appeal*, p. 42): "I am of the opinion that at the time of the seizure of the *Gul Djemal* she enjoyed no immunity from such restraint, as diplomatic relations between the United States and Turkey were then severed, and that, therefore, the comity and courtesy due from this country to Turkey did not, in the absence of appropriate suggestion from the state department of this Government require the extension of such immunity."

Counsel argued (*Brief of Appellant*, p. 37) "that it would be a very dangerous doctrine to hold that a breach of diplomatic relations not followed by war abrogates the respective rights of the Governments involved, and justifies their courts in disregarding the ordinary international immunities and privileges included in the rule of comity."

dicts nothing that the Department of State has said or done, creates no conflict between the departments.[108] If it places limits on the effectiveness of a particular foreign policy, that merely testifies that the claims of foreign policy are no more absolute than any other.

Immunities of an Unrecognized Power

At about this same time the New York Courts had before them an attempt to sue the R.S.F.S.R. for conversion of furs confiscated by it in Russia. The case was determined on a motion to dissolve an attachment. The trial court refused to dissolve the motion [109] and was upheld by the Appellate Division.[110] The R.S.F.S.R., said these courts, was a foreign corporation. Though unrecognized it notoriously existed as the government of a sovereign state. "The defendant had not been recognized . . . and for this reason had already been denied the right to maintain an action in our courts [citation of decision of Appellate Division in *Cibrario* case,[111] not yet decided by Court of Appeals]. For the same reason, it likewise is not entitled to immunity from suit." [112] ". . . The right of immunity of

[108] Quincy Wright, *loc. cit.* (*supra*, note 64) at 744, has suggested as one objection to allowing an unrecognized government to recover funds, "that if this government never achieves general recognition, a subsequent government which does will be likely to consider third states responsible for property of the state turned over to such usurping authority." This suggestion does not seem well taken. A subsequent government is bound by the acts of previous governments whether they were or were not recognized. Great Britain *v.* Costa Rica (the Tinoco Arbitration), (1924) 18 A. J. 147 (1923). Cf. Republic of Peru *v.* Peruvian Guano Co., 36 Ch. D. 489 (1887). Great Britain recognized *de facto* a revolutionary Peruvian government. The defendant effected a compromise with this government of a controversy over a contract. The subsequent *de jure* government repudiated the settlement and sued the defendant for performance of the contract. *Held*: subsequent government is bound by the acts of the recognized government. Internationally, the only question is whether the government was in fact in control.

Thus (by way of reply to Wright's argument), the court should not allow recovery to an unrecognized government unless its control is beyond dispute.

[109] Wulfsohn *v.* Russian Socialist Federated Soviet Republic, 118 Misc. 28; 192 N. Y. Supp. 282 (1922); affirmed, 202 App. Div. 421; 195 N. Y. Supp. 472 (1922); reversed, 234 N. Y. 372; 138 N. E. 24 (1923); writ of error to United States Supreme Court dismissed for want of jurisdiction, 266 U. S. 580 (1924).

[110] *Supra*, note 109.

[111] Russian Republic *v.* Cibrario, 198 App. Div. 869; 191 N. Y. Supp. 543 (1921).

[112] 202 App. Div. at 423; 195 N. Y. Supp. at 474.

a foreign government from suit is not based upon absolute right by virtue of its sovereignty but upon international comity." [113]

For this proposition the Court was able to cite eminent authority from Marshall in *The Schooner Exchange* [114] to Brett in the famous case of *The Parlement Belge*.[115] But in this case the Court of Appeals would have nothing to do with comity. "They [the courts] may not bring a foreign sovereign before our bar, not because of comity, but because he has not submitted himself to our laws. Without his consent he is not subject to them." [116]

And so for the very reason that the R.S.F.S.R. is admittedly and notoriously a sovereign it cannot be sued. This metaphysical assertion seems quite hollow. The property attached had certainly been submitted to our laws. Furthermore, some courts — in Belgium, Italy, Egypt [117] — have apparently in certain cases allowed suits against states, and the "nature of things" does not seem to have been offended.

Putting aside this formula, what are the merits of the question? The Court of Appeals said:

> But whether recognized or not the evil of such an attempt would be the same. "To cite a foreign potentate into a municipal court for any complaint against him in his public capacity is contrary to the law of nations and an insult which he is entitled to resent." In either case to do so would "vex the peace of nations." In either case the hands of the State department would be tied. Unwillingly it would find itself involved in disputes it might think unwise. Such is not the proper method of redress if a citizen of the United States is wronged. The question is a political one, not confided to the courts but to another department of government. Whenever an act done by a sovereign in his sovereign character is questioned it becomes a matter of negotiation, or of reprisals or of war.[118]

Noël-Henry finds these reasons unconvincing.

> Not only [he says] does the refusal of immunity fortify the government of the state of the judge in its attitude toward the unrecognized government, but it is a rule necessary to the good administration of justice. A recourse ought to be open to the injured party. Now, when it is a question of an unrecognized government the diplomatic avenue is closed; it is necessary, then, that the judicial path be open.[119]

[113] *Id.* at 422; N. Y. Supp. at 474.

[114] 7 Cranch 116 (1812).

[115] 5 P. D. 197, 217 (1880).

[116] *Supra*, note 109, 234 N. Y. at 376; 138 N. E. at 26.

[117] See De Visscher, *Les Gouvernements Étrangers En Justice*, 3 Rev. de Droit Int. (3rd Série) 149, 300, at 303 *et seq.*

[118] *Supra*, note 116.

[119] Noël-Henry, p. 130: "Non seulement le refus de l'immunité fortifie le

The first point is typical of Noël-Henry's general thesis. He insists that an unrecognized government has no personality. Yet, he is not at all at a loss to allow it to be sued as the representative of the state, and apparently to pay judgment from state funds, though how it can do either of these things if it has no personality is something of a mystery. In truth, all of his elaborate logic is merely so much dressing of the idea that the court should do everything in its power to help the foreign office, not short of embarrassing and thwarting the unrecognized government if it gets a chance. This extreme view, unpalatable to most American writers, probably reflects the great importance and value set upon foreign affairs in a country situated as France is.[120] However, it is the argument of the New York Court of Appeals that to *allow* suit would embarrass the foreign office even more than to reject the suit. On this point Noël-Henry seems to have the best of the argument. To deny suit means that the injured plaintiffs will bring pressure on the government for recognition so as to constitute diplomatic channels for the settlement of claims; and as for "vex[ing] the peace of nations" by irritating the unrecognized government, it is a little difficult on this

gouvernement de l'État du juge dans son attitude à l'égard du gouvernement non reconnu, mais c'est une règle nécessaire à une bonne administration de la justice. Un recours doit toujours être ouvert à la personne lésée. Or, quand il s'agit d'un gouvernement non reconnu, la voie diplomatique est fermée; il faut donc que la voie judiciaire soit ouverte."

And see *accord*, Pergler, *Judicial Interpretation of International Law* (1928), p. 64: "Public policy and justice would point to the conclusion that a non-recognized foreign government should not be permitted to take advantage of its culpability both in international relations and with reference to the injured party, by the application of what is a rule of comity to which the unrecognized government has not been admitted and is not deemed fit to be admitted by recognition."

[120] Furthermore, the French courts (i.e. the civil, not the administrative, courts) hold very strongly to the idea that they cannot and must not reflect upon or evaluate administrative action; and that to do otherwise would violate the principle of the separation of powers. See, for example, the manner in which they handle the interpretation of treaties (*supra*, pp. 66–71). And cf. Ghose, *Comparative Administrative Law* (1918), p. 96: "At the inception of the French Revolution, this traditional jealousy of the French people toward the Civil Courts was deepened by their reactionary attitude. This explains the strange uses to which the doctrine of 'separation of powers' . . . was put by the leaders of the Revolution. The administrative authorities were made completely independent of the judiciary and the judges were forbidden on pain of forfeiting their position to interfere in any way whatsoever with the acts of the officers of the administration or to cite them before them for the performance of their duties."

head to distinguish between denying it the right to bring its agents to justice and to collect its funds as the Court did in the *Cibrario* case, and requiring it to answer for its torts, if they can be proved to be such.

Now, it is on the point of liability that in the *Wulfsohn* case the Court seems to be on the solidest ground. The action sounded in tort for an act of confiscation by the Government in its own domain. If Wulfsohn were a national of the United States, this may have been a wrong to the United States under rules of international law; and the United States was not a party to the action. But it is difficult to see how it is a tort to the plaintiff under any law. There can be no doubt of the evil effect were the courts of one country to presume to regulate by the laws of the forum the internal order of a foreign state, whether recognized or not. Noël-Henry in his zeal seems to have completely overlooked this.[120a]

Now as to Noël-Henry's second point, that since diplomatic channels are closed, the judicial ones should be open, it strikes us that this is very good sense. It would have no application in the *Wulfsohn* case, since there was no liability except possibly to the United States. But a state may, under its own laws or under the laws of other states in which it acts, incur liability. The distinction between acts of *puissance publique* and acts *de gestion* is one of the bloody battlefields of jurisprudence today.[121] The validity of a distinction between governmental and non-governmental action may be open to doubt, but there is a feeling that when states engage in activities in competition with private citizens the usual rules of law and of liability should be applied.[122] The courts of both England [123] and the United States [124] have declined to modify the rule of im-

[120a] See Appendix A for an account of the recent New York case of Salimoff *v.* Standard Oil Co., in which judgment is based on the ground taken in the text.

[121] *Loc. cit.* (*supra*, note 117).

[122] *Research in International Law. Harvard Law School, Drafts of Conventions Prepared for the Codification of International Law* (1932), "Competence of Courts," (art. 12): "A State may be made a respondent in a proceeding in a court of another State when, in the territory of such other State, it engages in an industrial, commercial, financial or other business enterprise in which private persons may there engage, or does an act there in connection with such an enterprise wherever conducted, and the proceeding is based upon the conduct of such enterprise or upon such act."

[123] The Gagara, [1919] P. 95; The Porto Alexandre, [1920] P. 30.

[124] Berizzi Brothers *v.* S. S. Pesaro, 271 U. S. 562 (1926). In an earlier stage of this case Judge Mack decided otherwise, The Pesaro, 277 Fed. 473 (S. D. N. Y. 1921).

munity on the basis of this distinction. But where the defendant is an unrecognized government so that diplomatic relief is not open to the plaintiff, suit might well be allowed in proper cases.

In this light should be considered the recent case of *Voevodine* v. *Government of Commander-in-Chief of Armed Forces in the South of Russia.*[125] The plaintiff sold goods to the Denekin Government, which at the time of the suit had become non-existent. The plaintiff joined as defendant a commercial agent of the Denekin Government in America, in possession of funds of that government. The Court was asked to appoint a receiver of these funds, which it is alleged were being dissipated. In this situation, which ought to have appealed strongly to the husbanding instincts of a judge, the Court was able to find the most sweeping reasons for doing nothing at all, providing a spectacle of appalling impotence.[126] First it was said that there can be no cause of action against a government; its promise to pay creates a mere moral obligation. Then, a sovereign government cannot be sued, and *a fortiori* one that no longer exists. As to appointing a receiver until recognition, that was unthinkable. "That hour may be far distant; it may not happen for years or centuries. Meanwhile this court would be engaged in holding and protecting this property." [127]

This case suggests the question of whether the property of an unrecognized power is immune from attachment in an action *quasi in rem*. The reasoning of both this and the *Wulfsohn* case, in which there was an auxiliary attachment and an application for a receiver, indicates that it is immune, regardless of the nature of the cause of action. Yet the curious rule of *Ex parte Muir,*[128] which denies the immunity of state property unless the suggestion comes from the Department of State or unless the ambassador of the interested country joins as a party, would result in a denial of immunity to the

[125] 232 App. Div. 204; 249 N. Y. Supp. 644 (1931), affirmed. 257 N. Y. 557; 178 N. E. 793 (1931).

[126] This case was governed in some degree by Nankivel *v.* Omsk All-Russian Government, 237 N. Y. 150; 142 N. E. 569 (1923), reversing 203 App. Div. 740; 197 N. Y. Supp. 467 (1922). That was a supplementary proceeding against Kidder, Peabody and Co., garnishee, on a judgment secured by default against a government which, at the time of the judgment, was no longer in existence. It was held that the garnishee could attack the judgment collaterally, and that this judgment was void. "Acquiescence will not be inferred from the silence of the dead." *Id.*, N. Y. at 158; N. E. at 571.

[127] *Supra,* note 125, App. Div. at 209; N. Y. Supp. at 650.

[128] Ex parte Muir, 254 U. S. 522 (1921). See Chapter I, note 133.

property of an unrecognized government, where, as in suits against a ship, the government does not appear as a formal party. In fact in the *Gul Djemal*,[129] a libel against a Turkish ship, this very thing has happened. That was a case where Turkey was without diplomatic representation in America; the Secretary of State refused to make any suggestion of immunity. The suggestion of the master of the ship was held to be of no effect. However, in the recent case of *Banque de France* v. *Equitable Trust Co.* [130] a Federal court refused to allow an action *quasi-in-rem* against the funds of the Russian Soviets on bank in America. The Court was not troubled by the absence of a suggestion of immunity from the Department of State. Since the plaintiff garnished the funds as the funds of a foreign government, by the very force of the allegation they were immune. Liability was predicated on confiscation of the plaintiff's funds by the Soviet. The Court adverted to the French recognition of the Soviets and advised the plaintiff, a French national, that if it had been wronged it was the business of its government to secure redress.

In *The Annette* [131] an English Court took jurisdiction of a libel to determine title to a ship which had been sequestered by the Provisional Government of Northern Russia. The government had hired out the ship to a cooperative for commercial uses, retaining a residual control. The Court decided that England had not yet recognized the Provisional Government as the government of a sovereign state. A motion to dismiss the writ was refused.

"I must be satisfied before I can recognize the Provisional Government of Northern Russia as a sovereign state for the purposes of this case, that the British Government so recognize it." [132]

Thus, the immunity of the ship is made to turn on recognition. Furthermore, this in effect was a suit against the state itself to try its asserted title and the validity of its governmental acts.[133]

Interesting to compare with this case is the decision of [134] an Egyp-

[129] 264 U. S. 90 (1924), discussed *supra*, note 107.

[130] 33 F (2d) 202 (S. D. N. Y. 1929).

[131] [1919] P. 105.

[132] *Id.* at 111.

[133] The Court also took the ground that since the ship had been placed in the hands of private parties, the arrest of the vessel interfered with no sovereign right of government by compelling "the Government to submit to the jurisdiction, or to abandon its possession." *Ibid.* This seems to be the general rule. See Fraenkel, *Juristic Status of Foreign States, etc.*, 25 Col. L. Rev. 544, 559 (1925).

[134] National Navigation Cie. *v.* Tavoularidis et Cie. (Trib. Alexandrie 1927), 19 Gazette des Tribunaux Mixtes 251.

tian tribunal discharging an attachment on a ship of the Russian Soviet. The ship, Costi, at the time of the Revolution a Russian-owned vessel, had been commandeered by force of arms while on the high seas by Soviet agents, who had shipped as members of the crew. The owners (an Egyptian firm to whom the Russian firm had sold it) of this ship sought in this suit to attach *another* Soviet ship and make it answer in damages for the alleged conversion. In this respect, the case differs from *The Annette.* There it was the title to the ship which was involved, and the question was whether the act of government was effective to pass title, not whether it created liability. Answering the argument that since the Soviet regime was unrecognized its acts upon the high seas were no better than piracy, or at least unauthorized by any law which the court could recognize, the judge said:

> These facts, though they may bring about consequences of a political and diplomatic nature between the two governments do not, however, authorize judges to deny to the Soviet State the prerogatives which it exercises in fact as a sovereign State, nor its undeniable existence, recognized by a number of foreign States, above all when they are asked to pronounce a decision against the Soviet Government, as representative of the Soviet State.[135]

What is "the Law" of an Unrecognized Power?

There seem to be no cases holding a state or its property liable for its acts solely because it or its government is unrecognized. As we have already remarked, where such acts have taken place in the territory of the state itself or, as in the Egyptian case, on the high seas, there does not seem to be any law to create liability in favor of a private party. Noël-Henry would say that there is; that until recognition the court must assume that the old law, in force before the advent of the new government, is still in force, and that the new government is no better than a pack of pirates or robbers who at the

[135] *Id.* at 252: "Ces considérations, si elles peuvent entraîner des conséquences d'ordre politique et diplomatique dans les relations des deux Gouvernements, ne peuvent cependant autoriser les juges à méconnaître à l'État Soviétique les prérogatives qu'il exerce du fait comme État souverain ni son existence indéniable et d'ailleurs reconnue par nombre d'États étrangers, alors surtout qu'ils sont invités précisément à prononcer des decisions contre le Gouvernement Soviétique comme représentant l'État Soviétique."

But cf. Mayafis *v.* National Navigation Cie. (Trib. Comm. Alexandrie, 1929), 19 Gazette des Tribunaux Mixtes 249, in which in a suit by next of kin for the death of one employed by the Egyptian operators of the Costi, those who attacked the ship in the name of the Soviets are called "pirates."

best can only be dignified by the name of a *force majeure*. Undoubtedly, there are statements without end in the books that until recognition the court must regard the old state of things as continuing. These statements, however, derive from the early cases in which the question of rebel organizations was at issue, and they should be limited to that situation. Yet in 1930 Chief Judge Cardozo in the *Petrogradsky* case, speaking of the Soviet decrees nationalizing banks, said: [136] "They are exhibitions of power. They are not pronouncements of authority." Consequently these decrees would *ipso facto* have no effect on the life of a banking corporation which they purported to terminate.

"Conceivably *the law will* declare it at an end when marauders have brought frustration to the purpose for which personality was given. That is another question. What is not to be lost sight of is that even so it is the law and not merely an assassin that must pronounce the words of doom." [136a] (Word "will" italicized in originals; other italics mine.)

And what is *the law*? It is the law of the last recognized government, dead, gone, and buried. Contrast with these words, those of Judge Andrews speaking for the same court in the *Wulfsohn* case seven years earlier:

> Whether or not a government exists, clothed with the power to enforce its authority within its own territory, obeyed by the people over whom it rules, capable of performing the duties and fulfilling the obligations of an independent power, able to enforce its claims by military force is a fact, not a theory. . . .
>
> We have an existing government, sovereign within its own territories. There necessarily its jurisdiction is exclusive and absolute. It is susceptible of no limitation not imposed by itself. This is the result of its independence. It may be conceded that its actions should accord with natural justice and equity. If they do not, however, our courts are not competent to review them.[137]

To be sure, in the *Wulfsohn* case the Government itself was being sued; in the *Petrogradsky* case the effect of Soviet action arose in a suit between private parties. But the general point of view in the two statements is in complete contradiction. As with the question of the right to sue, we are up against a fundamental problem of

[136] Petrogradsky Mejdunarodny Kommerchesky Bank *v.* The National City Bank of New York, 253 N. Y. 23, 28, 30; 170 N. E. 479, 481, 482 (1930).

[136a] But see the more recent New York case of Salimoff *v.* Standard Oil Co., Appendix A.

[137] Wulfsohn *v.* Russian Socialist Federated Soviet Republic, 234 N. Y. 372, 375; 138 N. E. 24, 25 (1923).

starting points. How are the acts and laws of an unrecognized government to be regarded in foreign courts; what effect is to be given to them; are they to be ignored; are they to be put to the test of the laws of the supplanted authority? Cardozo (and a majority of courts) seem to answer the last two questions in the affirmative, qualifying the answer with what has been called an "inverted exception." [138]

> Limitations upon the general rule may be appropriate for the protection of one who has been the victim of spoliation, though they would be refused to the spoliator or to others claiming under him. We leave these questions open. At the utmost they suggest the possibility that a body or group which has vindicated by the course of events its pretensions to sovereign power, *but which has forfeited by its conduct the privileges or immunities of sovereignty*, may gain for its acts and decrees a validity quasi governmental, if violence to fundamental principles of justice to our own public policy might otherwise be done.[139] (Italics mine.)

To us the italicized phrase is rather a shocking presumption. It would appear that because our Department of State has refused to recognize the Soviet, that body has forfeited the privileges and immunities of sovereignty, which in this case means the power to govern in its own land. Andrews, on the other hand, speaks of the Soviet as "capable of performing the duties and fulfilling the obligations of an independent power." [140] In other words the laws of the Soviet are to be respected because it is the government, and the only one, capable of performing the function, and obliged to perform the function, of keeping order in its own bailiwick. Order in Russia is not only a national but an international necessity, and it seems presumptuous indeed for a court to impugn that order because the Department of State believes the Soviet is "unworthy of a place in the Society of Nations." [141] It may be that there are certain acts and laws of the Soviet to which we will not give credit

[138] Hervey, p. 145: "The genesis of the inverted exception of justice and public policy in recent years is to be found in Judge Cardozo's" rule that the laws of an unrecognized power will be disregarded unless their enforcement is necessary to "the public order" of the forum. Thus the phrase "the inverted exception," since under the Civil War cases the acts by the *de facto* government were *prima facie* valid until proved contrary to public policy. See Habicht, *The Application of Soviet Laws and the Exception of Public Order*, 21 A. J. 238 (1927).

[139] Sokoloff *v.* National City Bank, 239 N. Y. 158, 166; 145 N. E. 917, 919 (1924).

[140] *Supra*, note 137.

[141] Sokoloff *v.* National City Bank, N. Y. at 165–166; N. E. at 919.

because it would violate our public policy to do so. With this we have no concern, since that would be equally so after recognition.

The problem of what effect is to be given to the acts and laws of an unrecognized government has caused the courts immense concern, and has been raised in an acute form both by reason of the world-wide refusal to recognize the Soviets and by a repugnance to their laws. We have seen that with respect, at least, to unrecognized states Lord Eldon arrived finally at the conclusion that an unrecognized power must not even be mentioned in the court; that to hold otherwise would be to destroy the unison between the courts and the King's foreign office. This nominalism continues to pop up every so often. It will be said that a court has no means of knowing what the government of another state is or whether any such state exists. This sort of talk, however, has fairly passed out of the decisions; where the fact of the existence of an unrecognized government is involved only collaterally, courts have no difficulty in allowing the fact to be established. Where, however, an act or law of the government is the basis of a suit or defense the question lies deeper.

It is convenient to divide the field into acts of the government whether under laws or by executive fiat, and transactions between private parties under general law. There is no inherent logic in this distinction and the two merge into each other, but some have thought that there should be a difference in result. Broadly, the whole matter boils down to the question of whether there is anything in our conflict of laws which makes the recognition of a government of the least significance.

Noël-Henry in radical and doctrinaire fashion would deny the existence of any effective Soviet law whatsoever. The courts of France are to apply the old Imperial law to everything concerning Russians taking place either in France or Russia, including marriage.[142] Where due to the *force majeure* of Soviet rule this is impossible, the court may make modifications in the old rules to adopt them to changed circumstances.[143]

It is hardly conceivable that the French courts would carry out

[142] Noël-Henry, §§ 122–129. The legislation of an unrecognized government ought to be rejected "en bloc." *Id.* at 143.

[143] Noël-Henry, § 102. The Petrogradsky case (*supra*, note 136) is a very striking instance where the Court, assuming the old Russian law to be *still applicable to "nationalized" corporations*, adapted it largely by means of generous infusions of American law to meet the radically changed circumstances.

this formula in the doctrinaire manner proposed by Noël-Henry, but behind it is an idea of the conflict of laws different from the Anglo-American. When a foreign law is applied, it is conceived that the sovereign force of the foreign state is being given extension into the territory of the forum, or is being given effect by the court of the forum. Thus, it is very easy to view the application of the foreign law as something akin to the "comity" of which the New York Court spoke in the *Cibrario* case. Thus Professor Ténékidès says:[144] "All conflict of laws is only a conflict of sovereignties, and that ought to mean mutually recognized sovereignties, for only between such can there be normal international relations." The learned professor admits,[145] however, that theoretically this would bar out only unrecognized states, and is somewhat puzzled to arrive at the apparently desired exclusion of the laws enacted by an unrecognized government. However, the courts who wish to arrive at that result have found a formula. Thus, an Italian court has said:

> Since we do not recognize in the Russian Government the legitimate exercise of political sovereignty, we must equally not recognize any manifestations of this sovereignty in the legislative domain, because the political recognition of a foreign State is an indispensable condition of the exercise of its judicial activity in its relations with other States.[146]

In other words Russian law is recognized, but no power now existing there to change it.

Clearly the classic Anglo-American view of the conflict of laws[147] is different. In every case it is conceived that the law of the forum is being applied. In the interest of convenience or to fulfill just expectations, the court may look to other laws. A writer in the *Harvard Law Review*[148] says that the foreign law to which our courts

[144] See Ténékidès, *Les lois successorales soviétiques et l'ordre public en Grèce*, 52 J. D. I. 1143, 1144 (1925): "Tout conflit de lois *n'est qu'un conflit de souverainetés* (italics in original) et cela ne doit s'entendre que des souverainetés mutuellement reconnues entre lesquelles seules il peut se former des rapports internationaux normaux."

[145] *Id.* at 1144 n. 2.

[146] Katsikis *v.* Società Fati Tvoroni di Pallone, 50 J. D. I. 1021 (1923) (Trib. of Genoa, 1923).

[147] See Beale, *Treatise on Conflict of Laws* (1916), §§ 68, 100, 106. However, as Dickinson remarks, the differing views of conflict of laws do not necessarily require difference in the result here. But the continental view does offer some conceptual hurdles to taking account of the law of the unrecognized state which the Anglo-American view should not. *Recognition Cases 1925–1930*, 25 A. J. 214, 224 (1931).

[148] Note 38 Harv. L. Rev. 816 (1925).

look is usually the law of a "sovereign";[149] that before we can apply a law we must first find who the sovereign is, and "an American court can accept no evidence to establish the identity of a foreign sovereign but the statement of the federal executive department."[150] But, says the writer, we might associate law with organized social control rather than with sovereignty. Well, what is that but beating the devil around the stump? It seems that when the politically organized group passes a law regulating marriage, that is "organized social control"; when they pass a law confiscating property, that is "sovereignty." This is merely using a big word to cover up the fact that without recognition there are some laws which the writer believes should be given effect and some which should not.

Indeed the essential thing is just this organized social control rather than the mystical essence called sovereignty.[151] The function of a conflict of laws is to coordinate the many spheres of social control, to assign to each the objects best suited to be controlled by it, and by the same principle to exclude others. It is a broad application of the principle of the division of labor. To apply the law of another state is not to do that state a favor or to grant it a privilege because we approve of it or have welcomed it into our exclusive coterie; it is to recognize the universal need for order and predictability, to realize that in a given portion of the globe the privilege and obligation of maintaining that order is committed to one organization and not to some other, to appreciate that the maintenance of that order must be "respected" to a certain extent if it is to fulfill its function. We may not like that order, but to ignore it or suppose that some other exists is to produce an entirely useless anarchy and confusion. A German writer has said:

> In Germany the question of the recognition or of the non-recognition of the Soviet Government presents no interest for our problem. . . .

[149] *Id.* at 817, citing Beale, *op. cit.* (*supra*, note 147), § 101. [150] *Id.* at 819.

[151] See a book review by H. A. Smith in 12 British Year Book of Int. Law (1931) at 224: "'Sovereignty' is not a legal principle, but merely a descriptive word intended to describe certain political conditions if and when they exist. . . . If we try to formulate it as a legal principle, we find at once, first, that we are driven to all kinds of tortuous expedients in order to fit the facts into whatever formula we may choose to adopt. If, on the other hand, we recognize that the question is really one of fact, then we can readily argue that facts may vary almost infinitely, that sovereignty may be present in one place and absent in another, that it may be limited or unlimited, divided or undivided, that it is subject, in a word, to every influence that governs the relations of men."

The sole inquiry is what law is in force in Russia at the moment of judgment.

The application of abrogated law is quite clearly "non-sense."

Law is progress. A law whose perfecting has ceased at a certain epoch, which has become through non-application in its own country a veritable mummy has ceased to live.[152]

We may not agree with the Hegelian dictum that "law is progress," but surely this writer is correct in believing that law is a function of a living organism, the expression of an existing reality.

There are a number of well-known cases in which this, what we might call the *de facto* principle, was applied. During the War of 1812 the English forces occupied the port of Castine in Maine and collected import duties. After the war the United States collector sought to compel payment of the duties again. The claim was rejected. Mr. Justice Story said:

By the conquest and military occupation of Castine, the enemy acquired that firm possession which enabled him to exercise the fullest rights of sovereignty over that place. The sovereignty of the United States over the territory was, of course, suspended, and the laws of the United States could no longer be rightfully enforced there, or be obligatory upon the inhabitants who remained and submitted to the conquerors. By the surrender the inhabitants passed under a temporary allegiance to the British government, and were bound by such laws, and such only as it chose to recognize and impose.[153]

Now, the United States had never said or admitted through the Department of State that Britain, and not it, was sovereign in Castine. There was nothing equivalent to a recognition. Sovereignty, says the court, is merely equivalent to possession and ability to enforce the law. The collection of taxes, a so-called "sovereign" act, was held to be as effective as any other act in law. The case, of course, differs from the recognition cases. At the time of the decision the war was over, there was no question of our current relations with Britain. Divorced then from all fortuitous questions of policy, the case is grounded solidly in the conception that "sovereignty" is a function of political control as it exists in fact. And though we may challenge the rightfulness of control or refuse to "recognize" it, the fact persists.

The same moral is pointed by *Keene* v. *McDonough*.[154] In that

[152] Freund, *Le point de vue de la Jurisprudence Allemande* (translated from the German), 51 J. D. I. 51, 52 (1924).

[153] United States *v.* Rice, 4 Wheat. 246, 254 (1819).

[154] 8 Peters 308 (1834). But cf. Davis *v.* Policy Jury of Concordia, 9 How. 280 (1850). After the signing of the Treaty of Ildefonso, by which Spain ceded

case the defendant based his title on the decree of a Spanish court in Louisiana, given after the date of cession, but before actual delivery of possession to the United States. The adjudication was held binding. "The country, although ceded, was, *de facto*, in the possession of Spain and subject to Spanish laws." This, said the Court, it knew from history. Here again, be it noted, we have in question an act of political authority; to make binding judgments between citizens is one of the highest acts of state. As in the *Rice* case, the Court was not troubled by controversial questions of foreign policy. In other words, these cases show us that the *de facto* principle has found a place in the law; they do not show us how this principle operates when there are powerful reasons against recognizing the *de facto* situation.

The much-cited Civil War cases present a more intricate problem. The *de facto* principle is usually invoked as the source of an independent and self-sufficient political authority. In that form it was not applicable to the Confederate rule of law, when asserted in the courts of the United States, since these courts could not admit the validity of any order within the United States which denied the primacy of the Constitution. In 1861 Lincoln declared his famous blockade of the rebel ports. It is often said [155] that this constituted

Louisiana to France, but while Louisiana was still in Spanish possession, the Spanish governor granted an exclusive ferry franchise. The grant was held void. After such a treaty, the Court argued, the law of nations recognizes in the ceding nation prior to delivery no "other exercise of sovereignty than that which is necessary, for social order and for commercial purposes. . . ." *Id.* at 294. Grant of a franchise did not fall within such exercise. It was important that Congress had passed an act declaring void concessions of land made by the Spanish governor, and the executive had declared to the same effect. The Court treated this stand as applicable to the Spanish grants of franchises. *Id.* at 288.

[155] This was the view of Earl Russell given in defending the Queen's Proclamation of Neutrality. Moore, *Digest*, I, 190. Oppenheim (*International Law* [4th ed. 1926], vol. II, § 56) contends that the Civil War was a true war, and the Confederate states belligerents *seriatim*, because they were suzerains of the United States rather than mere political divisions. He also speaks (*ibid.*, § 59) of the parent state recognizing the "belligerency" of the rebels, but he does not say just what will be such a recognition.

But Noël-Henry (p. 19) believes that such a recognition of belligerency is not truly such, but merely a declaration by the parent state that the penal laws against treason will not be applied against the rebels and that the rules of international warfare will be observed. This view does better represent what was decided in the Civil War decisions considered here, though it would not be impossible for the parent state to recognize the rebels as true belligerents. Cf.

a recognition of the "belligerency" of the Southern states, and so gave the Confederacy status as an independent, international unit. But a blockade is addressed to other nations, and of itself gives no status to the party blockaded. The law of nations allows a state to blockade a rebel port, whether considered as an act of war or of domestic discipline,[156] so that in the eyes of the nations the rebels are still considered to be subject to the control of the parent law. Nevertheless, so powerful is the force of fact, and the compulsion of reality, that within limits the *de facto* principle received an application by analogy in the Civil War cases.

The cases are of two periods, those during the war and those after it. Most interesting of the first is *U. S.* v. *Greathouse*.[157] This was a prosecution for treason of one who sought to sail a ship out of San Francisco in aid of the rebellion. It was argued that the rebels had been recognized as belligerents and so no longer owed the duties of citizenship. Mr. Justice Field (on circuit) in his charge to the jury said:

> As a matter of policy and humanity, the government of the United States has treated the citizens of the so-called Confederate States taken in open hostilities as prisoners of war and has thus exempted them from trial for violation of its municipal laws. But the Courts have no such dispensing power; they can only enforce the laws as they find them upon the statute book. They cannot treat any new government as having authority to issue commissions or letters of marque which will afford protection to its citizens, until the legislative and executive departments have recognized its existence. The judiciary follows the political department of the Government in these particulars. By that department, the rules of war have been applied only in special cases.[158]

In the *Greathouse* case, the defendant had operated within the federal lines. The case would have been much more pertinent if he had been acting in the Confederate territory. In *U. S.* v. *Baker* [159] the defendant had operated on the high seas under letters of marque granted by the Confederacy. The indictment was not for treason but robbery on the high seas, which the statute punished as piracy. As in *The Ambrose Light*,[160] the Court was of the opinion that unless

remark in Ford *v.* Surget, 97 U. S. 594 (1878): "The Confederate States were belligerents in the sense attached to that word by the law of nations."

[156] Cf. Rose *v.* Himely, 4 Cranch 241 (1808); Hudson *v.* Guestier, 6 Cranch 281 (1810). But cf. preceding footnote.

[157] 2 Abb. C. C. 364, Fed. Cases No. 15,254 (C. C. Calif. 1863).

[158] *Id.* at 380.

[159] 5 Blatch C. C. 6, Fed. Cases No. 14,501 (S. D. N. Y. 1861).

[160] 25 Fed. 408 (S. D. N. Y. 1885). See *supra*, pp. 138–139.

the taking of property on the high seas was under the sanction of a "recognized" belligerent or *de facto* government it was piracy. To endow an organization with *de facto* political power would infringe on the prerogatives of the executive. In this wise the Court instructed the jury, which fortunately disagreed. In *The Lilla* [161] a Confederate prize court had condemned and sold a Yankee ship to a Britisher. The Court refused to recognize the decree.

"Treating the Confederates in some respects as belligerents was not an abandonment of sovereign rights. . . . Most assuredly I shall not recognize the Southern Confederates as a nation or as having a government competent to establish prize courts." [162]

The *Greathouse* and *Baker* cases were between the United States and its rebellious citizens. *The Lilla* raises a doubt; against Great Britain we claimed, by blockading the Confederacy, rights usually associated with war; perhaps her citizens should have been entitled to rely on the power of both warring factions to exercise the usual prerogatives of war. However, as we should expect during a time of rebellion, *de factoism* is not very popular with the parent state.

After the war the courts had a considerable body of litigation in which questions arose as to the validity and effect of laws and acts in the rebellious territories during the period of the war. In this respect there may be a distinction between the individual states on one hand which continued to function internally in the same manner as they had done under the Union, and the Confederacy on the other. Thus, the acts and laws of the states could be treated as growing from the same sources of power as in the past; and acts in aid of rebellion would simply be treated as unconstitutional. There are some statements in the cases taking this distinction.

Thus in *Williams* v. *Bruffy* [163] the Court says:

> Whilst thus holding that there was no validity in any legislation of the Confederate States which this court can recognize, it is proper to observe that the legislation of the States stands on a very different ground.
>
> The same general form of government, the same general laws . . . remained. As far as the acts of the States did not impair, or tend to impair, the supremacy of the national authority, or the just rights of citizens under the Constitution, they are in general to be treated as valid and binding.

In *Keith* v. *Clark* [164] the Court held that the State of Tennessee could not, after the war, repudiate the bills of a state-owned bank

[161] 2 Sprague 177, Fed. Cases No. 8,348 (D. Mass. 1862).
[162] *Id.* at 186.
[163] 96 U. S. 176, 192 (1877).
[164] 97 U. S. 454 (1878). Cf. City of Richmond *v.* Smith, 15 Wall. 429 (1872).

issued during the war under an arrangement between the bank and the state whereby the bills were to be legal tender for the payment of taxes. The Court said that since 1796 the State of Tennessee had always been one and the same political body.

There has been perpetual succession and perpetual identity.[165]

It is a mere chimera to assert that one State of Tennessee conquered by force of arms another State of Tennessee, and imposed laws upon it; and, finally, that the logical legerdemain by which the State goes into rebellion, and makes, while thus situated, contracts for the support of the government in its ordinary and usual functions . . . and then, by reason of being conquered, repudiates these contracts, is as hard to understand as similar physical performances on the stage.[166]

However, in *Texas* v. *White*[167] it was said by Chief Justice Chase that though Texas remained a state of the Union, its government was unlawful, its acts unlawful. Yet its acts and laws necessary to peace and good order would be treated as valid. In the case of *Thorington* v. *Smith*,[168] decided about the same time, the same judge distinguished between *de facto* governments such as Cromwell's which completely supplant the old authority, and governments of paramount force, which only partially supplant it, such as the Confederacy.

Its distinguishing characteristics are (1) that its existence is maintained by active military power within the Territories, and against the rightful

(a promise by the city to indemnify for destruction of liquor to keep it out of federal hands held enforceable).

[165] *Id.* at 461 (per Mr. Justice Miller).

[166] (*Id.* at 459.) To the argument that the state governments were false usurping governments whose acts were not binding on the present government Mr. Justice Miller replied: "We cannot agree to this doctrine. It is opposed by the inherent powers which attach to every organized political society possessed of the right of self-government, it is opposed to the recognized principles of public international law. . . ." There was a vigorous dissent by Justices Waite, Bradley, and Harlan, who contended that the rebellious state governments were illegal and usurping; that all their acts were void unless ratified by the restored government; and that the issue of bills having contributed to the support of the state during rebellion could not in any case be ratified or made legal.

See distinction made by Noël-Henry (p. 10) between a general *de facto* government, one which completely supersedes the old government and whose acts bind the state, though it is itself overthrown, and a local *de facto* government which supersedes the old government in only part of the territory of the state and whose acts are nil unless it succeeds. The rebel states were "general"; the Confederacy "local."

[167] 7 Wall. 700 (1869).

[168] 8 Wall. 1 (1869).

authority of an established and lawful government; and (2) that while it exists, it must necessarily be obeyed in civil matters by private citizens who . . . do not become responsible as wrongdoers.[169]

In other words, it could be said of both the Confederacy and the individual states that their governments were unlawful but that their acts and laws in so far as they were devised to promote peace and good order would be respected. It is true that the legislation of the states came off slightly better, and that some of the acts of the Confederacy were given credit, not as the acts of that body, but as they were found reflected in the legal structure of the various states. But a few cases will show that no very clear lines were drawn in actual decision.

A state corporation law,[170] a contract payable in Confederate notes (the only available currency of the time) were held valid.[171] A Confederate army officer confiscating property on grounds of military necessity was not liable in tort.[172] On the other hand, acts, whether of the Confederacy or of the states which in the opinion of the Supreme Court were in support of the rebellion, failed to produce the intended legal consequences. A Confederate law compelling debtors, under pain of penalty, to pay debts owing to Northerners into the Confederate treasury did not work a release of the debt.[173] A sale of goods by the Confederacy passed no title to the buyer. The grounds were that the transaction was illegal and that, in any case, the Confederacy was not an entity capable of holding title.[174] Consequently, the buyer seeking the return of the property under the Captured Property Act was denied relief.[175] And so it

[169] *Id.* at 9.

[170] United States *v.* Insurance Companies, 22 Wall. 99 (1875).

[171] Thorington *v.* Smith, 8 Wall. 1 (1868). But cf. Hannauer *v.* Woodruff, 15 Wall. 439 (1872), in which a note given for Confederate bonds was held unenforceable.

[172] Ford *v.* Surget, 97 U. S. 594 (1878).

[173] Williams *v.* Bruffy, 96 U. S. 176 (1877).

[174] In United States of America *v.* McRae, 8 L. R. Eq. 69 (1869), and United States of America *v.* Prioleau, 2 H. and M., Ch. 559 (1865), the United States claimed title to certain goods by succession to the Confederacy. The complaint presupposed that the Confederacy was capable of holding title. Relief was denied because the United States refused to perform the contracts under which the goods were deliverable.

[175] Sprott *v.* United States, 20 Wall. 459 (1874). The dissent of Mr. Justice Field seems more in accord with the purposes of the Captured Property Act and the Proclamation of Pardon and Amnesty. He distinguishes between upsetting executed transactions and enforcing unexecuted contracts. In the latter case,

was with the acts of the states. A sale of securities by the rebel State of Texas passed no title; after the war the state was allowed to recover them.[176] The war was over when these decisions were made; many of them appear quite narrow and unnecessary. It seems particularly purposeless for the court to have upset executed transactions [177] on the ground that they were in aid of the rebellion and sometimes rather remotely so.[178] However, with the content of this exception to the general rule of validity we are not primarily concerned. The important thing is that there was a presumption in favor of *de facto* governmental activity, and that to overcome it there must be positive reasons of policy.

M. Noël-Henry [179] contends, with some force, that the Civil War cases have no bearing on the problem of *de factoism* and non-recognition. The rebel states continued to be states of the Union, and certainly *after* the war they were part of the United States.[180] Thus,

the objection that they were in aid of rebellion might be properly urged, citing Hanauer *v.* Doane, 12 Wall. 342 (1820), and Hanauer *v.* Woodruff, 15 Wall. 439 (1872). Both of these were actions on notes, one given for goods to be supplied to the Confederacy, the other for Confederate bonds.

[176] Texas *v.* White, 7 Wall. 700 (1869). Grier dissented. He argued that it is admitted that Texas was acting through a responsible government; that she sold her bonds and received value; that there was no point in disturbing an executed transaction. This dissent seems wholly convincing.

[177] Texas *v.* White (*supra,* note 176); Sprott *v.* United States (*supra,* note 175).

[178] In Lamar *v.* Micou, 112 U. S. 452 (1884), a guardian was denied credit for investment in Confederate bonds; it was said that they had no legal value and could not be regarded by United States courts as lawful trust investments. *Accord*: Horn *v.* Lockhart, 17 Wall. 570 (1873). But by 1898 the Court was anxious to distinguish these cases, and did so on a very slim distinction indeed. Baldy *v.* Hunter, 171 U. S. 388 (1898).

[179] Noël-Henry (p. 103) criticizes Judge Cardozo for making use of the Civil War cases in Sokoloff *v.* The National City Bank, 239 N. Y. 158, 165; 145 N. E. 917, 919 (1924): "Après la guerre de Sécession, le juge Americain statuait comme juge interne, dans la sphère des affaires intérieures: aucune question de politique étrangère n'était en jeu; il n'était donc pas tenu à la reserve et il lui appartenait, à defaut des pouvoirs politiques, de faire les discriminations jugées par lui utiles à la meilleure administration de droit."

[180] In Texas *v.* White, 7 Wall. 700 (1869), a question arose as to the status of Texas on February 16, 1867, at which time it brought this original suit in the Supreme Court. On March 2, 1867, Texas was declared by Congress to be a "rebel state" and a military government was provided for it until a republican state government could be legally provided. Could Texas sue on February 16 as a state? The majority held "yes"; that it had never ceased to be a state, and that whatever government was in fact in power could bring the suit. Three

the court was serving as *juge interne*; in that capacity it is the duty of a court, in the absence of Congressional action, to find and apply the rules best fitted to promote the internal order.

The judge is the guardian of the internal legal order, the preserver of its continuity. In the silence of the political organs, he must devise rules of law, even at the risk of running counter to their policies. Thus, the courts were responsible for maintaining the continuity of the legal order in the erstwhile Confederate states, which were, and in legal contemplation had never ceased to be, part of the United States. But where the judge is asked to apply the law of another state, it is a very different matter. Here he sits as *juge tiers*. He has no duty, no concern to maintain the continuum of a foreign legal order,[181] unless his Government by entering into relations with another state thereby manifests its good will toward that state. "The 'juge tiers' acts in the sphere of exterior affairs and he cannot enfeeble the diplomatic position of his government by deciding in its place." [182] The motivation for this dogma appears in the statement that "it is useful to reinforce the diplomatic action of the government." [183]

The ideas behind these statements we have already attacked: the unreal insulation of the internal from the external order; the idea that the law of another state is applied out of friendship for that state; the assumption that the courts of justice are an annex to the foreign office.

It is true that between the non-recognition and the Civil War cases there are substantial differences. The principal one is that in the latter the disputed political controversy was in the past, as in the *Rice* [184] and *Keene* [185] cases. And there was, as Noël-Henry points out, the need of preserving the continuity of the internal order, which is the court's first concern. But the cases have a value for us in their reliance on *de factoism* as a broad principle needful for the conservation of the social order.

judges dissented. Grier said that as a "political fact" Texas for eight years had not been a state of the Union. Wayne believed that Congress had declared that Texas was not a state and that was final.

[181] Noël-Henry, p. 92: "Peu importe au juge tiers qu'il y ait une solution de continuité dans l'activité des États étrangers."

[182] *Ibid.*: "Le juge tiers agit dans la sphère des affaires extérieures et il ne saurait affaiblir la position diplomatique de son gouvernement en statuant à sa place."

[183] *Ibid.*, pp. 90–91.

[184] United States *v.* Rice, 4 Wheat. 246 (1819).

[185] Keene *v.* McDonough, 8 Peters 308 (1834).

Legal Effect of the Acts of Unrecognized Powers

In *Luther* v. *Sagor* [186] the King's Bench Division held that a confiscation of property by the unrecognized Soviet Government (R.S.F.S.R.) did not pass title. The expropriated owner, a Russian citizen, was declared to be entitled to the goods as against a purchaser from the Soviet. Said the Court:

> I am not satisfied that His Majesty's Government has recognized the Soviet Government as the Government of a Russian Federative Republic or of any sovereign state or power. I therefore am unable to recognize it, or to hold it has sovereignty, or is able by decree to deprive the plaintiff company of its property.[187]

Similar decisions have been given by Italian [188] and French courts,[189] the latter holding the action of the Soviet was equivalent to a theft or fraudulent abstraction (*soustraction frauduleuse*). There is an indication in Judge Cardozo's opinion in the *Sokoloff* [190] case that the same result might be reached.[190a] On the other hand, in the recent *Banque de France* [191] case the Court stated that the rule of *Luther* v. *Sagor* was not followed in this country. That was a case

[186] Aksionairnoye Obschestvo Dlia Mechanicheskoyi Obrabotky Diereva A. M. Luther *v.* Sagor, [1921] 1 K. B. 456. Reversed an appeal ([1921] 3 K. B. 532) on new evidence showing that in the interim the R. S. F. S. R. had been recognized. Roche, J's, opinion in the Divisional Court was spoken of with approval.

[187] *Id.* at 477.

[188] Fédération italienne Consorzi agrari di Piacenza *c.* Commissariat pour le Commerce étranger de la République socialiste des Soviets de Russie (Civ. Trib. Rome 1923), 51 J. D. I. 257 (1924). This case involved confiscation of the goods of an Italian national. Cf. Nomis di Pollone et Svarano Fotis *c.* Cooperativa Garibaldi Federazione italiana Lavoratori del Mare (Trib. Rome 1924), 52 J. D. I. 227 (1925). Court refuses to allow defendant in action of conversion to set up title of Soviets in nationalized ships which apparently were abroad at time of the confiscation.

It seems that on December 26, 1921, Italy and R. S. F. S. R. had concluded a commercial accord. In the first case above it was said that since the accord had not been ratified by Parliament, it could not change the public order exception; in the second case ratification had taken place, but the Court held that the treaty was not a *de jure* recognition, that it merely looked to recognition in the future.

[189] Héritiers A. Bouniatian *c.* Société Optorg (Trib. Civ. de la Seine 1923), Gazette du Palais, 1re Sem. 1924, 97, 51 J. D. I. 133 (1924).

[190] Sokoloff *v.* The National City Bank, 239 N. Y. 158, 166; 145 N. E. 917, 919 (1924).

[190a] Since this was written, the New York Court has refused to follow Luther *v.* Sagor. See Appendix.

[191] 33 F (2d) 202 (S. D. N. Y. 1929).

where a French bank, basing its action on the confiscation by the Soviet of its gold on deposit in a Russian bank, garnished Soviet gold in America, claiming title to it as the very gold confiscated. On a motion to strike out the garnishee's defenses the Court held that the title of a foreign government could not be questioned; at least not where one of our own nationals claims under that title. In this instance the garnishee banker might be laid open to double liability if he could not rely on the Soviet's title.

In *O'Neill* v. *Central Leather Co.*[192] the Court upheld a title to personal property derived from the Villa military organization in the Mexican Civil War of 1913–1914. Letters from the Department of State were before the Court advising that neither faction was recognized as a government or as a belligerent. However, said the Court, the President had declared our neutrality and thus recognized the existence of a civil war. It was well known that there were two political bodies, each exercising *de facto* authority over persons within a determinate territory. The President "has thus left it open — in fact made it necessary — for the courts in a proper case to determine whether a particular territory was in control of one party or the other." [193] A military occupant may make levies to support the army and operate a temporary government.[194] To allow this is preferable to pillage.

In other words, government, however rudimentary, is preferable to anarchy. If the Department of State does not positively specify what the government of a given territory is, then the Court must find out for itself. President Wilson had shown himself extremely hostile to military dictators. Up to this time he had refused to recognize Huerta and later Carranza, and there is no reason to suppose that he had any love for the bandit Villa. The decision is thus a remarkably broad recognition of the *de facto* principle. The Texas courts [195] refused to follow it, not, however, because of non-recognition, — in fact recognition of belligerency was assumed by the Court to have been given, — but simply because they conceived it

[192] 87 N. J. L. 552, 94 Atl. 789 (1915). Affirmed on writ of error by the United States Supreme Court *s. n.* Oetjen *v.* Central Leather Co. 246 U. S. 297 (1918); but in the interim the Carranza government in Mexico had been recognized by the United States.

[193] *Id.* N. J. L. at 557; Atl. at 791.

[194] Cf. Ford *v.* Surget, 97 U. S. 594 (1878) (Confederate officer not liable in tort for confiscating property to keep it out of Federal hands).

[195] Cía. Minera Ygnacio Rodriguez Ramos, S. A. *v.* Barthsville Zinc Co., 115 Tex. 21; 275 S. W. 388 (1925).

to be too dangerous to allow a rebel military commander "exercising paramount force" to confiscate property. If the commander is defeated and was never at any time in control of the government of the State, there will be no one responsible to nationals of other states for wrongful confiscation.

The doctrine of *Luther* v. *Sagor* has been treated to severe whippings by a number of writers.[196] On appeal the case was reversed, because the Soviet had been recognized by Britain in the interim. Obviously a doctrine which thus plays fast and loose with titles may work considerable havoc in a closely integrated world. The Soviet sells confiscated goods to *A* in a recognizant country. His title is good. *A* takes his property to a non-recognizant country; his title is bad. If by chance *A* had secured a judgment in the recognizant State, his title would probably have been perfected everywhere. And there is a suggestion in the *Banque de France* case that if the state of the expropriated party has recognized the expropriating state, the title cannot be questioned;[197] *a fortiori*, if the expropriated person was a national of the expropriator. However, *Luther* v. *Sagor* was the latter case. And under the reasoning of that case, the result should be the same if the property had been taken for taxes, since the levying of taxes is as much a "sovereign" function as confiscation, from which it differs only in degree.

Now there are other doctrines in the law by reason of which a title good in one place is bad in another. But one unfortunate rule is not an argument for another, and the rule of *Luther* v. *Sagor* is a

[196] See Dickinson, *Recent Recognition Cases*, 19 A. J. 263, 267 (1925): "The foreign decree ought not to be ignored. It is enough for the courts to subordinate themselves in matters of recognition to the decisions of the political departments. They are not required to assist the subjects of unrecognized *de facto* governments at the expense it may be of nationals, in thwarting the operation of such *de facto* government's decrees."

Fraenkel, *The Juristic Status of Foreign States*, 25 Col. L. Rev. 544, 563 (1925): "A rule of law producing results so variable in time and space should not be persisted in."

[197] 33 F (2d) 202, 206 (S. D. N. Y. 1929). In James *v.* Second Russian Ins. Co., 239 N. Y. 248; 146 N. E. 369 (1925), the argument was made that the claim of plaintiff (a British citizen) against defendant (a nationalized Russian insurance) was merged in the trade accord between Great Britain and the Soviets, the two nations being substituted for the private parties. The Court decided that passing "the question whether such agreement, if made, would be disregarded by our courts because of our refusal to recognize the existence as a government of one of the parties to the compact"; that in fact the accord looked forward to an agreement settling claims, but was not in itself such an agreement. N. Y. at 258; N. E. at 371.

threat on an unusually large scale. True, if there is some policy served by the rule, the suffering of individuals is the just price they pay for the general good. The apparent demands of "justice" in a specific case may blind us to the larger issues which lie dimly and less insistently in the background. The record, the lawyer's device for focussing the issues, may work a dangerous distortion. "Justice" includes more than, and may even result in a denial of, fair treatment to the immediate parties. This writer can only hope that he has resisted the appeal of particular litigations for satisfying but short-sighted solutions. For *Luther* v. *Sagor* the argument has been made that it creates an extreme embarrassment to the unrecognized government and may bludgeon it into meeting the conditions of the foreign office.[198] This cannot be denied, and if it is the business of the courts to minister unto current foreign policies, the case of *Luther* v. *Sagor* is correct, and tearful objections as to the harm it may do to our nationals and to the symmetry of the universal order of titles are undoubtedly wide of the mark. But we do not believe that a state should play the part of dog in the manger toward the unrecognized government. In considering the privilege of such a government to protect by suit the state's private rights, we gave our reasons for rejecting the policy of obstruction.[199] The reasons apply here with greater force, for in the matter of suit, the courts are being asked to give positive aid; whereas here the Court is being asked merely not to interfere with the orderly processes of government, which have already taken place in the territory of a foreign state. The attitude of the English courts is made unpleasantly evident in *The Lomonosoff*.[200] That case was a libel for services rendered as salvage in rescuing the ship from the imminent clutches of the Soviet authorities, unrecognized by England at the time. In allowing the claim, the Court remarked:

> It is obvious that this court respecting the comity of nations would never treat as a meritorious service the act of persons who in defiance of the laws of an established government recognized by and in friendship with this country took a ship out of the lawful control of such a government. But at Murmansk on February 21, there was no government recognized by this country and indeed no established government at all.[201]

If the last phrase is true, the case may be justified, but the very evident implication that a court will reward those who defy a gov-

[198] Noël-Henry, p. 139.
[199] *Supra*, p. 155.
[200] [1921], P. 97.
[201] *Id.* at 105.

ernment, even an unrecognized one, and subvert its laws is shocking. It is a further illustration of the insular notion that so far as the court is concerned the need for law and order stops at the boundary lines.

There has been an immense body of litigation on the status of the old Russian corporations, almost all of which the Soviet has "nationalized." Their assets in Russia have been confiscated, and their debts declared cancelled. Their shareholders and directors have been scattered over every portion of the globe. Some have established new headquarters in London, in Paris, either for doing business or for liquidation and distribution. The problem is a vast one, and has been treated voluminously by scholars. Most of it is not germane to this inquiry. If, for example, the court decides that since the Soviets are unrecognized, the decrees terminating the corporate existence are to be ignored and the old law is to be applied, many questions arise as to how to adopt these laws to the changed circumstances. If the Soviets have been recognized and the decree dissolving the corporation is given effect, liquidation offers its problems, for regardless of recognition foreign courts will not allow confiscation decrees to operate on assets situated outside of Russia; or it may be decided, as the House of Lords has done, that the decrees were not intended to dissolve the corporations,[202] and that they still may function as such outside of Russia; or it may be found that the corporation has established a new domicile, and on the basis of some free association theory exists without benefit of a creating act.[203]

In fact, by a variety of routes and without regard to recognition the courts have succeeded in giving full effect to their hearty distaste for Soviet legislation and a minimum of effect to the legislation itself.[204] Many of these corporations had foreign branches and

[202] Russian C. & I. Bank *v.* Comptoir d'Escompte de Mulhouse, [1925] A. C. 112; Banque etc. *v.* Goukassow, [1925] A. C. 150.

[203] The entire matter has been elaborately considered in Nebolsine, *The Recovery of the Foreign Assets of Nationalized Russian Corporations*, 39 Yale L. J. 1130 (1930); Wohl, *Nationalization of Joint Stock Banking Corporations in Soviet Russia*, 75 U. of Penn. L. Rev. 385 (1927).

[204] Thus, many students have been troubled by the wholesale disregard of Bolshevist legislation, even in recognizant countries, on the ground that to apply it would disturb the "public order." See André-Prudhomme, *La reconnaissance en France du Gouvernement des Soviets et ses consequences juridique*, 52 J. D. I. 318 (1925); Ténékidès, *loc. cit.* (*supra*, note 144); Habicht, *The Application of Soviet Laws and the Exception of Public Order*, 21 A. J. 238 (1927).

operated in foreign parts, substantially in the manner of domestic corporations. In such cases it is quite proper to resist the intended effects of the Soviet laws, in so far as that would mean the destruction of substantial vested interests in properties located outside of Russia; but all this has nothing to do with recognition, since recognizant states have treated the question of substantial interests in the same manner as the non-recognizant states.[205]

Now, it is the generally accepted rule in both the Anglo-American and Continental systems that corporate personality is in the first instance an act of creation by the law of some one state, and that this same state has the power of life and death over the corporation.[206] This law is sometimes called the law of the domicile or the principal place of business. To this there are certain exceptions in some systems. The corporation by acquiring a new principal office and losing its old one may be reborn at the new domicile. This seems to be the French law,[207] and there are suggestions of it in the English cases.[208] Corporate personality persists for liquidation regardless of the original creating law. The general rule is undoubtedly a convenient device, just as are the rules governing the place of principal and ancillary administrations, for securing uniformity in the handling of complex international phenomena in a world where no one man is king.

It is interesting to inquire what possible connection recognition or non-recognition has with the validity and use of these devices. A Swiss court has answered quite simply, "None." [209] Thus, the Swiss branch of a Russian bank sued in a Swiss court. Because of the nationalization decrees it was held to be without standing, fol-

[205] In Russian State *v.* Compagnie Ropit (Ct. Appeals Aix 1925), 53 J. D. I. 667 (1926), it was held that though France had recognized the U. S. S. R. her confiscation decrees did not affect property abroad, nor could it prejudice the rights of French creditors in the corporate assets. The defendant company, a nationalized Russian corporation, was held to have secured a domicile in France, at least for liquidation, by appealing to a French court for justice.

See Nebolsine, *loc. cit.* (*supra*, note 203) at 1139–1142, for the English law.

[206] Chief Judge Cardozo in Petrogradsky, etc. Bank *v.* The National City Bank, 253 N. Y. 23; 170 N. E. 479 (1930), considers the prevailing theories of corporate personality and gives elaborate citations.

[207] Russian State *v.* Compagnie Ropit, *supra*, note 205 (acquisition of new domicile for liquidation); Nebolsine, *loc. cit.* (*supra*, note 203) at 1142–1144.

[208] Nebolsine, *loc. cit.* (*supra*, note 203) at 1141–1142.

[209] Banque internationale de Commerce de Petrograd *c.* Hausner (Trib. fédéral de la Suisse 1924), 52 J. D. I. 488 (1925).

lowing the orthodox rule that corporate life depends on the law of the original creating state.

> Non-recognition of the Soviet Government has merely this consequence, that in the relations of international law, this government has no standing to represent Russia in Switzerland either in public or private matters. But this does not hinder Russian law from existing and producing effect.

This view is far too simple for the French and American courts. In the much-discussed case of *Pelzer* v. *United Dredging Company*,[210] the Supreme Court of New York denied the capacity as an administratrix of one so appointed by a Mexican court, on the ground that the Mexican Government was unrecognized. The Court said:

> The administratrix plaintiff is an officer of a foreign court. . . . It is syllogistically true that if the foreign court has no recognized power here she may not assert a right derived through her appointment therefrom. . . . The Mexican government is not *de facto* here, since recognition alone can make it so. . . .
>
> Its power as a government remains nil without our patent of recognition. As the parent of the court it cannot have notice either judicial or administrative, and surely the creature cannot be possessed of a power not given its creator. The duty to declare the legal incapacity to sue is paramount to a consideration of the evils attendant upon the failure of justice resultant [211] upon this policy of international relations.

Thurman Arnold [212] has recently had something to say on this judicial trick of blaming "the failure of justice" on some other department of the government. A more useless result than arrived at in this decision is hard to imagine. Indeed the use of the word "syllogistically" is a give-away; it is only too evident that a jejune conception prevailed over good sense.

For a few years the New York courts seemed to be in some doubt

[210] The case is unreported. A copy of the decision appears in Dickinson, *The Unrecognized Government or State in English and American Law,* 22 Mich. L. Rev. 29, 30 n. (1923). But cf. Keene *v.* McDonough, 8 Peters 308 (1834) (*supra,* note 154, and text).

[211] The administratrix secured appointment in New York, but was denied the right to amend the original complaint and continue the suit in her new capacity. Pelzer *v.* United Dredging Co., 200 App. Div. 646; 193 N. Y. Supp. 676 (1922).

Final disposition of the matter is not of record, but Dickinson assures us that there was in fact no miscarriage of justice (*loc. cit.* [*supra,* note 210] at 134 note).

[212] Arnold, *The Rôle of Substantial Law and Procedure in the Legal Process,* 45 Harv. L. Rev. 617, 629 (1932).

on the status of the nationalized corporations. In *James* v. *Second Russian Insurance Company*[213] a "nationalized" company was sued. It raised the defense of dissolution by the Soviet decree. Judge Cardozo said:

> The shades of dead defendants do not appear and plead. . . . The decree of the Russian Soviet government nationalizing its insurance companies has no effect in the United States unless, it may be, to such extent as justice and public policy require that effect to be given. . . . Justice and public policy do not require that the defendant now before us shall be pronounced immune from suit . . . we find it profitless to consider whether the decree was intended to put the nationalized companies out of existence altogether. . . . Our concern is not so much with the consequences intended by the authors of the decree as with those that will be permitted in other jurisdictions where the intentions of its authors are without effect as law.[214]

A recent writer has approvingly heralded this view as new: namely, that personality and capacity depend on the law of the forum.[215] But it has always been the position of our conflict of laws that the decrees of other jurisdictions are "without effect as law," that the forum determines the rules to be applied. The question is what will be the rule; ordinarily the rules of the domicile govern, presumably for the very reasons of "justice and public policy" of which the Court speaks, and there is nothing in this decision which tells us why justice here requires something else.

In *Russian Reinsurance Co.* v. *Stoddard*[216] the Court wavered. This was a bill in equity brought by a "nationalized" insurance company, no longer doing business in America, to secure the refund from the depository of a guaranty fund required by the New York law as a prerequisite to the writing of insurance. The suit was conducted by an agent appointed by six of the eight directors incumbent at the advent of the Soviet regime. Since 1917 no meeting of shareholders had been held, and a majority of the directors had been exiled in Paris, where they met in 1923 and executed the power of attorney to bring suit. The trial court held the corporation defunct and dismissed the bill. The Appellate Division[217] reversed the trial court. To give effect to the Soviet decree would be

[213] 239 N. Y. 248; 146 N. E. 369 (1925).
[214] *Id.*, N. Y. at 254; N. E. at 370.
[215] Nebolsine, *loc. cit.* (*supra*, note 203) at 1137–1138.
[216] 240 N. Y. 149; 147 N. E. 703 (1925).
[217] 211 App. Div. 132; 207 N. Y. Supp. 574 (1925).

to "give the recognition which our government has thus far withheld." The Appellate Division was in turn reversed by the Court of Appeals on a variety of grounds: the possibility that in a country recognizing the Soviets the courts would give effect to the confiscation decrees and allow the *Soviets* to recover from the defendants, the doubt as to whether distribution to the shareholders could be made at the time.

> The primary question . . . is not whether the courts of this country will give effect to such decrees [nationalization decrees] but is rather whether within Russia or elsewhere outside of the United States, they have actually attained such effect as to alter the rights and obligations of the parties in manner we may not in justice disregard, regardless of whether or not they emanate from a lawfully established authority.[218]

The Court seemed troubled by the artificiality of its conception that the laws of Russia were the laws of the old Imperial regime.

> Our view of what is the law of Russia rests upon a juridicial conception not always in consonance with fact. . . .[219] The plaintiff, if it exists at all, is an artificial entity. . . . It is in fact without existence in Russia, which has given it birth. . . . It exists here solely by force of the juridicial conception which we have pointed out should not be carried beyond the limits of common sense and justice.[220]

The opinion makes this important point:

> It [the Department of State] cannot determine how far the private rights and obligations of individuals are affected by acts of a body not sovereign, or with which our government will have no dealings. That question does not concern our foreign relations. It is not a political question, but a judicial question.[221]

But in the *Petrogradsky* [222] decision all such doubts were banished. A "nationalized" Russian bank sued the National City Bank for deposits. The suit was brought by the only three directors left from pre-Soviet times. Under the by-laws they constituted a quorum. These directors were doing business in Paris with the corporate funds and voting themselves substantial salaries. Next door to the Paris offices of the corporation, the directors had opened a new bank with a similar name, confessedly trading on the corporation's good will. The shareholders were dispersed, their whereabouts

[218] *Supra*, note 216, N. Y. at 156; N. E. at 704.
[219] *Id.*, N. Y. at 162; N. E. at 707.
[220] *Id.*, N. Y. at 164; N. E. at 707.
[221] *Id.*, N. Y. at 158; N. E. at 705.
[222] 253 N. Y. 23; 170 N. E. 479 (1930).

unknown. The trial court held [223] that the decrees of the Soviet had destroyed the plaintiff and denied recovery. The directors, the Court said, might petition for the appointment of a receiver to conserve the assets.

This was reversed, Chief Judge Cardozo writing an elaborate opinion. Its original premise is that the decrees of the Soviet Republic "are not law in the United States, nor recognized as law." This no one would deny. But following this is the curious *non sequitur*, "They are exhibitions of power. They are not pronouncements of authority." [224] It proceeds: a corporation is

> a *persona ficta*, the creature of the State. . . . The personality created by law may continue unimpaired until law rather than might shall declare it at an end. Conceivably the law *will* declare that end when marauders have brought frustration to the purpose for which personality was given. That is another question. What is not to be lost sight of is that even so it is the law and not merely an assassin that must pronounce the words of doom.[225]

The Court, putting aside "as irrelevant the fiat of the Soviet Government," purports to look to the law of the Imperial and Provisional Governments to determine whether the corporation is dead. Contemplating the nearly complete extinction of its milieu and its functions, the Court nevertheless concludes from an examination of *American* cases that "the corporation abides as an ideal creation impervious to the shocks of these temporal vicissitudes"![226]

The Court admits that the requirement for visitation of banks can no longer be carried out; that the Imperial law compelled dissolution where a bank loses one quarter of its assets; that there has been an entire paralysis of action. But it replies: "They have yet to show that as a consequence of this paralysis of action *the very law that has been flouted* multiplies the misfortunes of the victim by taking back the concession of juristic life." [227] (Italics mine.)

This amazing statement seems to imply that the Soviet is even now violating the laws of Russia. Indeed, in answer to the opinion of a witness that the plaintiff is without corporate capacity *in*

[223] *S. n.* Banque Internationale de Commerce de Petrograd *v.* The National City Bank of New York, 133 Misc. 527; 233 N. Y. Supp. 255 (1928); affirmed without opinion 226 App. Div. 866; 235 N. Y. Supp. 862 (1929). The Court relied on the Stoddard case, also on the Swiss case cited *supra*, note 209.

[224] *Supra*, note 222, 253 N. Y. at 28; 170 N. E. at 481.

[225] *Id.*, N. Y. at 30; N. E. at 482.

[226] *Id.*, N. Y. at 32; N. E. at 482.

[227] *Id.*, N. Y. at 34; N. E. at 483.

Russia the Court replies that this opinion is based on "the notion that the Soviet decrees have the authority of law"! [228]

Here indeed is the very apotheosis of the constitutive theory of recognition. Not only do we refuse to apply the legislation of the unrecognized government, but we declare that it is illegal in its own land. [228a]

The result of the case seems as doubtful as the language. These directors did not, as was the situation in many of the other Russian corporation cases, hold proxies from any of the shareholders. They were responsible to no one. To these objections the Court optimistically replies: "It will be for the courts of the French Republic, if the fund is sent to France, to devise and apply the process and the remedies that will insure an administration of the assets in conformity to justice." [229]

Thus every objection is waved aside by a whirl of words, all driving toward the apparently desired goal of somehow getting rid of the embarrassment of husbanding these funds. To be sure the problem is of great and unprecedented difficulty. Here are these assets, homeless, drifting idly, their ownership in doubt, their owners scattered over the face of the globe. The Soviet purports to have confiscated them; this claim is indignantly rejected. But what shall be done? Are they to be stored up awaiting the day when the entire body of shareholders shall sit represented in the courts of New York? Every day that eventuality becomes more improbable. And now a few persons come into court who, at least, bear some relation to these assets, who are doing business in Paris — the capital of the dispossessed White Russians; why not turn the assets over to these people and hope for the best? Where the directors hold a fair number of proxies or where the corporation is being liquidated by the French courts, this course has much to recommend it. Where the business has become newly domiciliated with the shareholders' consent, it is perhaps better to release the funds to business uses. But none of these things were true in the *Petrogradsky* case. At least, the Court might have said to the directors: Go out and get proxies, give us some assurance that we are not making you a personal gift of these funds. In an earlier memorandum decision [230] directors of a nationalized company were allowed

[228] *Id.*

[228a] The language of this decision has recently been repudiated by the New York Court. See Appendix. [229] *Id.* N. Y. at 37; N. E. at 484.

[230] First Russian Insurance Co. *v.* Beha, 240 N. Y. 601; 148 N. E. 722 (1925).

to recover a guaranty fund from the Superintendent of Insurance. Judge Pound dissented as he did in the *Petrogradsky* case.

The corporation is a mere simulacrum. If we regard facts rather than legal technicalities, its funds now belong in equity to its policy holders, creditors, and stockholders to be administered under the Insurance Law (section 63) or otherwise in accordance with the public policy of the State and the United States.

The Insurance Commissioner must have taken the hint; he put five leading Russian insurers having assets in the United States into liquidation.[231] After paying domestic creditors and policyholders in whose behalf the liquidation was undertaken, the question arose as to the distribution of the surplus. The Insurance Commissioner proposed to retain the funds until such time as the United States recognized Soviet Russia or some regime which would recognize the parent company as existing, so as to allow of distribution at the domicile. In most instances the list of shareholders and books of account were in warehouses in Russia. The Appellate Division approved of this plan.[232] It relied on the *Stoddard* case, which had pointed out the impossibility of a distribution at the domicile and had emphasized the need of protecting the interests of individuals. These decisions were all reversed by the New York Court of Appeals, Chief Judge Cardozo delivering the opinion.[233]

[231] These companies were the First Russian Insurance Co., the Second Russian Insurance Co., the Northern Insurance Co. of Moscow, the Russian Reinsurance Co., the Moscow Fire Insurance Co. They were put into liquidation under sec. 63 of the Insurance Law (Cons. Laws c. 30), on the ground that further transaction of business would be hazardous to the policyholders, the creditors, and the public. People ex rel. Beha, Second Russian Insurance Co., 243 N. Y. 524; 154 N. E. 590 (1926).

[232] The plan was presented for all the companies named in note 231, *supra*. People ex rel. Beha, Northern Insurance Company of Moscow, etc., 229 App. Div. 637, 243 N. Y. Supp. 35 (1930). The Court rejected two other plans, one to organize a local company and appoint trustees to hold the stock for unidentified interests, the other to transfer the funds to the state comptroller to be held against eventual distribution. The Second Russian Insurance Company was insolvent; an assignment for the benefit of creditors was allowed. People ex rel. Beha, Second, etc. Co., 255 N. Y. 436; 175 N. E. 121 (1931).

[233] People by Beha *v.* Russian Reinsurance Co. etc.; People by Beha *v.* First Russian Ins. Co., 255 N. Y. 415; 175 N. E. 114 (1931). In re People by Beha. In re Moscow Fire Ins. Co. In re Northern Ins. Co., 255 N. Y. 433; 175 N. E. 120 (1931). In re People by Beha. In re Second Russian Ins. Co., 255 N. Y. 436; 174 N. E. 120 (1931).

The Appellate Division also had forbidden all suits by foreign creditors

Russian directors, chosen by Russian shareholders in accordance with Russian law, must work out for themselves their problems of internal management. . . . Our administrative machinery should be no longer clogged, our liquidator no longer burdened, our courts no longer vexed, with problems not our own.[234]

Here, indeed, we find at last the real motive behind the *Petrogradsky* case. But in that case, since it was left obscure and unexpressed, since a hollow formula, based on non-recognition, was allowed to dictate the result, no provision was made for what might be very legitimate domestic interests, not to mention interests of the shareholders. This was forcibly pointed out by Judge Pound in *First Russian Ins. Co.* v. *Beha.*[235] In these later liquidation cases domestic interests, at least, had been taken care of. As to the distribution of the surpluses the ideology of the *Petrogradsky* case produced a curious result. In the matter of the Russian Reinsurance and First Russian Insurance Companies, the surplus was released without condition to the hold-over directors, who constituted in each case a quorum. These directors held proxies in one case for 8,000 out of 12,000 shares, in the other for 3,700 out of 10,000. Now, in the matters of the Northern and Moscow Insurance Companies, there were no longer quorums, the Moscow having one director, the Northern two. The funds were turned over to these men as conservators, but they were required to give bond; failing this, the funds were to be banked. In the *Petrogradsky* case the whereabouts of the shareholders seemed to be entirely unknown, but there were three directors, a quorum. So it turned out that if there were only two directors, a bond must be put up to protect the shareholders; if there were three, the old law of Russia (in its Anglo-

against the Superintendent of Insurance or the corporate assets. This ruling was reversed, and it was suggested that before turning the funds over to the directors, the Superintendent should hold them a few months to give foreign claimants an opportunity to be satisfied. People by Beha *v.* Russian Reinsurance, etc. Co., *ibid.* During liquidation such claimants, among whom would be American policyholders who had taken out their policy in other than an American branch (People ex rel. Stoddard, Norske Lloyd Ins. Co., 242 N. Y. 148; 151 N. E. 159 [1926]) were enjoined from suit. People ex rel. Beha, Second Russian Ins. Co., 244 N. Y. 606; 155 N. E. 916 (1927). An alien enemy was not entitled to share with domestic creditors in the liquidation. People ex rel. Beha, Second Russian Ins. Co., 256 N. Y. 177; 176 N. E. 133 (1931).

[234] People by Beha *v.* Russian Reinsurance Co., 255 N. Y. 415, 427; 175 N. E. 114, 118 (1931). Also: "It [the Appellate Division] did not solve the problem. It adjourned it sine die." N. Y. at 421; N. E. at 115.

[235] *Supra*, p. 187.

American reincarnation) pronouncing this to be a quorum, no protection was needed. There is nothing in the realities of the situation to account for this important difference in treatment. It may be said that this all follows logically from the proposition that the Soviet Government is a usurper, that the law of old Russia governs the Soviet itself and everything Russian; if this is so, it would seem only to confirm the contention that the starting point is unfortunate.

The courts of Europe have had a large mass of litigation over the status of Russian émigrés. The particular solutions are not of importance in this inquiry,[236] but a word as to the general basis of treatment is in order.

The problem is more acute in Continental countries than in Anglo-American ones, since personal relations, under the Continental conflict of laws, are governed by nationality even in the forum of the domicile. The French, Italian, and Egyptian courts have stoutly maintained that prior to recognition the Soviet law must be ignored. Thus, an Egyptian court has said of the law governing Russians:

> . . . that this law (*ce statut*) can not be that of the new legislation, that legislation emanating from an authority which, by the very fact of its non-recognition, has been denied the power to legislate, exclusive attribute of a legitimate government, and by the same consequence has been denied power to abrogate the old law; that thus . . . by an irreproachable application of principles . . . non-recognizant States have continued to treat the old law as always in force. . . .[237]

[236] The matter has been treated in Noël-Henry, p. 134; Grouber et Tager, *La révolution bolchévique et le statut juridique des Russes: le point de vue de la jurisprudence française*, 5 J. D. I. 8 (1924); Ténékidès, *loc. cit.* (*supra*, note 144); Freund, *loc. cit.* (*supra*, note 152); Connick, *The Effect of Soviet Decrees in American Courts*, 34 Yale L. J. 499 (1925).

[237] Gross *v.* Gretchenko et al. (Trib. Comm. Alexandrie, 1924), 14 Gazette des Tribunaux Mixtes, 234 at 237: "Que ce statut ne peut être celui de la nouvelle législation, cette législation émanant d'une autorité à laquelle, par le fait seul de son non-reconnaissance, sont contestés le pouvoir de légiférer, attribut exclusif d'un gouvernement légitime; et par voie de conséquence le pouvoir d'abroger les lois anciennes; qu'ainsi c'est à juste raison et par une application irréprochable des principes que les États qui n'ont pas reconnu le gouvernement des Soviets ont continué à considérer l'ancienne loi russe comme toujours en vigueur et comme constituant le seul statut national applicable à tout ressortissant russe réfugié sur leur territoire."

In all of these cases, of course, the Court ignores the Soviet decrees denationalizing the émigrés. Treating them as still citizens of the "Russian" state, it applies the old Russian law. *Ibid.*; also Noël-Henry, pp. 45, 134.

But at least one Italian court,[238] while admitting that Soviet law cannot be applied, has objected as well to the application of the old law. To do so would be to "resuscitate for a moment a legislative corpse. One cannot, by using words and with a doctrinal serenity, feign to be ignorant of the incontestable existence and real consequences of an historic fact." [239] In other words, the Soviet power can and has abrogated law, but it cannot create it. The distinction seems a doubtful one. What law, then, is the Italian Court to apply? The Court found the relevant Italian law too narrow, and finally decided [240] to apply the general principles *du droit*. The case involved the contractual relations between crew, captain, and owners, and, as one commentator has said,[241] it would not have been artificial in this instance to apply the old law under which the contract was entered into, as the Egyptian Court has done in like cases.

In a recent Egyptian case, *Charalambos Papadopoulos* v. *Monastery of Mount Sinai*,[242] the Egyptian Court in the handling of a claim in contract has shown more flexibility. At issue were two loans contracted in Russia to be used by the defendant for one of its monasteries in Kiev. One of the loans was made before the war, the other on the eve of revolution with a stipulation for repayment after the establishment of regular government. The plaintiff wished to recover the original gold ruble value of his loans. But the Court held that the contract being made in Russia was governed by Russian law; that the demonitization decrees were in Russia both law and fact; that the Soviet had fixed the rate of exchange at 500 milliards of old rubles for one new gold ruble. As a makeweight the Court added that defendant's monasteries had been confiscated and its debts cancelled. This, however, was advanced probably to negative the alleged unjust enrichment of the defendant should recovery be denied rather than to establish a formal cancellation of the debt. Thus in this case the Court made no attempt to set its face against the living facts.

[238] Katsikis *c.* Società Fati Svoroni di Pallone (Trib. de Genoa, 1923), 50 J. D. I. 1021 (1923).

[239] *Id.* at 1024: "Il ne serait licite, en effet, de ressusciter pour un instant, un cadavre législatif. . . . On ne peut davantage en se payant de mot et avec une sérénité doctrinale, feindre d'ignorer l'existence incontestable et les conséquences réelles d'un fait historique."

[240] *Id.* at 1026. The French is a translation of the Italian judgment.

[241] *Id.* at 1030.

[242] (Cour d'appel, 1927), 17 Gazette des Tribunaux Mixtes 293.

By a curious procedure, the New York Court of Appeals in a recent case,[243] though it purports to reason in the same fashion as the Egyptian Court, arrives at a nearly contrary result. In the earlier and famous *Sokoloff*[244] case the Court had decided that a contract made in New York, but performable in Russia, could not be discharged by Soviet decree even though the creditor was a Russian national.[245] That was a case in which the plaintiff had banked money with the defendant, all of whose Russian assets had been confiscated. The Court held that the contract was broken when as a result of the Soviet decree the Petrograd branch ceased to function, and that the damages were to be "measured according to the value of rubles as of that date in Petrograd, measured in dollars in New York City,[246] where the remedy was sought." In a

[243] In re People by Beha. Claim of Dougherty, 255 N. Y. 428; 175 N. E. 118 (1931).

[244] Sokoloff *v.* The National City Bank, 239 N. Y. 158; 145 N. E. 917 (1924).

[245] To the question of whether a state can confiscate a credit when the *creditor* is a national the Court replied hypothetically: "If there is jurisdiction in these conditions to confiscate the incorporeal right, no power short of sovereignty in all its plenitude has a competence so high." *Id.* N. Y. at 169; N. E. at 920. And, of course, it is the doctrine of the New York cases that the Soviets have no "sovereignty" at all, until recognized by us. But see recent case, Appendix A.

[246] This was decided in a later stage of the litigation after trial of the case. 250 N. Y. 69, 82; 164 N. E. 745, 750 (1928). But cf. Pirojnikoff *v.* National City Bank of New York, 133 Misc. 536; 233 N. Y. Supp. 219 (1929), in which the Court takes May, 1924, at which time defendant notified plaintiff of its desire to close plaintiff's Petrograd account, as the date at which the ruble value of the account was to be calculated, and dismissed the action because there was nothing in the record to indicate the value of rubles (recovery had been asked for in dollars paid in New York to establish the credit, which accounts for the absence of evidence).

[247] Dougherty *v.* Equitable Life Assur. Soc., 228 App. Div. 624; 238 N. Y. Supp. 824 (1929).

The trial court had decided the other way: "It is clear that defendant has lost all of its assets in Russia against which was written the policy in suit. Such policy was a Russian contract, made and to be performed there. Plaintiff's assignor was a Russian citizen, amenable to its laws, and subject to the rights, privileges, and liabilities caused by a change of the form of government." 135 Misc. 103, 110; 236 N. Y. Supp. 673, 682 (1929). The Court believed that the Stoddard case showed a veering in this direction, a thought very generally held until the Petrogradsky case distinguished the Stoddard case clean away.

In Buerger *v.* New York Life Assurance Co., 43 T. L. R. 601 (1927), the Court of Appeals in England arrived at the same conclusion on the ground that the People's Commissariat of Justice charged with the interpretation of the Soviet laws had decided that the decrees cancelling policies did not apply where

subsequent case [247] the Appellate Division held that the *Sokoloff* decision was applicable to a contract of insurance not only to be performed but also made in Russia. This, too, was a case in which the Soviet had confiscated all of the defendant's assets, had itself assumed the defendant's debts, and had later cancelled them. It was a case [248] very similar to the latter one which recently came before the New York Court of Appeals. Plaintiff proved a claim against the First Russian Insurance Company for 5,921 rubles. The breach of contract was in June, 1923. In October, 1922, the Soviet decreed that the chervonetz should be the standard of value, redeemable in a fixed amount of gold. For convenience the word "ruble" was used to designate a given part of a chervonetz having a gold value equivalent to about 50¼ cents. The depreciated paper was left in circulation, and as seen in the Egyptian case a ratio of exchange was fixed between it and the gold chervonetz. The Court of Appeals held that the 5,921 rubles were equivalent to that number of gold rubles. "The Soviet decree restoring the gold standard is to be ranked with those 'everyday transactions of business or domestic life' that 'are not subject to impeachment though the form may have been regulated by the command of the usurping government'." [249]

But of course this is a complete perversion of the Soviet decree, which decidedly did not put the old paper rubles on a gold basis of one for one, but, as we saw in the Egyptian case, of 500 milliards for one gold ruble. Furthermore, the new unit of value is a chervonetz. The ruble is merely a convenient division of the chervonetz, and has no connection other than name with the old ruble. The result of these decisions is that cases in contract are decided very much as if time had turned backward in her course, and the Czars were still on their throne.

Of remarkable interest is the attempt by the New York legislature to relieve the insurance companies of the liabilities which the courts were insisting must be met. The New York and Equitable Life Insurance Companies — the only American companies en-

the insurer had assets abroad not reached by the confiscation decrees. Otherwise it is assumed by the Court, the Soviets having been recognized, that the decrees confiscating the credits of Russian nationals would be given effect.

[248] In re People by Beha. Claim of Dougherty, 255 N. Y. 428; 175 N. E. 118 (1931).

[249] *Id.* N. Y. at 432; N. E. at 120. The English Court in Buerger *v.* New York Life Assurance Co. (*supra*, note 247) arrived at the same result (Scrutton, L. J., dissenting).

gaged in the Russian business — had written some $80,000,000 in policies.[250] The Soviets decreed the insurance business to be a government monopoly, confiscated the assets of the companies, and later cancelled the policies written out of the Russian offices. This was all done in 1917, and it was not until 1924 that it occurred to the Russian policyholders to collect from the companies. Perhaps it was the *Sokoloff* decision which put the idea into their heads — or into the heads of enterprising attorneys. The Soviet itself took the lead in gathering up the policies and establishing an agency for litigation on a wholesale scale. It charged a substantial fee for its service — 25 to 45 per cent of the recovery.

Out of the blue, the companies found themselves suddenly threatened with a deluge of claims and litigations [251] — mostly of Soviet origin, but interspersed with a goodly number from Poland, Finland, Latvia, Lithuania, and Paris, the capital of White Russia.[252] Sliosberg, an émigré, brought suit against the New York Company. The company moved for a dismissal on the basis of a clause in the policy which, it argued, made the Petrograd Court

[250] Defendant's Reply Memo. Citations here and below are to the record in Sliosberg *v.* New York Life Ins. Co., 244 N. Y. 482; 155 N. E. 749 (1927).

[251] Transcript of Record, f. 128; Brief of Superintendent of Insurance (*amicus curiae*), 5.

[252] There was considerable dispute between the parties as to how extensive was the Soviet interest in the policies. The companies (and the Superintendent of Insurance) maintained that the Soviet "Credit Bureau" (organized to bring suit on the policies) held nearly all (put by the Superintendent at 90 per cent, Brief, 2) of the 35,000 Russian policies, in which the Soviet contingent interest was 25 per cent to 40 per cent (Transcript, ff. 65–72, 134). It was said by the defendants that this was "admittedly" a move on the part of the Soviet to force recognition by our Government, and that in any case the Soviet would draw out of the country a large sum of money. (Counsel for the Equitable, *amicus curiae*, spoke of the Soviet's plan as a "nefarious plot," Brief, 9.) Thus, our non-recognition policy would work in favor, rather than against, the Soviet. This was a ground in policy for allowing the legislature to pass the stay law. It is true that one number of the official "Izvestia" had rather loosely linked recognition and collection of insurance. Thus: "Step by step, we must follow up our demands of judicial justice, and even reach the White House, so that we might hear from the American Senate a reply to our direct demand: Why do you not pay on your insurance obligations?" (Transcript, ff. 94–99). But it is not clear whether the alleged plan here is to force recognition or merely payment.

The plaintiff argued that whatever the "sinister" purpose of the Soviet, he was an émigré, and his case could not be controlled by such considerations. The non-Soviet claims were numerous, though representing but a small part of the whole (Transcript, ff. 367–369).

alone competent, and, in the alternative, for a stay until such time as conditions in Russia made available the records for an adequate defense. The Court denied both,[253] and the defendant appealed. Before the matter could be heard, the New York and the Equitable prevailed upon the legislature and the Governor (Smith) to pass a law in the following terms:

> § 169–a. *Stay of action on insurance contract payable in Russian roubles.* Whenever in any civil action or special proceeding now or hereafter pending in any court of this State, it shall appear that . . . any cause of action, counterclaim, set-off, or defense is founded upon or grows out of any contract of insurance made or entered into prior to November seventh, nineteen hundred and seventeen,[254] by any insurance company organized under the laws of any state of the United States and expressed to be payable in Russian roubles or to be performed in whole or in part [255] within the territorial confines of the former Russian Empire, such action or special proceeding, upon application, as hereinafter provided, shall be stayed by order of the court in which the same is pending until the expiration of thirty days next following the recognition *de jure* of a government of Russia by the government of the United States.[256]

That this bill was passed for the benefit of the interested insurance companies — they are mutual companies, and at that time had 700,000 shareholders in New York State alone — it would have been absurd to deny. But the companies maintained that they were justly entitled to the relief, and in this they were joined by the state Superintendent of Insurance, who sponsored their cause before the legislature and before the Court as *amicus curiae.*[257]

[253] Sliosberg *v.* New York Life Ins. Co., 125 Misc. 417; 211 N. Y. Supp. 270 (1925).

A clause in the policy provided that "any claim and suits that may arise under the present insurance are acknowledged by both sides as being subject to the jurisdiction of the St. Petersburg Courts only." The plaintiff, a former Russian attorney, swore an affidavit that this provision applied only if suit were brought in Russia (Transcript, ff. 416, 417). The Court held that it would be unjust to apply it where the company no longer could be sued in Russia nor had assets there.

[254] Date of the Bolshevist revolution. No insurance was written in Soviet Russia after this date.

[255] Since the policies were secured on the general credit of the company, as well as special Russian reserves, the policies were understood to be performed elsewhere than in Russia.

[256] Laws of 1926, c. 232, C. P. A. § 169–a.

[257] It does not appear from the Record what the relations of the companies and the Superintendent were. An officer of the defendant swore an affidavit that "the bill was actually promoted in large part by the Superintendent of Insurance, who appeared in support thereof before the Senate Committee and

Each company had done business in Russia under a *pravila* — a regulatory decree — which, to some extent, made the Russian branch a separate business and economic unit. The policies were countersigned and issued in Russia. The companies agreed to be bound by Russian laws and by decisions of Russian tribunals, and, above all, to maintain in Russia in specified securities a fund sufficient to cover current liabilities on the policies. Recovery, however, was not limited to these assets; the policies were backed by the general assets of the companies. At the time when the Soviet took over the business, the funds on hand in Russia far exceeded the current policy liability. By the initial Soviet decree, the insurance business was declared to be "the State monopoly," and a Commissary for Insurance was set up. By a subsequent decree, the life insurance contracts were cancelled, and it was provided that all those who were thereby deprived of insurance were entitled to Soviet protection.

The companies argued that these were Russian contracts, primarily payable out of the Russian funds; that the Soviet had worked a novation of the companies' liability and had, by expropriating the fund, in effect discharged the liability of the contract;[258] that it was not fair to the stockholders outside of Russia to saddle them with the payment of policies when company assets, more than enough to cover them, had been taken over by the government which represented those policyholders. Since, however (the argument continued), the force of the Russian decrees could not, according to the decisions of the Court, be given effect by reason of the non-recognition of the Soviet, the legislature had passed the stay law to "preserve" the companies' defense until such time as it could be set up. Surely, where the unfortunate and unforeseen result of the policy of non-recognition was to injure citizens of this country, the legislature was not powerless to relieve them.

The plaintiff replied that the contracts were charges on all the assets of the company; that the obligation of the contract ran wherever the company had assets or could be served, and, above all, in New York, the home office; that the Soviet decrees — whether the Soviet was or was not recognized — could not extinguish liability

made the principal argument in his capacity as guardian of the interests of the New York policyholders" (Transcript, f. 140). We do not have to believe that he received the idea spontaneously, however much he may have been convinced of its justice.

[258] This was the reasoning that prevailed in the lower court in Dougherty *v.* Equitable Life Assur. Soc. (*supra*, note 247).

outside of Russia; and that, as a consequence, the stay law, practically washing out the remedy, impaired the obligation of contract, and was unconstitutional.[259] As for the alleged hardship on the company and its shareholders, the amount of all the Russian policies was not even equal to the sum available for dividends for one year.

The Court adopted the plaintiff's argument and declared the law unconstitutional. Whether the defense of payment or cancellation would be available in case of recognition, the Court did not trouble to decide. Assuming that it might be, it indignantly replied:

> The defense will be that the unpaid policyholders have lost their causes of action by virtue of decrees, then having legal sanction, which arbitrarily cancelled their obligations against such companies without compensation and without substitution of other obligors having the will or the duty to pay. We do not think that the public weal required that honest creditors should be made to abide the time when a law, inherently unjust and confiscatory, enacted by a governmental power, then regarded as barbarous, might become an effective weapon of defense, through the recognition of that power as a worthy member of the society of civilized nations.[260]

Here, again, we are treated to another of those displays of virtuous horror which have been a feature of the New York decisions. There would seem to be nothing "inherently" unjust in a law which cancels insurance contracts, takes over funds earmarked for their payment, and substitutes a scheme of social insurance. To be sure, the scheme is of no help to an émigré, and to be sympathetic to his claim is natural, especially when, as counsel pointed out, pay-

[259] The technical argument on the contract clause turned on the question whether a state which had not created the contract could impair its obligation by denying a power to sue on it. Was the obligation of a contract the right to sue (generally accorded in all jurisdictions) or the right created by and enforceable at the place of making? The plaintiff seemed to have the best of the argument on this score. The contract clause was adopted to protect (*inter alia*) foreign creditors from local legislatures. Cf. Beard, *Economic Interpretation of the Constitution* (1915), pp. 179 ff. It would make little difference where the debt was contracted. It may be important that the state imposing the challenged law be the domicile of the debtor, since there both he and his assets are normally most available. It was on this ground that the Court of Appeals in the *Sliosberg* case invoked the contract clause. The only case directly in point which counsel could find was Western National Bank *v.* Reckless, 96 Fed. 70 (C. C. N. J. 1899), and that decision may turn on a provision in the New Jersey Constitution forbidding laws depriving a party "of any remedy for enforcing a contract which existed when the contract was made."

[260] Sliosberg *v.* New York Life Ins. Co., 244 N. Y. 482, 498; 155 N. E. 749, 755 (1927).

ment of the claim would, at the most, reduce a single dividend for each shareholder.[261] In previous cases, the court had said in effect, "The decrees are fearfully wicked, and, anyhow, since the United States does not recognize the Soviet, it is our duty to ignore them." Now, the legislature has answered (at the behest, it is true, of the companies), "It seems unfortunate that our citizens should pay a debt which, if it were not for the fortuitous fact of non-recognition, may not be owing. You must stop the actions until you can decide on the merits." To which the Court replies, "If you had not issued this 'fiat,' a remedy would exist. We have said so (non-recognition forbidding us to consider the validity of the defense). If we obey your order and wait until we can consider the defense, the remedy may be indefinitely postponed, or there may be none at all. Ergo: you are attempting to impair the obligation of contracts."

The Court might have broken through this flimsy circle by asking first whether, indeed, recognition would have ripened the defense. If not, then quite obviously there was no sufficient reason to stay the action indefinitely. The company, it is true, suggested the stay also on the ground that they could not prepare defenses for non-payment of premiums, breach of condition, etc., until their records were available; but we would not quarrel with the Court for deciding that this was not sufficient to justify an indeterminate stay. But if the defense would have been good after recognition,[262] the question is not one of impairing the obligation of contract but our old one of what course of action the executive policy of non-recognition imposes upon other governmental organs. The New York courts have decided that they are compelled to ignore or deny the governmental capacity of an unrecognized government. [262a] Is the New York legislature interfering with the Federal prerogative in foreign affairs by commanding the courts of New York to act as if the Soviet may in the future have capacity? The plaintiff argued that it was, but the Court found it unnecessary to consider the case

[261] Respondent's Brief, 12.

[262] It seems not at all improbable that a decree by a government confiscating debts owing to its own nationals will be given effect in other countries. According to counsel for the companies in the Sliosberg case, the German courts have so decided with respect to these same decrees in the case of Meyer *v.* New York Life Ins. Co. (Appellant's Brief, 12–13). Cf. Buerger *v.* New York Life Ins. Co., 43 T. L. R. 601 (Eng. Ct. of Appeals, 1927), discussed *supra*, note 247. The New York Court expressly left the question open in the Sokoloff case. See *supra*, note 245.

[262a] But see Appendix.

from this point of view. If the position taken by the New York courts in non-recognition cases had been forced upon them by an inexorable constitutional compulsion, if any other decision would unquestionably have been a usurpation of the constitutional powers of the organ of foreign affairs, then it would seem that the New York legislature could stand no higher than the New York court, and there would be some warrant for the holding that the stay law was an unconstitutional intrusion into a Federal sphere. But it seems to us that the very highest ground upon which the New York court can place its position is that the judiciary, as a matter of sound statesmanship, of good governmental policy, should not give judgments which weaken the foreign policy of the executive, and that, in its opinion, this is such a case. So put, it is judicial self-limitation, and no more. Now, ordinarily, the legislature can dictate to its courts upon matters of policy unless it interferes with constitutional limitations or with "inherent" judicial capacities,[263] and neither seems to be involved here. Baldly, the psychology behind the *Sliosberg* decision seems to have been: "We, the Court, have already decided what we think best. The defeated parties have prevailed upon the legislature to force us to change our minds. We shall not allow it. The law is unconstitutional."

Apparently the general question of the relation between non-recognition and the conflict of laws has not been much before the courts in Germany, since it was among the earliest to recognize the Soviets. We have already quoted from the article of Professor Freund that private German international law is unconcerned with recognition: the sole inquiry is what law is in force in Russia at the moment of judgment. There was, however, in view of the early recognition, no scope for trying out the principle. The Swiss courts have probably adopted this view, and we believe that it is the proper one. The aim of courts everywhere should be to maintain the continuum of order and harmonious relationship between the various competences each responsible for order in its sphere. In certain cases, as in refusing an unrecognized government the right to sue, a particular policy may override these considerations, but generally to equate foreign law with recognition seems to us grounded in a false and unreal conception of what law is.

[263] Indeed, the lower Appellate Division agreed that the stay law interfered with inherent judicial power to exercise discretion in the granting of stays. 217 App. Div. 67; 216 N. Y. Supp. 215 (1926). The Court of Appeals did not pass on the point.

CHAPTER IV

RECOGNITION AND THE COURTS

Must Recognition be "Explicit"?

"As to international affairs such as the recognition of a foreign government, or of the diplomatic character of a person claiming to be its representative, they [the Courts] may inquire of the Foreign Office or the Department of State." [1] To this Noël-Henry adds that recognition by the government must be explicit: "The fiction of non-official (*officieuses*) relations is precisely destined to permit a state to enter into relations with a foreign government without recognizing it." [2]

The corollary to this is that the court is not to allow to a state any capacity as such unless there has been explicit "recognition." But the whole matter rests on the shifting sand of what is meant by recognition. Mr. Baty [3] would say there is no such thing as "officious" relations; that if you deal with a state or government as a ruling power you have recognized it. We have seen, however, that this is not the understanding of diplomats today, and that to them "recognition" is the prerequisite of but one, the most complete it is true, type of interstate relations.

To this shift from a literal to a special meaning of the word "recognition" is due some of the misapplication of early authorities,

[1] Jones *v.* United States, 137 U. S. 202, 216 (1890); McNair, *Judicial Recognition of States and Governments, and the Immunity of Public Ships*, 2 British Yearbook of Int. Law 57, 65 n. (1921–22) lists five procedures whereby the court may receive information as to the status of a foreign power: (*a*) it may direct an officer of the court to apply to the foreign office; (*b*) the law officers of the Crown may initiate proceedings; (*c*) the court may invite the law officers to appear and address the court; (*d*) where status of a foreign power is notorious, the court may take judicial notice *meru motu*; (*e*) letters addressed to the litigants from the appropriate department may be put in evidence.

[2] Noël-Henry, § 88: "La fiction des relations officieuses est précisément destinée à permettre à un État d'entrer en rapports avec un gouvernement étranger sans le reconnaître."

[3] Baty, *So-Called De Facto Recognition*, 31 Yale L. J. 469, 470 (1921); and see *supra*, pp. 120–123.

and the current confusion. In the early case of *The Helena*,[4] often cited as a case of "recognition," Lord Stowell does not even use the word, and certainly did not have in mind our present conception. He held that a decree of the Dey of Algiers was entitled to respect, and adverted to a long course of treaties between England and Algiers "acknowledging and confirming to them [the African States] the relations of legal states."[5] In short, the question at issue was the power of Algiers as a state, and this England had acknowledged.

And in the early cases dealing with recognition of belligerency, the courts were interested in finding out whether the legal relation of neutral to belligerent existed rather than with what the foreign office called it. Monroe in his message of December 2, 1817 said:

> It was anticipated at an early stage that the contest between Spain and the colonies would become highly interesting to the United States. . . . Through every stage of the conflict the United States has maintained an impartial neutrality, giving aid to neither of the parties in men, money, ships, or munitions of war. They have regarded the contest not in the light of an ordinary insurrection or rebellion, but as a civil war between parties nearly equal, having as to neutral powers equal rights.

In *Palmer* v. *United States*[6] counsel argued that

> nothing short of an act of the whole legislature, a treaty, a proclamation of the President, or the public reception of an ambassador from a new state ought to be considered as a recognition of independence. . . . Nothing should be left to inference and conjecture; because, such a course might lead to a usurpation by the courts of the high prerogative of making war and peace, . . .[7]

This was a case of prosecution for piracy of agents of one of the South American rebel states. Chief Justice Marshall said: "It may be said, generally, that if the government remains neutral, and recognizes *the existence of a civil war*, its courts cannot consider as criminal those acts of hostility which war authorizes. . . ."[8] (Italics mine.)

In 1858 Secretary of State Cass said: "By what public act, whether proclamation or otherwise, this recognition must take place, I have not found laid down. I am not aware that, in this

[4] 4 Robinson Adm. 3. (1801).

[5] *Id.* at 5. The case has been discussed *supra*, p. 113.

[6] 3 Wheat. 610 (1818).

[7] *Id.* at 623–625.

[8] *Id.* at 635.

country, any solemn proceeding, either legislative or executive, has been adopted for the purpose of declaring the status of an insurrectionary movement abroad." [9]

Judge Benedict, however, in *The Conserva* (1899), said: [10]

> Various documents issued from the Department of State have been put in evidence, containing certain expressions which the Court is invited to examine in order to find therein an implied recognition of the faction of Legitime as representing the Government of Hayti. I do not think that in a case like this the court is required to deal with uncertain implications contained in such documents as have been here presented. The fact of public recognition of any prince, as a belligerent is one to be made known to all men by public proclamation from the Executive or some public act by necessary implication equivalent to such a proclamation.

As a matter of fact, the Secretary of State had said in regard to the Hayti contest of 1889 that neither of the parties had been recognized as belligerents, but that *de facto* relations were kept up with Legitime.[11] The question in *The Conserva* was whether our Neutrality Act should be applied. As has been said already,[12] there was no need for making the operation of this act turn on recognition of belligerency. Here is a case where the mere *fact* of civil conflict should suffice; to look to the political department for formal acts to establish such a fact is a characteristic exaggeration of the doctrine of self-limitation held by the courts [13] in anything even remotely connected with unrecognized powers.

The Ambrose Light [14] has already been discussed.[15] Judge Brown took the extreme view that war vessels of an unrecognized political group were piratical. But he extricated himself from this unnecessarily embarrassing position by an expedient which has drawn down on him considerable criticism.[16] The United States had in-

[9] Moore, *Digest*, I, 182. See Beale, *Recognition of Cuban Belligerency*, 9 Harv. L. Rev. 406, 409–411 (1896), to the effect that recognition of belligerency takes no particular form. [10] 38 Fed. 431, 437 (E. D. N. Y. 1889).

[11] Moore, *Digest*, I, 201. [12] *Supra*, pp. 134–138.

[13] Even Noël-Henry, who states the incompetency of the courts in most absolute terms, insists that the judges are capable of determining and should determine the existence of war or of an unrecognized government in the "material sense" (*au sens matériel*) just as long as they do not by their judgment endow the unrecognized power with juridical personality (*personnalité juridique*). Pp. 107, 186.

[14] 25 Fed. 408 (S. D. N. Y. 1885).

[15] *Supra*, pp. 138–139.

[16] See Noël-Henry, p. 54; 33 Alb. L. J. 125 (1886) (note on The Ambrose Light by Francis Wharton, at the time Solicitor for the Department of State).

formed the Government of Colombia that it would not recognize a decree forbidding trade with the port of Cartagena held by the insurgents. The Department of State had written to Colombia:

> A decree by a sovereign power closing to *neutral* commerce ports held by its *enemies*, whether foreign or *domestic*, can have no international validity, and no extraterritorial effect in the direction of imposing any obligation upon the governments of *neutral powers* to recognize it.[17] (Italics by the Court in quoting statement.)

The Court argued that our stated position was in effect a recognition of the insurgents as "belligerents," since the port was treated by us as in the possession of an enemy and not subject to the law of Colombia; a real blockade we would recognize, but that would proceed from Colombia's rights as a belligerent rather than as a sovereign.[18] However, in answer to an inquiry by one of the parties the Secretary of State had replied:

> A state of war has not, *in a formal sense*, either before or after April 20, 1885 been recognized by the government of the United States as existing in the United States of Colombia; nor have the insurgents now in arms against the latter government been recognized by the United States as belligerents.[19] (Italics by the Court in quoting statement.)

The Court replied that though there may have been no recognition "in a formal sense," there was in a real sense, as shown by our diplomatic position. Thus the Court gets itself into a tight place by undue deference to the foreign office, and then gets itself out again by contradicting it. Mr. Wharton, the then Solicitor for the department, severely criticized [20] the opinion at the time. He maintained that not even in legal effect was there a recognition of the insurgents as "belligerents." There was what he calls a recognition of "insurgency"; apparently by this is meant that we do not accord to the insurgents any status, as we do to a "belligerent," but that as between us and the parent government the relation is that between a belligerent and a neutral.[21] Furthermore, the Court's contradic-

[17] The Ambrose Light (*supra*, note 14) at 444.

[18] However, in Rose *v.* Himely, 4 Cranch 241 (1808), and Hudson *v.* Guestier, 6 Cranch 281 (1810), the Supreme Court seemed to be of the opinion that a blockade might be used as a measure of domestic discipline. See *supra*, pp. 169–170, for the significance of the Civil War blockade as it related to recognition of the Confederacy.

[19] The Ambrose Light (*supra*, note 14) at 443.

[20] 33 Alb. L. J. 125 (1886). Reprinted in Moore, *Digest*, II, 1100.

[21] Noël-Henry (p. 110) says that "the North American notion of a recogni-

tion of the Department was, in any view of the matter, unprecedented.

Nevertheless, the Court's position, though unfortunately formulated, is basically sound. To declare that the Government had recognized belligerency when it expressly stated otherwise was clearly wrong. But it was quite proper to examine the action of the Government to determine whether the insurgents were treated as having the characteristics of a political organization of such a nature as to repel the charge of piracy (assuming, as the Court did, that it was necessary to find this fact to negative piracy). Lord Stowell in *The Helena* did not bother himself about recognition, but inquired simply whether England had treated Algiers as a state. This point is of first-rate importance. It presents a position half way between that already advanced in this work and the extreme one against which the bulk of criticism has been directed.

The argument is this: the court will not take testimony to determine whether a state is independent and has the necessary characteristics of a state, nor will it heed common or notorious report; it will not conduct an investigation concerning the capacity of an unrecognized government; it will await the verdict of its foreign office. But this verdict need not be labelled. It need not fit into the category of some type of "recognition," since the question at issue is not "recognition" as such, but the things that recognition implies, statehood, governmental power, all of them facts which the government may make manifest in other ways, by the creation of lesser relations than those constituting recognition. Thus, as Lord

tion of insurgency is a useless complication." It grants no status to the insurgents, it merely announces the *fact* of a civil war, and is in no sense a "recognition," i. e. a declaration creating status. But such a declaration does create a status between the declaring "neutral" and the *parent state*. On one hand, the neutral insists that he is entitled to trade with the insurgents in the absence of a blockade, thus denying to the parent state a portion of its sovereign rights over the insurgents; in return he concedes that the parent state may exercise "belligerent" rights such as blockade, search, and seizure on the high seas. There is, however, very little mention of the recognition of insurgency in the textbooks, and Hyde (1 International Law, § 50) speaks of it as merely "a reckoning with a state of facts." But it is submitted that the position of the United States in the affair here under discussion, the letter of Mr. Cass in re The Vivanco Insurrection in Peru (Moore, *Digest*, vol. I, § 64, and 9 Op. Attn'ys Gen'l 140 [1858]) and of Hay in re Bolivia insurgency (Moore, *Digest*, I, 243) are cases in which there is something more than a mere acknowledgment that fighting exists and something less than a recognition of belligerency; and that the term "recognition of insurgency" might be applied to such a situation.

Stowell decided, the making of a treaty would suffice to establish the fact of statehood, and of governmental capacity as well; nor should it matter whether the treaty were bilateral or multilateral. There is good reason to believe that this was all that was intended by the early American cases. As has been pointed out, most of them dealt with the touchy question of recognizing the independence of rebel colonies, and it was assumed that recognition by the parent state was as effective as recognition by the court's own government. Marshall derived the "belligerent" character of these communities from the fact that the executive spoke of them as engaged in a "civil war," not as deriving from a particular formal process. This view divorces the entire question from the shifting and uncertain practice of recognition, from the impossible attempt to define the meaning of recognition; it proceeds on the premise that if the political department treats a foreign organization as a state,[22] a foreign power as a government, it is a state, it is a government. This does not mean that if our government has manifested a hostile attitude toward such a power, it could not be denied certain rights. Just as, far from denying the existence of an enemy, we yet forbid it the right to sue in our courts.

The English courts, however, have implicitly rejected this view. In *The Annette*,[23] discussed above, in which state immunity of the libelled ship was set up and denied, the Court had before it the following communication from the Foreign Office.

> In reply I am to inform you that the Provisional Government of Northern Russia is composed of Russian groups who do not recognize the authority of the Russian Central Soviet Government established at Moscow. The seat of the Government is Archangel, and it extends its authority over the territory surrounding that port and to the west of the White Sea up to the Finnish frontier. As the title assumed by that Government indicates, it is merely provisional in nature, and has not been formally recognized either by His Majesty's Government or the Allied Powers as the Government of a sovereign independent state. His Majesty's Government and the Allied Powers are however at the present moment cooperating with the Provisional Government in the opposition which that government is making to the forces of the Russian Soviet Government, who are engaged in aggressive military operations against it, and are represented at Archangel by a

[22] Cf. the interesting suggestion in the recent Egyptian case of National Navigation Co. *v.* Tavoularidis et Cie (Trib. Alexandrie 1927), 19 Gazette des Tribunaux Mixtes 251, discussed *supra*, p. 161, that if the Egyptian Government allows a Soviet ship to drop anchor in harbor, it will be taken that it intends to allow the usual privileges granted to state-owned ships.

[23] [1919] P. 105. Discussed at p. 161.

British Commissioner. The representative of the Provisional Government in London is Monsieur Nabokoff, through whom His Majesty's Government conducts communications with the Archangel Provisional Government. . . .[24]

Hill, J., says:

I have here a mere negative statement that the Provisional Government of Northern Russia "has not been formally recognized by His Majesty's Government." I am asked to infer from that that it has been "informally recognized" as a sovereign state. I do not think I ought to draw that conclusion. I must be satisfied before I can recognize the Provisional Government of Northern Russia as a sovereign state, for the purposes of this case, that the British government so recognize it.[25]

It was clear that "recognition" had not been extended; but the Foreign Office refrained from declaring categorically the status of the Provisional Government. The Government presented the Court with facts admitted by it to be true from which the Court might itself decide, not the question of recognition, but of statehood. The Court might have examined and construed these facts as did Lord Stowell in *The Helena*; if they spelt statehood, immunity should have followed. Against such a conclusion there were no reasons of policy, since England was making common cause with the Provisional Government. This decision is one more of the mechanical and meaningless applications of the formula that recognition is for the political branch of the government.

Practically the same line was taken by Justice Roche in *Luther* v. *Sagor* [26] at *nisi prius*. The question was whether the Soviet Government was a sovereign, capable of transferring title to property by confiscation.

The Court was furnished with a letter from the Foreign Office:

I am to inform you that for a certain limited purpose, His Majesty's Government has regarded Monsieur Krassin as exempt from the process of the Courts, and also for the like limited purpose His Majesty's Government has assented to the claim that that which Monsieur Krassin represents in this Country is a State Government of Russia, but that beyond these propositions the Foreign Office has not gone, nor moreover do these expressions of opinion purport to decide difficult, and it may be very special questions of law upon which it may become necessary for the Courts to pronounce. I am to add that His Majesty's Government has never officially recognized the Soviet Government in any way.[27]

[24] *Id.* at 107.

[25] *Id.* at 111.

[26] [1921] 1 K. B. 456.

[27] *Id.* at 460.

The Court said:

> I am not satisfied that *His Majesty's Government has recognized* the Soviet Government as the Government of a Russian Federative Republic or of any sovereign state or power. *I therefore am unable to recognize it,* or to hold it has sovereignty.[28] (Italics mine.)

Here of course, as so often, the Court mixes up the literal and special meanings of the word "recognize." The Court says it is "unable to recognize." Of course it is. Under no circumstances do courts "recognize" foreign powers.

The misuse of the word may be significant. Still lurking unformulated in the minds of some judges seems to be a feeling that to take account of a foreign government is to accord it a true recognition, on which it may rely. This notion seems to have carried over from the times of Eldon, when the word had not yet acquired a "technical" meaning and was used interchangeably with "take notice of" and "acknowledge," of which "recognize" is a literal but not a technical equivalent.[29]

It is just as clear here as in *The Annette* that there has been no recognition by the Government. But the Foreign Office admits that it is dealing with Krassin as the representative of a government or state. Surely it would not undertake to negotiate a trade agreement with the representative of a debating society.

Lord Sumner in his excellent opinion in *Duff* v. *Kelantan* [30] puts neatly and comprehensively something akin to what we have here called the middle ground. It bears quotation as conclusion to this topic:

> There may be occasions when for reasons of State full, unconditional or permanent recognition has not been accorded by the Crown, and the answer to the question put has to be temporary if not temporizing, or even where some vaguer expression has to be used.[31] In such cases not only has the

[28] *Id.* at 477. The decision is based on an assumption (*id.* at 474) that because the courts "must recognize the sovereignty" of *recognized* powers, the Court "cannot, or at least need not, or ought not to, take notice" of *unrecognized* powers. The only cases at all in point which he cites for this proposition are the early cases before Eldon and Shadwell, discussed *supra*, pp. 124–129. The case of Republic of Peru *v.* Dreyfus, 38 Ch. D. 348 (1888), cited by the Court is, as the Court notes, a case of the binding effect of recognition; the Court in that case rehearses the old cases, but only to show that they are not applicable rather than to approve them.

[29] See *supra*, p. 129.

[30] [1924] A. C. 797, 824.

[31] Citing The Annette, [1919] P. 105. Discussed *supra*, p. 161.

Court to collect the true meaning of the communication for itself, but *also to consider whether the statements as to sovereignty made in the communication and the expressions "sovereign" or "independent" sovereign used in the legal rule mean the same thing.*[32] . . . I conceive that, if the Crown declined to answer the inquiry, as in the changing and difficult times policy might require it to do, the Court might be entitled to accept secondary evidence in default of the best.[33] . . . (Italics mine.)

The Extent to Which Recognition Concludes the Courts

"If a foreign government is recognized by the government of this country the Courts of the country may and must recognize the sovereignty of that foreign government and the validity of its acts." [34]

On its face this is a doctrine that commands a ready assent. But in recent years there have been cases when dubious political tactics have abused the protection afforded by the rule. Probably the well-known case of *Duff* v. *Kelantan* [35] is such an instance. Duff, under an agreement with the Government of Kelantan, at great expense and after much litigation secured against Kelantan an arbitration award. This Government then refused to pay the award. Duff levied execution. The Secretary of State for the Colonies then informed the Court that the Sultan of Kelantan "exercises without question the usual attributes of sovereignty," and that "His Majesty the King does not exercise or claim any rights of sovereignty or jurisdiction over Kelantan." In addition

[32] Citing Best, C. J., in Yrissari *v.* Clement, 3 Bing. 432, 438 (1826), that if there is no recognition yet given, the independence becomes matter of proof.

[33] Lord Sumner goes on to say that this rule is "subject, of course, to the presumption that, in case of a new organization, which has de facto broken away from an old State, still existing and still recognized by His Majesty, the dominion of the old State remains unimpaired until His Majesty is pleased to recognize the change." This sounds very much like a conclusive "presumption."

[34] Aksionairnaye, etc. Luther *v.* Sagor, [1921] 1 K. B. 456, 474. A classic and much quoted statement of the same idea is found in Jones *v.* United States, 137 U. S. 202, 214 (1890): "All courts of justice are bound to take judicial notice . . . of its [the government's] recognition or denial of the sovereignty of a foreign power, as appearing from the public acts of the legislature and executive. . . ."

[35] [1924] A. C. 797. The criticism of the Foreign Office here set forth is garnered from Allen, *Bureaucracy Triumphant* (1931), pp. 14–17. The heat of the author's indignation has caused many to doubt his tales of horror. This, however, makes no difference in our use of his material, since here we employ it simply as an illustration of the possible.

he transmitted to the Court documents which showed that Kelantan had once been a dependency of Siam and that Siam had transferred its rights to Britain. By an agreement between the Sultan of Kelantan and Great Britain, the Sultan "had engaged to have no political relations with any foreign power except through the medium of His Majesty the King of England and to follow, in all matters of administration (save those touching the Mohammedan religion and Malay custom) the advice of an adviser appointed by His Majesty." [36] Viscount Cave argued inconclusively that despite these agreements Kelantan might be an independent state,[37] but Lord Carson stated flatly that he would find the greatest difficulty in coming to any such conclusion, if the question were open for decision.[38]

Yet all the Lords agreed that the Court was bound by the declaration of the Secretary that Kelantan was a sovereign and independent state. Lord Sumner said that this followed not from "the mere obligation of deference to any statement made in His Majesty's name" but because the best evidence of sovereignty came from the office whose business it was to recognize sovereign states.[39] With this form of statement Viscount Finlay did not agree. "Such information," he said, "is not in the nature of evidence; it is a statement by the Sovereign of this country through one of his Ministers upon a matter which is peculiarly within his cognizance." [40]

Mr. Allen, in his stirring little tract *Bureaucracy Triumphant*, has said of the conduct of the Colonial Office in this case: "It may well be doubted whether in any other case a Crown department has, at every turn, so frankly avowed its intention to obstruct justice by any dishonourable means in its power." [41]

Mr. Allen,[42] in what has already been noted as characteristic in those whose ire is aroused by "the bureaucracy," [43] completely absolves the Court of all blame in the matter: they could do

[36] [1924] A. C. at 807.

[37] *Ibid.*

[38] *Id.* at 830.

[39] *Id.* at 823.

[40] *Id.* at 813.

[41] *Op cit.* (*supra*, note 35) at 14, and comment.

[42] *Id.* at 16.

[43] *Supra*, Chapter III, note 212, and p. 182. See remarks of Bewes, in a discussion on *Recognition*, 15 Trans. of the Grotius Society 76 (1930): "With regard to the recent case of the *Kelantan Government* . . . considerable dissatisfaction arose because the question of sovereignty was withdrawn from the Courts on the *ipse dixit* of the Foreign Office — that is, of its officials. There was a

nothing; they were bound hand and foot by the nefarious Department on one hand, and the altogether sainted precedents on the other.

Was there no escape from this decision? It will be remembered that in *The Ambrose Light* Judge Brown examined the position of his Government and determined its relations to the insurgents not by what the Government had said, but by what it did. It was, indeed, unfortunate that the Court labelled the insurgents "belligerents" when the Department of State had denied the label. It was a tactical error; the same result could have been reached without using the word at all. But that case was far easier than *Duff* v. *Kelantan*. The Government in *The Ambrose Light* case merely denied that a certain relation existed between it and the insurgents. In the *Kelantan* case the Government claimed the existence of a positive relationship between it and Kelantan, a relation which under ordinary circumstances requires mutual and meticulous respect, as conceived by the law of nations. Yet there is one thing on which the Court might properly have fastened. It was abundantly evident from the documents submitted by the Secretary himself that here was not the usual relation between nations. And (to borrow a phrase from common-law pleading) specific allegations govern general allegations. The Court might simply have decided that whatever name was given to the status of Kelantan, it appeared that it was not such as to require the application of the rule of sovereign immunity.

Lord Phillimore in *The Charkieh*,[44] in determining the status of the Khedive of Egypt and whether his ships were entitled to sovereign immunity, looked to four things: "1. The general history of the Government of Egypt. 2. The firmans which contain the public law of the Ottoman Empire on this subject. 3. The European treaties, which concern the relations between Egypt and the Porte. 4. The answer which the Foreign Office has furnished to an inquiry which I thought it my duty to make." [45] This answer was "that the Khedive has not been and is not now recognized by Her Majesty as reigning sovereign of the State of Egypt." "He is recognized by Her Majesty's government as the hereditary ruler of the province of Egypt under the supremacy of the Sultan of Turkey."

feeling that recognition should be decided on judicial and not on administrative principles."

[44] L. R. 4 A. & E. 59 (1873).

[45] *Id.* at 74.

Courts and writers have heaped criticism [46] on Phillimore because he presumed to form his own opinion independently of the Foreign Office, though he arrived at the same conclusion. This criticism proceeds from the indiscriminate adherence to the words of foreign offices which has already been pointed out in the later cases, to the automatic attachment of consequences to the presence or absence of the terms "sovereign" and "recognition" in official communications coupled with a complete disregard of the surrounding circumstances, even where, as in the *Duff* case, they appear from the Secretary's communication. Now what foreign relation was at issue in *The Charkieh*, and in what manner would the possible alternatives of judgment affect it? In the first place, the Foreign Office denied, rather than asserted, a relation between itself and *Egypt*. It did, however, state that Egypt was under the supremacy of the Sultan of Turkey; and since England recognized and maintained relations with Turkey, it could be said that the statement bore on an essential element in that relationship. Phillimore, however, did not presume to investigate the fact of Turkey's supremacy; he did not suggest for a moment that there was any question about it. He sought to determine the exact relation between the Khedive and the Sultan: whether it was suzerainty, vassalage, or mere provincial governorship. The Foreign Office had by no means made this clear; it had said the Khedive was "hereditary ruler" "under the supremacy of the Sultan." Phillimore's question was: Can the Khedive be called a sovereign in the sense that his property is entitled to sovereign immunity? His critics have said that he cannot ask any such question, because the Foreign Office in its letter said that he is not "the sovereign of Egypt." Truly this is to stick in the bark of words.

In *Duff* v. *Kelantan* there was even more reason than in *The Charkieh* for adopting Phillimore's technique. What, after all, in terms of the administration of justice is the question before a court when a claim of sovereign immunity is made? It is whether the controversy should be settled by a court or through diplomatic channels. Initially, at least, it is a problem of the proper distribution of function. If the court allows the claim of immunity, it normally makes the assumption that the disappointed plaintiff can press his interests through the foreign office. But it is just the contention of the plaintiff in the *Duff* case that there are no independent diplo-

[46] Lord Esher disapproved in Mighell *v.* Sultan of Johore, [1894] 1 Q. B. 149, 158, and it has been the fashion ever since. See Hervey, pp. 74–76.

matic relations between Great Britain and Kelantan; and the treaty which, mind you, not the Foreign Office but the Secretary of State for the Colonies transmitted to the Court showed quite conclusively that this contention was true. It was the British administration itself which had thwarted satisfaction of this claim, and which, driven back from ditch to ditch, had finally stepped out and said, "We're not the enemy, you know. It's the Sultan of Kelantan. You can't fight *him*" — and at this donned a mask of oriental countenance; the comedy was complete. Nothing left for the plaintiff but to appeal to His Majesty's Grace, a not very favorable prospect under the circumstances.

This, then, is a case where the doctrine of sovereign immunity would seem to have no place whatsoever. But the Court has been informed that the Sultan of Kelantan "exercises without question the usual attributes of sovereignty." Cannot the Court say: "We do not deny that the Sultan of Kelantan is a sovereign; if the administration wishes to so regard it, that is their affair, but the legal relations between Kelantan and Britain are such that the rule of immunity is not applicable; the rule of immunity assumes the existence of foreign relations between the sovereign claiming immunity and the sovereign of the forum, and it is undisputed that no such relation exists"?

It will be argued in reply that the court must accept without subtraction every result that can possibly flow from the fact of a relation between sovereign states, since this is the effect intended by the administration, when it applies the title of sovereign to the state in question. Thus, it may be the policy of Britain to speak of dependent native rulers as "sovereigns" in order to keep these rulers happy, and so preserve the peace and order of the Empire. The courts, it would be said, must do nothing to disturb this pretense or any other like pretense which the Foreign Office chooses to keep up. As far as this particular case goes we believe that a contrary decision would have done little, if anything, to give the show away. The Court, as we have suggested, might have paid its respects to the sovereignty of the Sultan, and then gone on to hold that the special circumstances did not warrant the immunity; furthermore, if, as it appears, the Colonial Office was handling the case, it is more than likely that the Sultan would never know how the matter was decided — if, indeed, he knew of the case at all. But even if the policy of the Government may be weakened to some extent, we should want the court to feel that it can put limits to the type of action which the Government can take in carrying out that policy.

In dealing with non-recognition we have argued that however valuable a given executive or diplomatic policy may be, its claim is not absolute. We have found that this is true even where the defense of the realm is at stake; there will come a point where other interests — personal liberty, for example — will put limits to this most powerful of all executive competences. And allowing for differences in its application, we are now asserting the same generality with respect to the policies which may underlie a recognition or, more specifically, a recognition of an organization as a "sovereign" state or person. This does not mean that the court will put its nose into foreign or colonial policy; it does not mean that the court will compel the Government to expose its policy or that the court itself will assume the policy to be such and such and then attempt to gauge the effect that its decision will have on it. What it does mean is that the court will be in a position to say: "Whatever your policy, there are certain means of furthering it to which we will not lend our aid. We have no objection to your calling Kelantan a sovereign state, and we will not inquire why you do so or whether it is wise, but you cannot expect us to victimize this plaintiff in the interests of that policy, when it is quite clear that the reasons and the assumptions on which we base *our* rule of immunity are absent in this case." The occasions on which a court would exercise such a power would be very rare indeed; no court, we trust, will fail to appreciate the danger of putting the country in a position where it cannot perform its duties to a friendly foreign power, but aware of these dangers the court should not find it impossible to prevent the perversion of its own processes by an improper use of the recognition formula.

In the United States, our courts have had a question of the effects of recognition which in complexity and intrinsic difficulty far exceeds those already discussed. We refer to the so-called continuing "recognition" of the extinct provisional government of Russia. On July 5, 1917, the United States received Boris Bakhmétieff as the Russian Ambassador. He was accredited by the Kerensky provisional government. On November 7, 1917, the Bolsheviki swept the Kerensky government into the limbo of history, and it has not been heard from since. Yet until June 30, 1922, the Department of State certified unto all and sundry that this same Bakhmétieff was the duly accredited ambassador extraordinary and plenipotentiary of Russia. On December 18, 1917, one Khrabroff, acting for the once "Russian State," released to certain parties whatever interests this state might have in a contract claim against the American Can Company. Bakhmétieff certified to the Court in *Agency of Canadian Car* v. *American Can Company* [47] that Khrabroff was at the time of the release an agent of the Russian State. And the Department of State gave its usual certificate as to Bakhmétieff. Behind this, said the Court, it was not possible to go.

"Who is the sovereign de jure or de facto of a country is a question for the political department of the government. . . . The decision of the matter by the political departments is in this country conclusive upon the judges." [48]

But this pronouncement, however correct as an abstract proposition, states the effect of a line of decisions in which it was clear that the power certified to be sovereign had some pretense to that character, and in which it was assumed that the executive was testifying to the existing, contemporaneous character of the government; and since no case like this had ever before arisen, there had been no occasion to decide what should be done when the assumption was challenged. It is therefore significant that, as it appears from the record,[49] the defendant, instead of asking the Court to disregard the certificate of the Department of State, requested it to write to that Department for answers to the following questions (*inter alia*):

4. Did the Provisional Russian Government, that is the Kerensky Government, cease to exist in or about the month of November, 1917?
8. Is Boris Bakhmétieff now recognized by the United States as the representative of the Provisional Russian Government, that is the Kerensky Government?

The Court refused the request. Before probing the significance of this refusal, let us go on further. On July 23, 1918, was commenced [50] the famous litigation of "Russian Government," later "State of Russia," against Lehigh Valley Railway Company. To commence suit "the attorneys for the Russian Government" ob-

[47] 253 Fed. 152 (S. D. N. Y. 1918); affirmed 258 Fed. 363 (C. C. A. 2nd, 1919).

[48] *Supra*, note 47, 258 Fed. at 368, citing Jones *v.* United States, 137 U. S. 202, 212 (1890).

[49] This information appears from the *Transcript of Record* in Lehigh Valley R. Co. *v.* State of Russia, 21 F (2d) 396 and 406 (C. C. A. 2nd, 1927), on writ of error to the district court for the Southern District of New York. The references here and below are to action No. 2. See *Transcript of Record*, II, 389.

[50] *Id.*, II, 400.

tained authority from Bakhmétieff.[51] The cause of action would have been barred on July 30, 1918. The defendant moved to dismiss on the ground that there was not in existence "the Russian Government"; that there was no recognized government now entitled to represent the interests previously represented by the Imperial Russian Government up to the time of its overthrow; that the Kerensky government which had accredited Bakhmétieff was overthrown seven months prior to the initiation of the action. It appears from the record that counsel for the defendant had sought information from the Department of State as to the relations between the United States and "Russia." The Department replied (October 3, 1918) that it would not answer such inquiries except upon the request of the Court.[52] Thereupon counsel, upon moving for dismissal, requested the Court to make certain inquiries: specifically, what were the relations between the United States and "the people or sovereignty of the territory formerly within the confines of the Imperial Russian Government on July 23, 1918, when the suit was commenced" and what were they at the time of inquiry; did the United States recognize any government existing in Russia at the time; was Bakhmétieff the representative of an existing government? [53]

Now the certificate already in the case stated merely that Bakhmétieff had been received and was still recognized as "ambassador extraordinary and plenipotentiary of Russia." It did not provide answers to any of the above questions. The Court refused to make the inquiries: "The court will make official inquiry only for reasons

[51] *Id.*, II, 317, 537. See statement of Coudert, II, 401: "We are now acting in behalf of the Russian Government the successor of the Imperial Russian Government and we are taking our instructions from the representative in this country of such government recognized by the State Department."

[52] *Id.*, II, 409: "The Department has given careful consideration to your letter and, inasmuch as your inquiries relate to the diplomatic relations between the United States and Russia, of which it is understood courts take judicial notice, the Department prefers not to answer those inquiries except upon the request of the court."

But at a later stage of the proceedings and under the secretaryship of Charles E. Hughes, the Department did reply to an inquiry by the Attorney for defendant. And in the English cases it appears that the Foreign Office is willing to answer such inquiries. See, for example, Luther *v.* Sagor, [1921] 1 K. B. 456. The Department probably felt somewhat uncertain as to its position and seems to have been hedging.

[53] *Id.*, II, 411.

of an impelling character, especially where such inquiry may involve pending questions of the greatest delicacy." [54]

This solicitude for the delicate position of the Department of State seems misplaced, since the Department can itself decide what is demanded by the delicacy of pending issues and answer accordingly or not at all. It would be a most curious paradox that because of the delicacy of foreign affairs the courts must follow the executive, and that for the same reason they are not to make any inquiries from that source. It would seem that they should apply directly for information on all material issues.[55] It is probably the real significance of these cases that the Court did not consider the issues raised to be material; that, to use its own phrase, there were no "reasons of an impelling character" for making the inquiry. In other words, the Court considered it immaterial whether or not Bakhmétieff represented an existing government, that is to say whether he was responsible to any one for his conduct. The Court argued that there must be someone to carry on "governmental continuity," to assure that the property of the foreign state would not be lost. This reasoning would apply to the *Lehigh Valley* case, where there was a threat of the action being barred, but hardly to the *Agency of Canada* case, where rights of the foreign power were released.

Later stages of the *Lehigh Valley* case confirm this analysis of the earlier one. On March 27, 1922,[56] counsel renewed the motion for dismissal before Judge Mack on the ground of the plaintiff's cessation. In the moving papers counsel set forth a letter to him from the Department of State in which it is said (*inter alia*): "Mr. Bakhmétieff was received on July 5, 1917, and that he was accredited to the Government of the United States by the 'Provisional Government of Russia.'"

[54] Russian Government *v.* Lehigh Valley R. Co., 293 Fed. 133 (S. D. N. Y. 1919).

[55] This seems to be the view of the English courts. Lord Sumner in Duff *v.* Kelantan, quoted *supra*, p. 206, remarked that on occasions the Foreign Office might have to give "temporary or temporizing answers," but it has never been suggested that for this reason the courts should not ask the questions. It will be seen from the discussion below of White, Child, and Beney Ltd. *v.* Simmons, 127 L. T. R. 571 (1922), that Roche, whose views of deference to the executive were extreme, was unusually persistent in directing questions to the Foreign Office, even in the face of a reluctance to answer.

[56] *Supra*, note 49, II, 416.

He further set forth an extract from a message of President Wilson on December 7, 1921: "We do not recognize the Government of Russia."

From this it was quite clear that Bakhmétieff, whatever else he might be, was not the representative of *any* existing government. The motion to dismiss for lack of plaintiff was denied. In an unreported opinion Judge Mack said:

> Whether or not "The Russian Government" is the correct title of the sovereign power of which Boris Bakhmétieff is recognized by the Department of State as the ambassador, is not material on these motions. Clearly that sovereign power is the plaintiff. If its title be "Russia" or the "Republic of Russia," the misnomer can be corrected at the time of trial.[57]

Bakhmétieff retired on June 30, 1922. One Serge Ughet, a financial attaché, remained at his post. Of Ughet Secretary Hughes wrote in a letter to counsel for the Lehigh:

> The custody of the property of the Russian Government in this country, for which Mr. Bakhmétieff had been responsible, was, after the date of his retirement, considered to vest in Mr. Serge Ughet, the financial attaché of the Russian embassy, whose diplomatic status with this government was not considered to be altered by the termination of the ambassador's duties.
>
> In answer specifically to your questions, I may say that the United States has not recognized any other government in Russia since the fall of the provisional government. . . .[58]

It was clear from this that Ughet represented no government, and challenging his authority to continue the conduct of the suit, once more the defendant moved to dismiss, and the motion was again denied, this time by Judge Goddard, who said that the State of Russia was the plaintiff, that the manifold vicissitudes of changing governments did not destroy the State.[59] Counsel maintained that even admitting the State of Russia had persisted a state could sue only through a recognized government, and from the beginning of the suit down to that very moment there was none such. Ughet's standing to prosecute the suit was denied, since by the statement in Secretary Hughes' letter he was declared to have "*custody* of the property of the Russian Government *in this country*," a phrase which it was argued related only to tangibles with a locus here. A mere custodian could not prosecute an action.[60] But the letter was

[57] *Id.* II, 560.

[58] Quoted in Russian Government *v.* Lehigh Valley R. Co., 293 Fed. 135, 137 (S. D. N. Y. 1923).

For a franker and more recent statement by the Department of State see Appendix.

[59] *Supra*, note 49, II, 708.

[60] *Id.*, II, 320, 332.

interpreted, and it would seem correctly, to give Ughet the same status as Bakhmétieff to protect property interests. The final decision was sustained by the Circuit Court of Appeals; [61] certiorari was denied by the Supreme Court.[62] The Lehigh Valley was allowed to pay the judgment into court to protect it from suits by the Soviet Government.[63] The Soviet Government moved for the appointment of a receiver, which was denied. During the course of argument on this motion the Assistant United States Attorney presented a statement from the Secretary of the Treasury in the following terms:

> Mr. Serge Ughet is officially recognized by the United States as custodian of all property in this country belonging to the State of Russia. In pursuance of an arrangement with the Treasury under which Mr. Ughet has already paid on account of Russia's debt to the United States amounts aggregating in excess of seven million dollars, he has undertaken to pay the United States all sums after deduction of the expenses of litigation, recovered from the Lehigh Valley Railroad as a result of the judgments awarded the State of Russia.[64]

The newspapers reported that the money was paid to Mr. Ughet.[65]

There has been some failure to focus the issue in the *Lehigh* cases. Mr. Fraenkel has said witheringly, but without a complete understanding of the real issue: [66] "It would seem that here fiction has been carried to its logical extreme and a result obtained defensible upon no grounds whatever." It is true that the Court was somewhat responsible for the blurring, and indeed, up until the final disposition of the fund as set forth above, it was not clear where the decisions were leading.

Even as late as the appeal in 1925 the Court said: "*The recognized government* may carry on the suit, at least until the new government becomes accredited here by recognition." [67] (Italics mine.) But it was clear from the communications of the Department itself that there was no recognized government, and to trot out the

[61] 21 F (2d) 396 and 406 (C. C. A. 2nd, 1927).

[62] 275 U. S. 571 (1927).

[63] Hervey, p. 124. *New York Times*, December 23, 1927.

[64] Quoted in Barry, *Russian Insurance Funds — The Problem of Their Distribution*, 14 Virg. L. Rev. 243, 253 (1928).

[65] *Ibid.*

[66] Fraenkel, *The Juristic Status of Foreign States*, 25 Col. L. Rev. 544, 552 (1925).

[67] Lehigh Valley R. Co. *v.* State of Russia, 21 F (2d) 396, 401 (C. C. A. 2nd, 1927).

formula about the binding effect of recognition of a government and of its diplomatic agents obscured the issue. In the past, that formula has been grounded on the fact that by recognizing a diplomatic agent the Department impliedly or expressly declared that he was *responsible* to an existing power of some sort which had accredited him. Prior to the Hughes letter, the Court refused to inquire of the Department whether its certificate carried such an implication, and after it there was no need, since the letter itself denied it. The real issues, then, were these: first, in the absence of a government recognized as representing the interest of an already recognized state, may the executive appoint or acknowledge someone to protect these interests? And second, had the executive done so in this case?

The first of these issues is the prime one; it was never squarely faced. In the first place, it would seem that if such an appointment is to be respected by the court there must be an assurance of responsibility. The formula of certifying the agent as an ambassador of a foreign state must not be allowed to obscure the fact that the agency between the foreign power and the ambassador is dead and incapable of providing effective control. The only alternative is that the agent should be responsible to the certifying government, and that this government should stand ready and willing to enforce this responsibility. Is the mere certificate sufficient evidence that it stands ready? Perhaps it should be sufficient to allow at least the bringing and prosecution of the suit; but there should be a more positive showing, as there was finally in the *Lehigh* cases, before collection of the judgment that the Government of the forum is assuming ultimate responsibility. Such a requirement is valuable in putting the Government on record, and in awakening in it a sense of responsibility where it might hitherto have been lacking. Furthermore, it may tend, though not completely, to check vicious practices which the device may, and probably did, to some extent, allow; that is, the use of these state funds by an agent of an ousted régime to discredit and promote the destruction of the current one.

Following the downfall of the Kerensky government, the Russian funds in America were consolidated in the National City Bank; the Department of State exercised with the cooperation of the Bank an informal veto over withdrawals.[68] The funds were used principally

[68] A full account of the handling of the funds appears in Senate Document No. 86, 67th Congress, 2nd Session, under title "Loans To Foreign Governments."

to liquidate contracts for war materials made by Russia with American manufacturers, to meet interest on Russian indebtedness in America both to private parties and to our Government, and to maintain the embassies and consular staffs.[69] Some of the disbursements thus allowed were questionable: the maintenance of huge salaried staffs,[70] a fund of $100,000 to enable Bakhmétieff to represent "Russia" at the peace conference.[71] But raising most serious doubt was the permission given Bakhmétieff to use these Russian state funds to aid Kolchak in his attempt to overthrow the Russian Government.[72] But by 1925, when the *Lehigh* case was finally ready to pay, these improper leaks had, it seems, been stopped up.

The device, no doubt, is subject to abuse.[73] But it is preferable to a court receivership, which could only deal with the matter piecemeal, and which has not developed the machinery to handle a situation so rare and so closely bound up with political issues. In the last analysis the executive will have to account to the foreign state for the disposition of the funds, and it is good sense to permit him to assume responsibility over all funds from the beginning. The court should keep in mind that this, and not a superficial deference to the foreign office's certificates, is the issue; definitely located responsibility should be the determinate of judgment.

One difficulty with this device remains quite unsolved. It is clear that even though the Soviet should later be recognized, the courts of the United States will treat the judgment against the Lehigh as *res judicata*, and not allow a second recovery. But what if the Lehigh were, today, sued in Germany, where the U.S.S.R. is recognized as the representative of the old Russian interests? Conceivably the German courts might adopt the reasoning of our courts that the "State of Russia" was the owner of the claim, and that (at

[69] *Id.* at 96, 97. [70] *Id.* at 123. [71] *Id.* at 132.

[72] *Id.* at 162. Funds were released for the printing of paper money for the Kolchak government. It is true that on May 26, 1919 the Council of Four at Versailles had "recognized" the Kolchak faction, but it was clearly not an established or representative government, and it was improper to allow Russian state funds to be used for Kolchak's support.

[73] In an interdepartmental memorandum by Basil Miles to B. C. Leffingwell (*id.* at 100), Miles, urging that the funds should be taken from Bakhmétieff's control, says: "His whole policy is to carry on as though nothing had happened and hope that before the funds are exhausted the situation will have been reversed and his party be in power." He goes on to say that dissipation of the funds for purposes which might be regarded as inimical to the Russian people should not be tolerated.

least where the action was created by our law or the property was located in the United States) our Government was qualified to name an agent for suit and collection.

The defendant in the *Lehigh Valley* case claimed that if the Soviets were later recognized, such recognition would be retroactive, and place the Soviet in the position of having been at all times able to sue; thus, it could make the Lehigh pay over again. The Court answered: "It is only the acts performed in its own territory that can be validated by the retroactive effect of recognition." [74]

Much has been written about the so-called retroactivity of recognition, as if it were a magic formula. Thus, it is said [75] that it "validates" all acts of the state or government done within its territory from the time when its authority in fact began,—as if it took recognition by the United States to validate the acts of a foreign state! And Professor Dickinson [76] speaks of it as "the fiction of retroactivity," though withal a salutary one. But there is nothing fictitious about it. It may be that a court will give no effect to the laws of an unrecognized power, or will not allow it to sue, but this is not because its laws are invalid, or because it is not in fact a state; it is because for reasons of policy our courts believe they must ignore the state and its laws. Once the state is recognized, no such reasons of policy exist and the court need no longer assume a struthious posture. This is really neither fiction nor retroactivity.

In *State of Yucatan* v. *Argumendo*,[77] the then unrecognized Carranza régime brought suit to recover funds from an absconding rebel. A few days later the government was recognized. The Court refused to dismiss the suit. Mr. Hervey [78] says the case is wrong, that recognition retroacts to "validate" only acts taking place within the recognized state and thus governed by its law. But we believe that Yucatan had *capacity* to bring suit from the beginning, though in the absence of recognition the suit might have been dis-

[74] Lehigh Valley R. Co. *v.* State of Russia, 21 F (2d) 396, 401 (C. C. A. 2nd, 1927). Barry, *loc. cit.* (*supra,* note 64) at 252, takes the argument rather seriously.

[75] Fraenkel, *loc. cit.* (*supra,* note 66) at 548.

[76] Dickinson, *The Unrecognized Government or State in English and American Law,* 22 Mich. L. Rev. 29, 44 (1923).

[77] 92 Misc. 547; 157 N. Y. Supp. 219 (1915). The leading case in the United States on the "retroactivity" of recognition is Oetjen *v.* Central Leather Co., 246 U. S. 297 (1918).

[78] Hervey, p. 66, n. 36.

missed for political reasons. If, as in *Kennett* v. *Chambers*,[79] our neutrality law has been violated, or if, as in the *Lehigh* case, rights are adjudicated or determined, the results are of course in no way affected by recognition.[80]

Who is to determine when the newly recognized state or government first came into being as such? Is this a political question? [81] The point was raised in acute form in *White, Child, and Beney Ltd.* v. *Simmons*.[82] That case was tried shortly after the final decision in *Luther* v. *Sagor*,[83] and before the same Judge, Roche. The plaintiff sued on a loss policy, which excepted claims for "confiscation or destruction by the Government of the country in which the property is situated." The plaintiff had bonds and money on deposit with a Petrograd bank; on December 14–27, 1917 (old and new style), the properties of the bank were confiscated by a decree of the "Central Executive Committee," a Bolshevist-controlled organization which had seized power on November 7. On December 13 the Bolsheviki had dispersed the Constituent Assembly which had met to form a new Constitution. It proclaimed new elections for an assembly which met on January 18th of the following year, and which was dissolved by the Central Committee the next day, apparently because the elected delegates, as in the earlier assembly, were hostile to the Bolsheviki. The confiscation decree in question was issued as a decree of the "Provisional Worker and Peasant Government." Not until July, 1918, was there a government called the R.S.F.S.R., which was the government recognized in 1921 by Great Britain. Were plaintiff's assets confiscated by "the Government of the country"?

[79] 14 How. 38 (1852).

[80] Noël-Henry (§§ 153, 154) criticizes the conception of retroactivity as based on what he considers the erroneous notion that recognition is declarative rather than, as he contends, constitutive. In granting recognition, the political power "disposes" only for the future; laws have no retroactive effect unless expressly stipulated, and so with an executive constitutive act. However, he disagrees with none of the cases in which the concept was employed.

[81] De Visscher, *Les Gouvernements Étrangers En Justice*, 3 Rev. de Droit Int. (3rd Série) 149, 165 (1922), says it is. He contends that the formula in the Oetjen case (*supra*, note 77) that recognition validates all acts "from the commencement of its existence," is too absolute, giving the idea that such a moment is automatically or at least easily determinable. "Un Gouvernement insurrectionnel, aujourd'hui victorieux et reconnu, peut avoir eu les plus humbles origines."

[82] 127 L. T. R. 571 (1922).

[83] [1921] 3 K. B. 532.

In the first place it was assumed that the government must be the same one recognized by Great Britain. "It must be remembered that the Government which has been recognized by His Majesty's Government is the Russian Socialist Federal Soviet Republic and that the commencement or the identity of *that* Government is the point in issue." (Italics mine.) [84]

Roche would not for a minute have admitted that any government not recognized by His Majesty was *ever*, even in the non-controversial past, a government. Now, counsel had asked the Foreign Office for information as to when the R.S.F.S.R. was deemed by it to have come into power. The Foreign Office in its reply gave a great deal of valuable information on which to base a conclusion, but stated that His Majesty's Government could not "express any opinion as to how far, or over what area, the power of the Soviet Government was effective, the questions being also questions of fact for the courts to determine on the evidence laid before them."[85]

Roche considered this a "mistaken view," and had another letter addressed to the Foreign Office; again Lord Curzon replied that he was in no better position than the Court to decide the question and was "unable to take the responsibility" but felt sure that "the Court [was] fully qualified." [86] But Roche was not to be thus cajoled out of the conviction of his complete incompetency. "I regret that I do not feel either qualified or entitled, still less bound, to answer the question for myself. I may perhaps usefully indicate only a few of the difficulties which would seem to preclude me from venturing away from the functions of judicial decision into the realm of conjecture in the political and international sphere." [87] Roche then goes on to dilate on the difficulties involved in determining whether the government in December, 1917 was "the government of the country," and whether it was the government later recognized by Great Britain. He inclines to think it was not, because it had a different name, but he concludes that since the matter is obscure and "not being satisfied by any certificate or statement . . . from the executive" [88] he cannot decide; that, hence, the insurance company has failed to sustain the burden of proving the defense of "act of state."

The decision was reversed by the Court of Appeals. Bankes, L. J., said:

[84] *Supra*, note 82, at 579.2 (last number refers to column).

[85] *Id.* at 577.1.

[86] *Id.* at 579.1.

[87] *Ibid.*

[88] *Id.* at 580.1.

It does not seem to me that the sources of information with regard to the time when a particular foreign Government came into existence as a Government is a matter for the Foreign Office to determine. . . . Roche J. felt himself unable to decide when the Soviet Government came into existence, partly because the Foreign Office are unable to express any opinion. . . .[89]

This case has been set forth at some length, not because of the importance of the decision as law, but as an example of that almost unreasoning sense of incompetency to decide issues of international status and fact which seems to obsess some courts. Courts which do not hesitate to declare laws unconstitutional, courts which boldly announce that they "have rarely, if ever, felt themselves so restrained by technical rules that they could not find some remedy, consistent with the law, for acts, whether done by government or by individual persons, that violated natural justice," [90] — these courts seem to regard the power over foreign affairs as sacrosanct, as absolute and unlimited. And from this, like Roche, they derive a principle of such absolute incompetency that the court, even at the suggestion of the foreign office, can make no decision of a fact bearing on the status of a foreign nation.

Territorial Questions

A recognition of a state or government ordinarily supposes control over a given, defined territory, and a classic statement treats recognition of the state and determination of its territory as reverse sides of the same "political question."

Who is the sovereign, *de jure* or *de facto*, of a territory, is not a judicial, but a political question, the determination of which by the legislative and executive departments of any government conclusively binds the judges, as well as all other offices, citizens, and subjects of that government.[91]

It may be a "political question"; yet at least in the absence of legislative or executive determination our courts have decided such questions. When they arise in English cases, the courts resort very freely to the Foreign Office for information. Our courts, however, seem reluctant to do so, and have, on occasion, refused, when asked.[92] In the very interesting case of *In re Taylor* [93] the question arose

[89] *Id.* at 582.2.

[90] Harlan, J., in President, etc. of the Monongahela Bridge Co. *v.* United States, 216 U. S. 177, 195 (1909).

[91] Jones *v.* United States, 137 U. S. 202, 212 (1890).

[92] See *supra*, p. 213 and note 52.

[93] 118 Fed. 196 (D. Mass. 1902).

whether the South African Republic was, prior to Lord Roberts' proclamation, a part of the British Dominions. Great Britain was seeking extradition under its treaty with the United States for a crime committed in South Africa prior to the Boer War. The United States Ambassador at London certified that South Africa had been part of the British Empire at the time. It was argued that the Court could not go behind this. The Court replied:

> If the legislative or executive department of the Government of the United States has taken action regarding the diplomatic or international status of any place or country, this Court is ordinarily bound by that action. But it is bound, also, to inquire what that action has been. . . . The Court does not . . . refuse to take action for fear that its decision may not be approved thereafter by the legislative or executive department.[94]

The Court noted that, by Congressional enactment, consuls were sent to Pretoria, which was described as within the "South African Republic." The Department of State informed the Court that the exequatur was granted by the Republic. The Court studied the treaty relations between the Republic and Great Britain: the Republic was allowed to make treaties, Great Britain retaining a veto power. On this data the Court decided that the Republic was not part of Great Britain, and so it denied that Great Britain was entitled to extradition under the Treaty.

A like question appeared in more intricate and puzzling guise in a series of cases before the English admiralty during the Napoleonic Wars. They arose out of that fruitful source of litigations, the revolt in Santo Domingo against the French. In 1805 an American vessel, *The Happy Couple*, traded with Dessalines, leader of the revolt. The vessel was hailed before the Admiralty Court in Nova Scotia, which condemned it for carrying contraband to the enemy, i. e. the French. On appeal to England, the judgment was affirmed [95] with "much expressed reluctance." [96] Santo Domingo was a colony of the enemy, and whether in its control or not must still be considered as such by the Court until the Government said otherwise. Yet the contraband here in question was munitions for Dessalines with which to fight the French. The case is very different from *In re Taylor*, since the political considerations in *The Happy Couple* were of current moment, and touched on the conduct of a war. There might be a danger of the courts treating the terri-

[94] *Id.* at 197.

[95] The Happy Couple, Stewart 65 (Nova Scotia, 1805).

[96] The Manilla, Edw. Adm. 1, 3 (1808), per Sir William Scott.

tory as neutral while the Government treated it as enemy, though the danger was extremely slight.

In fact, however, at the time of the appeal, though not at the time of capture, the Government by Orders in Council had provided that whereas it would be expedient for British vessels to trade with such parts of the island as "are not or shall not be under the dominion and in the actual possession of His Majesty's enemies," certain authorities might license British vessels to trade with such places as were named in the license.[97] In *The Manilla* [98] Sir William Scott held that by reason of these Orders neutrals might, without a license, trade with portions of Santo Domingo not under French control. The Order in Council, he said, was "a positive declaration of the State that parts of Santo Domingo are neither in the possession nor in the dominion of France." [99] But no parts were specified, and who is to say which they are? Says Scott, the Court will determine that from notoriety. But by requiring a license did not the Government reserve that very power for itself? Scott says:

> If there are purposes and motives for these Orders which are inconsistent with this construction [i. e. the Court's] they are purposes and motives which are not expressed; and courts of justice are not to attend to latent motives and purposes in order to controul clear and definite declarations. Here is a positive declaration of the State that parts of Santo Domingo are neither in the possession nor in the dominion of France. The Court has to look no further than to see whether the port in question comes within that description; if it does, the Court is bound to apply all the consequences which belong to such a description. It cannot assume to say, it shall be good for one purpose but not for another. It is not necessary that this should amount to a perpetual recognition of the independence of these places. . . .[100]

In the uncritical estimates which have been made of this case, its significance has not been brought to light. It is a vigorous application of what we have spoken of as the middle view, the view not too tactfully exemplified in *The Ambrose Light,* that when the Government has declared or implied the existence of certain facts the court will treat this action at its face value and draw its own conclusions. In *The Helena,* already discussed,[101] Sir William Scott

[97] The Order will be found in Appendix A following p. 174 of Edw. Adm. Reports.

[98] Edw. Adm. 1 (1808). Followed in The Pelican, Edw. Adm., Appendix D.

[99] *Id.* at 5.

[100] *Ibid.*

[101] See *supra,* pp. 113, 200, 203.

deduced the statehood of Algiers from the fact that Britain has made treaties with it. Nowhere did he speak of recognition; here again he expressly declares it to be immaterial. The Government may not admit facts and yet hope to control the legal consequences which normally flow from them.

The case, however, is not free from doubt. The Order did not specify that any particular part of Santo Domingo was non-enemy, and the very function of the license seems to have been to determine that fact, which, depending on the fortunes of the rebellion, might change continuously. Perhaps the secret of the decision is that the licenses were restricted to British vessels, which was clearly unfair to neutrals. Sitting as a prize court with, as has been shown, an exalted idea of the international character of that tribunal, Sir William Scott found a way to remedy the injustice. It is always said that *The Manilla* does not overrule *The Happy Couple*, because in the interim the Government had declared the non-enemy character of ports of Santo Domingo. This may be, but it is quite evident that Scott disliked *The Happy Couple* and sought a "favorable distinction." [102]

In the last few years, three of our state courts have tackled a similar problem. All were suits by alien relatives for death benefits under workmen's compensation acts. The defense was the statute of limitations. Plaintiffs claimed that they had been alien enemies, debarred from suing during the course of the World War. All had been resident in and citizens of Austro-Hungary. In 1918 and 1919 the United States in concert with the Allied Powers "recognized" the new states of Jugo-Slavia, Czechoslovakia, and the kingdom of the Serbs, Croats, and Slovenes, all of which were located in various ill-defined portions of the Austro-Hungarian Empire, none of which were under the control of the new *soi-disant* national organizations. It was claimed by the defendants that from the moment of the "recognition" inhabitants of the territories later acknowledged to be within these states ceased to be alien enemies. The Minnesota Court accepted this view.[103] The courts of

[102] Edw. Adm. 1, 3 (1808): "There can be no doubt that the *strict* legal principle of that decision was correct; and yet at the same time, if circumstances can be pointed out in this case for a favorable distinction, the Court would not be disinclined to adopt it. . . .". (Italics mine.) Lawyers are familiar with this discreet fashion of expressing dislike.

[103] Kolundjija *v.* Hanna Ore Mining Co., 155 Minn. 176; 193 N. W. 163 (1923); cf. Waldes *v.* Basch, 109 Misc. 306; 179 N. Y. Supp. 713, affirmed 191 App. Div. 904; 181 N. Y. Supp. 958 (1919). Action by joint obligees, two of

Pennsylvania and Indiana refused to follow it. Said the Pennsylvania Court:[104]

> In the absence of adequate political action recognizing a change of boundaries, we cannot assume the place in question ceased to be enemy territory until the war ended. . . . There is . . . a distinction between the recognition of a revolutionary people and the territory which they may acquire.

The Indiana Court said:[105]

> It [the recognition] was intended merely as a recognition by appropriate diplomatic act of the existence of the new kingdom, and as an expression of readiness to enter into relationships such as the United States usually establishes with friendly powers. Recognition was extended before peace treaties had settled territorial and other rights in part, because of our relations with Serbia. . . . An act of recognition, within the powers delegated to the national executive, is conclusive in all courts in respect to everything which it actually decides, but no further.

These two decisions surely achieve a sound result. As Professor Dickinson[106] has pointed out, in the uncertain days of the war inhabitants of these places could not have been expected to know whether recognition had changed their citizenship. The Pennsylvania Court is probably a shade too dogmatic in its statement that in the absence of adequate political action a territory must be presumed to continue as enemy. The political action here was surely as pertinent as in *The Manilla,* and if justice had required, the Court might well have followed Sir William Scott in ascertaining by proof what territory was in fact under control of the recognized states.[107] The Indiana Court has given us the more exact analysis. It hints that recognition was premature, that it did not necessarily purport to affect the status of any particular territory, and that it would be unjust to the litigants to have required of them foresight as to the final outcome of the war.

them resident in Bohemia. Held not to be alien enemies after the "recognition" of Czechoslovakia. This case is correct; the war was over, the plaintiffs were not in fact enemies, no hardship was done as in the Minnesota case.

[104] Garvin *v.* Diamond Coal and Coke Co. 278 Pa. St. 469, 473; 123 Atl. 468, 469 (1924).

[105] Inland Steel Co. *v.* Jelenovic, 84 Ind. App. 373, 376; 150 N. E. 391, 392 (1926).

[106] Dickinson, *Recent Recognition Cases,* 19 A. J. 263, 266 (1925). Dickinson is quoted with approval in the Indiana case. *Supra,* note 105; Ind. App. at 378; N. E. at 393.

[107] Cf. Waldes *v.* Basch, *supra,* note 103.

A final question is whether a positive executive declaration as to the status of territory is conclusive on the courts. There is nearly, but not quite, a unanimous opinion that it is. One phase we have already discussed at some length.[108] Where the executive claims or exercises jurisdiction over a territory in the name of his own state, it would create a threat of disorder for the judiciary to deny the jurisdiction. In *The Fagernes* [109] the question arose whether the same rule was applicable to a disavowal of jurisdiction. The Secretary of State for Home Affairs informed the Court that "the spot where this collision is alleged to have occurred [in the Bristol Channel] is not within the limits to which the territorial sovereignty of His Majesty extends." Lawrence, L. J., and Atkin, L. J., thought that this was conclusive. Bankes, L. J., said that the information "given under such circumstances, and on such a subject, . . . does not in my opinion necessarily bind the Court in the sense that it is under an obligation to accept it." [110] The reasons for holding the statement conclusive are not so strong here as where sovereignty is asserted. Yet cases may arise (*The Fagernes* was possibly such a one) [111] where the court might put the foreign office in the position of having to justify to a foreign state an exercise of jurisdiction which the foreign office itself disclaimed.

Pearcy v. *Stranahan* [112] involved a curious situation betwixt and between those already considered. It concerned the status of the Isle of Pines after the Spanish-American War. The plaintiff brought suit for the return of custom duties on goods imported from the Isle of Pines into the United States. Now there was no question that both the legislative and executive departments were treating the Isle of Pines as temporarily subject to the *de facto* government of Cuba, which though still controlled by the United States was under previous decisions considered to be a foreign

[108] See *supra*, pp. 62–66.

[109] [1927] P. 311.

[110] *Id.* at 323: "This information was given at the instance of the Court, and for the information of the Court. Given under such circumstances [*et seq.* as quoted in the text]. . . ."

[111] At issue was the question whether a summons should issue under Order XI, r. 1 (e. e.), providing for service of personal summons outside the realm where the tort occurs within it. The defendant was an Italian company; conceivably, then, an improper exercise of jurisdiction could have been cause for the Italian Government to complain, though the chance of such a complaint would be remote.

[112] 205 U. S. 257 (1907).

country.[113] It was clear that for the collection of duties the Isle of Pines was understood to be in the same class. That, then, was a sufficient ground for rejecting the plaintiff's claim. However, the Court went further. There was in Congress and elsewhere at the time considerable debate as to the ultimate status of the island, and some claim that it should be (or was) a territory of the United States. In the Platt amendment one clause read:

"That the Isle of Pines shall be omitted from the proposed constitutional boundaries of Cuba, the title thereto being left to future adjustment by treaty."

Since that time and prior to the litigation a treaty relinquishing to Cuba our claim to the Isle of Pines had been rejected by the Senate.

The Court, under these circumstances, undertook to interpret the treaty of peace with Spain and to determine whether the Isle of Pines was intended to be part of Cuba, or was one of a number of unspecified islands ceded to the United States by Spain. On the basis of history and executive declaration it decided that the island was justly part of Cuba. In a concurring opinion Mr. Justice White, joined by Mr. Justice Holmes, criticized the Court for expressing any opinion on the *de jure* status of the island, since Congress had made it clear that the question was to be left open for future determination. White, characteristically, said that Chief Justice Fuller's dictum was in disregard of "the very principle upon which the decision is placed, that is, the conclusive effect of executive and legislative action." [114]

A treaty [115] ceding the Isle of Pines to Cuba was at last ratified in 1925, and it is interesting to notice that Secretary of State Hughes in recommending that the Senate consent to ratification referred to the opinion of the majority in *Pearcy* v. *Stranahan*.[116]

[113] Neely *v.* Henkel, 180 U. S. 109 (1901). For purposes of an extradition statute was Cuba a "foreign country"? *Held* Yes. Decision based on a consideration of executive and Congressional action and declaration showing that we had never expressed any intention of annexing Cuba, that it was our stated object to make it free. Followed in a customs case, Galban *v.* United States, 40 Ct. Cl. 495 (1905); affirmed 207 U. S. 579 (1907).

[114] 205 U.S. 257, 274 (1907).

[115] 44 Stat. 1997.

[116] Senate Document No. 166, 68th Congress, 2nd Session, pp. 13–14. Notice the very curious comment in the Encyclopedia Britannica (14th ed. 1929) showing the layman's point of view: "A decision of the United States Supreme Court which recognized it [the Isle of Pines] as a part of Cuba was

The question with which we are more directly concerned is the force of executive declarations on the status of foreign territories. In *Foster* v. *Globe Venture Syndicate Ltd.*,[117] Justice Farwell said that when a question as to the status of a foreign territory arises the proper course is to apply to the Secretary of State for Foreign Affairs for information. "I should, speaking for myself, not allow the answer, assuming it to be a direct answer in the affirmative or negative, to be questioned in any way." [118]

On that case plaintiff sought recission of a contract on the ground of misrepresentation. The defendant had stated that it had secured a trading monopoly from the independent tribe of Suss for the entire territory between the Atlas Mountains and the River Nun. There were two questions to be asked of the Foreign Office: (1) whether the tribes of Suss were independent; (2) whether the territory between the Atlas Mountains and the River Nun was within the dominions of the Sultan of Morocco or the tribes of Suss. Farwell conceived that the answers to both these questions, whether in the positive or the negative, would be binding.

Lord Sumner in *Duff* v. *Kelantan* [119] has analyzed Farwell's judgment acutely. If the Foreign Office had answered that the Suss tribes were not independent, but were vassals of the Sultan of Morocco, the question as to territory would, of course, need no answer. And the answer as given would undoubtedly be binding, for we have seen that the most delicate of recognition processes — the one out of which historically most of the formulas have sprung — is the treatment of claims to independence of portions of *recognized* states. If there is ever a case where the courts are to be bound absolutely by the foreign office this is surely it. Nor, as we have tried to show,[120] is the much-abused judgment of Lord Phillimore in *The Charkieh* [121] opposed to this view. The Foreign Office told Lord Phillimore that the Khedive of Egypt was not the "reigning sover-

finally ratified [!] by the United States Senate on March 13, 1925." In article on "Cuba — History — American Occupation" (p. 840).

[117] [1900] 1 Ch. 811.

[118] *Id.* at 813.

[119] [1924] A. C. 797, 823. Lord Sumner's opinion has already been considered in related matters. See *supra*, pp. 206–208. The opinion probably does not represent the thought of a majority of the Court, who lean toward a more absolute view of the incompetency. See opinion of Viscount Finlay (*id.* at 813).

[120] *Supra*, pp. 209–210.

[121] L. R. 4 A. & E. 59 (1875).

eign" but "the hereditary ruler of the province of Egypt under the supremacy of the Sultan of Turkey." It is true that Lord Phillimore did say that he had sought to determine whether the Khedive had the status of a sovereign prince in international law. But he at no time questioned the existing dependency of the Khedive. He sought to establish the exact relationship for the purposes of applying the rule of sovereign immunity. An even clearer example of the same situation is *Tartar Chemical Co.* v. *United States*,[122] already discussed as a case where the court refused to follow the executive interpretation of a treaty.[123] Under the treaty, France was given preferential custom rates. Did "France" include Algeria, which admittedly was under French sovereignty? The executive said that the word "France" was a geographical expression signifying continental France and nothing more; that furthermore Algeria was a colony. But it was shown that constitutionally Algeria was as much a part of France as Burgundy. The Court refused to follow the executive, and correctly distinguished the long line of authorities holding that the sovereignty of a territory is a question for the executive.

To return to the analysis of Farwell's opinion, let us assume that in answer to the first question the Foreign Office replies that the Suss tribes are independent. Under this circumstance, will an answer by it to the second question stating to whom the disputed territory belongs — Morocco or the Suss — be binding on the court? Lord Sumner says not. There may be cases of disputed boundaries where the Crown has no peculiar knowledge, where in fact no one can give a conclusive opinion. "I think such boundaries, *where no acts of the Crown with regard to them have been involved*, must depend on evidence given in the ordinary way." [124] (Italics mine.)

As far as we can find, no court has ever agreed with Lord Sumner; and Viscount Finlay, in the course of the same case, emphatically declared to the contrary.[125] The cases that may arise are of two sorts, depending on whether or not the government of the judge is involved in the controversy (if there be any). In *Williams* v. *Suffolk* [126] our Government had protested against the exercise by Buenos Ayres of jurisdiction over the Falkland Islands, asserting

[122] 116 Fed. 726 (C. C. S. D. N. Y. 1902).

[123] See p. 72.

[124] [1924] A. C. 797, 827.

[125] *Id.* at 813.

[126] 13 Peters 415 (1839).

that Spain was still sovereign of them. We have already discussed that case.[127] The methods for determining the controversy lay more in the realm of politics than in that of law; for that reason, and not because the judiciary must necessarily second the executive, the Court was wise to accept the executive's version of the dispute.

Even where the government of the judge is not interested, there are weighty reasons against the court determining the matter contrary to the foreign office. If the territory is in dispute between two countries, a decision either way may give offense and embroil the foreign office in a diplomatic quarrel. This consideration is entitled to more weight where, as in the question of territorial sovereignty, the solution lies beyond the range of evidence in the narrow sense given to the term in our courts. If, then, there may be a quarrel it is perhaps wise to let the foreign office name the side which it feels ready to uphold. And yet, even so, must we say that because in many, maybe most, cases the reasons for conclusiveness are weighty, the rule must be made absolute for all cases? To the rubric quoted by Farwell: "The Courts of the King should act in unison with the Government of the King," [128] Lord Sumner replied pithily, "This seems to be rather a maxim of policy than a rule of law." [129]

[127] *Supra*, pp. 65, 77.

[128] In Foster *v.* Globe Venture Syndicate, [1900] 1, Ch. 811, 814, quoting Vice-Chancellor Shadwell in Thompson *v.* Powles, 2 Simons 194 (1828).

[129] [1924] A. C. 797, 826.

CONCLUSION

Lord Sumner's reply may well serve as the *leit motif* for a brief conclusion to this paper. We have not sought a specific answer to any one question or group of questions. Our purpose has been to sketch an attitude or to indicate a method which the courts may use in approaching litigations in which matters of foreign affairs or foreign policy may conceivably be involved. To this end, writers and courts have sought to devise formal methods based on deduction from the express allocation of powers in the Constitution. The power to make treaties, to declare war, and to receive ambassadors is expressly vested in the "political organs" of the Government, and so it is said that any disputed questions logically related to or presupposed in the exercise of these powers are "political," and that by the same token they are withdrawn from the courts, whose constitutionally granted functions are a-political, i. e. judicial. This has been further reinforced with nineteenth-century notions of the "will" of the state as a moral entity. It is said that the expression of this "will" must be single, unified; apparently it must on any given matter abide continuously in a given organ. It must not be expressed by the executive one day and the courts the next. This is said to be a description of what is, and it is also a program of what ought to be. This scheme is thought to have absolute validity, because structurally and dynamically it is completely contained, in its formal aspect, within the Constitution; and the Constitution is given as the absolute and ultimate juridical norm.

But as we have sought to show, it is not a true picture of what is. Many matters relating to foreign affairs which under this logic would be "political" are, in fact, handled by the courts. Courts determine whether a claim of sovereign immunity is properly asserted; they interpret treaties; they determine whether Orders in Council relating to prize are in conformity with international law; they delimit and apply the duties of neutrality. They may do these things in the absence of relevant executive action, thus running the risk of future conflict and contradiction; they may do it in the face of executive action already taken.

We do not set down these facts defiantly as one who would take glory in the independence of the courts as an end in itself. We begin with the separation of the powers and the functions of governments into three large groupings. This should not mean that each organ feels obliged to pull in a different direction. No organ can function adequately or efficiently without the cooperation of the others. This was dramatically illustrated by *Worcester* v. *Georgia*,[1] in which the Supreme Court ordered the State of Georgia to release Worcester, but was impotent to directly accomplish that end in the face of Jackson's indifference. In the ordinary run of affairs no such conflicts will arise, because there will be no diversity of aim or purpose. And if there is likely to be conflict, since such conflicts shake the security of the State it is often the better part of wisdom to avoid them. But whose business is it to avoid them? In *Worcester* v. *Georgia* was it the Supreme Court's or Jackson's? Should the Court have said: "This is a 'political question'; it is up to the President to say whether Georgia can make laws for the Cherokees; he has not spoken and lest he disagree with us, we should refrain"? Or should Jackson have said: "The Court has spoken, it has pledged the dignity of the United States; even though I do not agree with the Court, I must sustain it"?

Undoubtedly there are a few axioms applicable to such problems. There is a presumption that if one organ has already acted, the others, if for no other reason than the avoidance of stress, should back it up. This applies to all organs equally; it does not suppose the superiority of any one over another. There is a second presumption arising out of the materials on which judgment or action is to be based. To each organ is assigned certain functions. It should be given the widest scope in handling the materials on which its action depends, both that it may function successfully and that responsibility may be located. *Prima facie*, another organ should not hinder it in the manipulation of these materials. This, then, is a presumption of deference, of abstention. In matters concerning foreign affairs it means that the court presumably will defer to the executive.

But neither of these presumptions is conclusive. It is of the very essence of the separation of power and function that each organ is primarily concerned with and responsible for the performance of its own function; and if in its opinion it must to perform it properly exercise a certain discretion or make a certain judgment it will do so regardless of these presumptive limitations. In the words of Lord Sumner they are "maxim[s] of policy" rather than "rules of law." The judiciary is charged with the decision of litigations

[1] 6 Peters 515 (1832). See *supra*, pp. 18–19.

brought before it in a given way. It decides these conflicts by a technique which it has developed by projecting particular litigations into the entire scheme of the legal and social order. The judiciary, of course, is not alone in its concern with the legal and social order. The executive and the legislature each in its own way have like aims and purposes, but there will surely be places where one mode of procedure offers larger gains than another, and in the last analysis it is for the particular organ to decide this. If its own mechanisms seem superior, it will and should ignore the presumptive limitations.

These conclusions, so far, have been based on the assumption of direct conflict between executive and judicial judgment. This is the case where the executive issues an order and the judiciary declares it void. But in the matters with which we have dealt that is rarely so. Particularly is this true in matters of non-recognition. If the executive refuses to recognize the U.S.S.R. but the courts give effect to a law of the U.S.S.R. or to a confiscation decree, or allow the U.S.S.R. to sue, there is no contradiction whatsoever, unless we devise a formula of recognition involving inevitable and logical consequences, — a formula which will not stand up under realistic scrutiny. There is simply what some people like to call "embarassment"; more exactly there is the chance that the effectiveness of a particular foreign policy as conceived by a given group of persons may be diminished.

Since there is neither direct contradiction nor the potentiality of it, the presumptive limitations of which we have spoken are not brought squarely into play; the policy behind them is applicable, but it operates with a lesser degree of force. This should mean that the courts will and should adhere more closely to the procedures, to the rules and doctrines applied by them normally: doctrines which were presumably devised because they promote the judicial function and which should be deflected only where the gains to be achieved have been formulated with some, if not perfect, precision.

We have pointed out that in the recognition cases the courts have developed a narrow and insular conception of their function. They have viewed it as definitely limited to the preservation of the national order, and have closed their eyes to the fact that the national order does not and cannot exist in a vacuum but is contingent upon and related to other national orders and the international order which is the sum of all these orders. This conception is contrary to the general attitude traditionally taken by our courts, well exemplified in the prize decisions, that the function of a national court is *ipso facto* international; and however this idea may be juristically formulated, whether it is said that international law is part of municipal law as such, or is merely a source of municipal law, this tradition does embody a realistically correct conception of the judicial function. We believe that if the courts had been more alive to this tradition they would have been less apt to posit the legal non-existence of non-recognized communities, and would not have displayed a deference and subserviency to executive policy which far exceeds their practice in other matters.

APPENDIX

APPENDIX

In its recent decision, *Salimoff* v. *Standard Oil Company,*[1] the New York Court of Appeals has repudiated the dogma of Soviet non-existence which in the *Petrogradsky*[2] case it spun out with such tenuous refinement. This was an action by Soviet ("Russian") nationals against the Standard and Vacuum Oil companies for conversion of oil from lands once owned by the plaintiffs, confiscated by the Soviet, and sold to the defendants; the case, then, of *Luther* v. *Sagor,*[3] in which the King's Bench gave judgment for the plaintiff. The English case was quietly rejected by the New York Court.

"A recovery said the Court in conversion is dependent on the laws of Russia. *Riley* v. *Pierce Oil Corp.*, 245 N. Y. 152, 154. When no right of action is created at the place of wrong, no recovery in tort can be had in any other state on account of the wrong. The United States government recognizes that the Soviet government has functioned as a *de facto* or *quasi* government since 1917, ruling within its borders. It has recognized its existence as a fact, although it has refused diplomatic recognition as one might refuse to recognize an objectionable relative although his actual existence could not be denied. It tells us that it has no disposition to ignore the fact that such government is exercising control and power in territory of the former Russian empire." [4]

This quotation reveals the skeleton of the juristic syllogism by which the Court arrived at its result. But the opinion goes much further; it challenges the fanciful conception of the Soviet as "an assasin," etc., so unfortunately developed in the *Petrogradsky* opinion.

"As a juristic conception [the Court proceeds] what is Soviet Russia? A band of robbers or a government? We all know that it is a government. The State Department knows it, the courts, the nations and the man on the street. If it is a government in fact, its decrees have force within its borders and over its nationals. . . . The courts may not recognize the Soviet government as the *de jure* government until the State Department gives the word. They may, however, say that it is a government, maintaining internal peace and order, providing for national defense and the general welfare, *carrying on relations with our own government and others.*" [5] (Italics mine.)

A number of factors are relevent to explain the repudiation of the dogma of the *Petrogradsky* case. The opinion in that case and the earlier *Sokoloff*[6]

[1] 262 N. Y. 220 (1933).

[2] Petrogradsky Mejdunarodny Kommerchesky Bank *v.* The National City Bank, 253 N. Y. 23; 170 N. E. 479 (1930), discussed *supra*, pp. 163, 184 *et seq.*

[3] [1921] 1 K. B. 456, [1921] 3 K. B. 532, discussed *supra*, pp. 4-5, 176-179.

[4] *Supra*, note 1 at p. 226.

[5] *Id.* at pp. 226-227.

[6] Sokoloff *v.* National City Bank, 239 N. Y. 158; 145 N. E. 917 (1924), discussed *supra*, pp. 164, 176, 191.

opinion were written by Judge Cardozo. Judge Pound, now successor to Cardozo as Chief Judge of the New York Court, dissented in the *Petrogradsky* case, and to the memorandum opinion in *First Russian Insurance Company* v. *Beha*[7] he entered a short but acute dissent. Chief Judge Pound wrote the opinion in the current case.

Furthermore the occasion was ripe for a change of front. The motivating conviction of our anti-Soviet policy has vanished. Very recently President Roosevelt has communicated directly with the Soviet,[8] a fact to which the Court adverts, apparently, in the words italicized in the quotation above. The recent attitude of the Department of State is reflected in the memorandum on the status of the Soviet government submitted by it to the Court in this case:

". . .

2. The Department of State is cognizant of the fact that the Soviet regime is exercising control and power in territory of the former Russian Empire and the Department of State has no disposition to ignore that fact.

3. The refusal of the Government of the United States to accord recognition to the Soviet regime is not based on the ground that that regime does not exercise control and authority in territory of the former Russian Empire, but on other facts."[9]

A comparison of this memorandum with that submitted in the *Lehigh* cases[10] shows that the Department has abandoned its painful attempt to intimate that somehow the erstwhile Russian Empire was being governed from the Russian Embassy in Washington by an obsolete ambassador.

[7] 240 N. Y. 601; 148 N. E. 722 (1925), discussed *supra*, p. 186.

[8] See *supra*, p. 118, for an account of this incident.

[9] *Supra*, note 1 at p. 224.

[10] Lehigh Valley R. Co. *v.* State of Russia, 21 F(2d) 396 (C. C. A. 2nd, 1927), discussed *supra*, p. 213 *et seq.* A portion of the Department's communication to the Court in that case is printed on p. 216.

TABLES

TABLE OF CASES

A. Anglo-American

B. Foreign and International

TABLE OF STATUTES, TREATIES, AND DIPLOMATIC CORRESPONDENCE

TABLE OF SECONDARY AUTHORITIES

INDEX

INDEX

Bei Fragen zur Produktsicherheit wenden Sie sich bitte an:
If you have any questions regarding product safety,
please contact:

Walter de Gruyter GmbH
Genthiner Straße 13
10785 Berlin
productsafety@degruyterbrill.com